1794

1794

America, Its Army, and the Birth of the Nation

Dave R. Palmer

PRESIDIO

Published by Presidio Press
505 B San Marin Dr., Suite 300
Novato, CA 94945-1340

Library of Congress Cataloging-in-Publication Data

Palmer, Dave Richard, 1934—
    1794 : America, its army, and the birth of the nation / by Dave R. Palmer.
      p.   cm.
    ISBN 0-89141-523-8
    1. United States—Politics and government—1789—1797. 2. Civil-military relations—United States—History—18th century. 3. United States. Army—History—18th century. I. Title.
    E311.P34 1994
    973.4'3—dc20   93-45935
                                                         CIP

Typography by ProImage
Printed in the United States of America

*In full appreciation
to a quartet of scholars from Duke University
who led me to understand why soldiers in a democracy
ought to have a sense of history.*

*John Richard Alden (deceased)
I. B. Holley, Jr.
Harold T. Parker
Theodore Ropp*

CONTENTS

CONTENTS

ACKNOWLEDGMENTS

By its very nature, a work of synthesis and analysis is indebted to every scholar who has contributed to the body of research upon which it is based. I readily express my appreciation to all those whose combined talents have created a solid foundation permitting me to write.

I am grateful, too, to several individuals for their direct assistance in one form or another. David Skaggs stands out among them for the breadth of his involvement. From encouragement to providing information, from helping with research to acting as a sounding board, he more than earned my utmost appreciation. Larry Nelson, Richard Manion, Mike Morell, and Philip Samsey gave graciously of their time to help me become familiar with the area of conflict in the Old Northwest. Robert Doughty and his fine stable of historians at West Point were helpful in more ways than they realize, and I am quite in their debt. James Stanton exhibited his usual patience and talent in preparing the maps.

An impressive team at Presidio Press helped in a thousand ways to make the final product a better one. Robert Kane provided the initial encouragement so necessary in any undertaking of this sort, and Dale Wilson was a model of tact and expertise in the editing process. They deserve much of the credit for whatever degree of quality the work possesses.

Finally, let me say a word about the four mentors to whom the book is dedicated—John Alden, I. B. Holley, Harold Parker, and Ted Ropp. Some thirty years ago Duke University was blessed with a coterie of outstanding historians and teachers. Their students over the decades

ACKNOWLEDGMENTS

went out to enrich the intellectual understanding of military history in colleges and universities across the land. They were thereby instrumental in helping to shape an entire generation of American scholars. Those four in particular had a lasting influence on me. They taught me to think in time, to look back in order to see forward, and to view the world with the South Pole uppermost. Dedicating this book to them is a way to tell them of my gratitude.

PREFACE

The United States has resorted often in its history to the use of armed force, in domestic disturbances as well as against foreign adversaries. Still, as a nation, we have never been comfortable with our military. In fact, evidence abounds suggesting that many Americans harbor an instinctive distrust of their military establishment.

Twice in recent memory, for instance, at moments of high trauma for our country, that deep-seated sentiment has bubbled dramatically to the surface. The first occasion came in 1974, when Richard Nixon resigned the presidency. Secretary of Defense James Schlesinger worked quietly behind the scenes to preclude any move by military units to take a hand in the matter. His action passed almost without notice in the coverage of the tumultuous event itself, but it did make the small print in the news. Incredible as it seemed to members of the armed forces—and as disappointed as they were at the lack of special trust and confidence displayed by certain senior civilian leaders—it did happen. Irrational the worries may have been, but they were real nonetheless. The second event occurred in 1981, shortly after President Reagan was shot by a would-be assassin. In the hubbub of the White House press room, with the president's ability to govern unknown and the vice president out of town, television commentators fell to wondering on the air whether anyone was in charge. Hearing that, Secretary of State Alexander Haig, the senior cabinet officer, rushed up the stairs from a meeting in the Situation Room to settle that issue at once. Out of breath from the rapid climb, he huffed, "I am in charge here." Media members there—and others watching around the country—gasped. Haig was a former general, a wearer of four stars whose last position had been commander of all NATO forces. The subliminal symbol, caught in a flash, was that of a "man on horseback." Again, inexplicable though it may always seem to Haig, the reaction was real.

Another example, less glaring but nonetheless quite illustrative, happened in late 1992. The Winter 1992–93 issue of *Parameters,* a quarterly publication of the United States Army War College, carried an article entitled, "The Origins of the American Military Coup of 2012." Entries in such a limited circulation journal generally escape national interest, especially when penned by so relatively junior an officer as the author of this one, Lt. Col. Charles J. Dunlap, Jr. This piece, however, gained nationwide attention, being highlighted prominently by print and television journalists, to include coverage on prime-time national news programs. Why? For only one reason: the fact that a person in uniform published something with that title. In his article, Dunlap described a successful military coup against the U.S. government, a takeover made possible by "massive diversions of military forces to civilian uses . . . and the insularity of the military community" beginning in the 1990s. That approach was simply a literary technique to dramatize the point he wanted to make. But it is newsworthy, nevertheless, for a soldier (an air force officer, in this case) even to put thoughts of coups into words. The mere idea is enough to cause a good number of Americans to shudder involuntarily.

Professor Charles C. Moskos, preeminent sociologist and long-time observer of the American military, once noted that "anti-militarism is the anti-Semitism of the intellectual." Those who might be thought of as intellectuals are found in virtually every walk of life, but by and large they are either on university faculties or they once were students on those campuses. Fortunately, higher education in this country is founded on the pursuit of truth. Just as most intelligent people reject anti-Semitism, so would most intellectuals resent being labeled as antimilitary. Still, one does not have to scratch deeply in American society to find ostensibly broadminded individuals who would fervently second Machiavelli's contention that "He who makes war his profession cannot be otherwise than vicious."

Given the great weight of evidence showing that soldiers in our society may actually be less inclined to employ force than are civilian leaders, and knowing that the record of the U.S. armed services is one of unshakable adherence to the principle of subordination to civil authority, one has to wonder why such deep—almost visceral—antipathy toward the military persists.

Pondering that phenomenon led me to this book. In searching for reasons, I was pulled increasingly back in time to the very beginnings of our nation. When the Founding Fathers wrote the military clauses for our Constitution, they were drawing on their personal experiences, their heritage, and their common sense. Determining what those Constitutional concepts would be, and turning them into practical policies, consumed a dozen years or so from the final months of the Revolution through 1794. That lengthy process permanently molded the core elements of America's military structure, elements which have endured for more than two centuries. The modern defense establishment of the United States emerged in embryonic but recognizable shape in the climactic year of 1794. Its very essence is revealed in three legacies from that era: philosophical and practical underpinnings, providing direction; codification in the Constitution, providing form; and early, precedent-setting experiences, providing substance. This book is about that beginning. It will probe what was behind the writing of the military clauses in the Constitution, how they were set down, and what subsequently happened to give them such lasting effect. Besides providing the answers I sought, the story itself is a prime part of our national heritage. It is a story quite worth the telling, for the federal government has one paramount responsibility: the defense of the republic.

The book's time frame encompasses our country's first postwar period. While no attempt is made to draw specific analogies among our numerous national experiences in transitioning from war to peace, history itself suggests some abiding similarities. It should not be surprising if readers find parallels between issues surfacing in the years following the American Revolution and those arising two centuries later after the end of the Cold War.

A word about form. Although unavoidably conditioned by my own background—more than three decades spent in balancing the sometimes disparate pursuits of army officer and military historian—I have tried to approach this work from neither perspective solely, but from somewhere in between. It might be that soldiers will see too much of the scholar, and historians too much of the practitioner—which could mean I have come close to finding the place where the two meld, where the story probably has most value for all citizens. That is the vantage point I have sought. The formative period in our nation's history has been richly recorded—in collections of research material, through a host of historical writings, by the publication of many primary sources. This book is indebted to that full and excellent body of work, particularly the recent contributions of modern scholars; it attempts neither to supplant nor to compete with any. Rather, building on the historical foundation already formed, I have turned primarily to synthesis and analysis. Seeking new insights by examining the evidence from my particular perspective, and striving to paint in broad strokes on a large canvas, I have been guided by the admonition of Henry David Thoreau: "Our life is frittered away by detail . . . simplify, simplify."

Thus, while this book is at end a work of history, indeed of military history, it is not for historians alone. Nor for military libraries only. It is for anyone wanting to know more about *why* our modern military establishment is the way it is—and particularly for those who aspire to be leaders in the arena of national security, whether uniformed or civilian.

PART 1
SENTIMENTS ON A PEACE ESTABLISHMENT

Where there is no vision, the people perish.

—King Solomon: Proverbs, Chapter 29, Verse 18.

CHAPTER 1
GUIDE THE TORRENT

It was a day indelible in George Washington's memory. The tenth of March, 1783. A cold Monday in Newburgh, New York. Frosted light filtered through the single window in the center room of the sturdy Dutch house built by Jonathan Hasbrouck in 1750, and serving in this last year of the Revolutionary War as the Continental Army's headquarters. Ice floes choked the nearby Hudson River. Any chill that might have been felt inside, however, rapidly dissipated with Washington's heated reaction to the astonishing contents of several sheets of paper handed to him by an excited aide.

Not since Benedict Arnold's treason, more than two years before, had anyone seen the Virginian so visibly upset. His large hands, trembling with tension, rattled the clutch of papers. Aides edged involuntarily away. "Inexpressible concern" creased the commander in chief's face as he read the anonymous call to mutiny circulating among the officers of the Continental Army encamped in the area. Incredible words poured forth from the pages, powerful and terrible at the same time: a blast against ungrateful public officials; an ultimatum for Congress; a cry to remain under arms should peace arrive; a threat to let the enemy ravage unimpeded if war continued. Barely able to concede the meaning of all he was reading, the thunderstruck general grasped instinctively that his officers were about to throw themselves and the country "into a gulph of horror." On the verge of winning the Revolution, the victorious officers stood poised to devour it. A smell of gunpowder hung in the air.

3

Astounded Washington may have been, yet not entirely surprised. Although he had in no way foreseen such an overt and blatant effort to turn the army against the country, he had been nervously anticipating some sort of an explosion. He and others had been aware of the deepening resentment harbored by officers of the Continental Army, and of recent attempts to incite them still further. The fuse had been smoldering for months, but it had been beyond even Washington's ability to extinguish it.

Ironically, the igniting spark had been the Battle of Yorktown in 1781, a high point for the Continental Army and a pivot point for the Revolution. That smashing American and French victory had led to a British decision to consider ending the war by granting the thirteen colonies independence. Negotiations soon began in Paris and London. By the time Washington and his army had returned from Virginia to settle into familiar positions in the Hudson Highlands of New York, those events had changed the American scene dramatically. When Continental soldiers left the banks of the Hudson to march south, war had provided the glue holding the United States together. But with peace a real and present possibility, that glue had begun to dissolve.

Washington had become worried right away. "My greatest fear," he wrote shortly after the Battle of Yorktown, "is that Congress . . . may think our work too nearly closed and will fall into a state of langour and relaxation." His concern had grown after the opening of negotiations. Knowing that the gains of seven years of fighting could be lost in as many days at the conference table, he had urged caution. In August 1782, he had spoken of pitfalls in this "critical and awful period when our hands are to be tried at the arts of negotiation." While the smoke of combat no longer swirled around the thirteen states, fighting had by no means ended in other theaters among other foes. The nation dared not let its guard down prematurely, Washington had warned. It could not risk losing the peace by celebrating too soon the winning of the war. Euphoria could undo everything. Elation was an enemy.

Certain members of Congress echoed the commander in chief's concern, but for rather different reasons. While the general fretted over preserving advantages won on the battlefield, a few somber men in Philadelphia were more worried about the shape of the peace. He worked to keep his army intact and ready; they wrestled with an emerging crisis as dangerous as any encountered in the long war. Both concerns—the military and the political—would combine in early 1783 to open a door on catastrophe.

Congress was bankrupt. Under the Articles of Confederation—the document of union ratified by the thirteen United States in 1781, not long before the Yorktown campaign—the separate states had retained the authority to tax. The Confederation government had no way to raise money if the states failed to meet their obligations to the overall effort. Slow to respond to federal levies even in times when British bayonets threatened, local governments had grown thoroughly unresponsive as peace beckoned. By the end of the summer of 1782, states had forwarded a mere $125,000 of a required $6 million. Consequently, Congress struggled just to conduct its daily business. It was patently unable to pay the interest on national loans or to meet the military payroll. For that matter, it could not pay its own members either. It survived on foreign grants and personal loans. Creditors who held national notes had the same chilling premonitions about the impact of peace as did destitute soldiers. Without some ability by the central government to raise funds, the creditors faced ruin. Nevertheless, the states were most reluctant to grant any such authority. Robert Morris, the superintendent of finances, lamented acidly that the Articles of Confederation gave Congress the "privilege of asking everything" while giving the states the "prerogative of granting nothing."

Making matters worse, many of the strongest leaders had long since quit Congress to work for their states or to pursue private enterprises, leaving the institution but a weak reflection of its former self. Historian John Alden noted, "After 1776 talent, integrity, and energy were not lacking in Congress; genius was." Henry Laurens, arriving in 1777 to fill a seat from South Carolina, took stock of his colleagues and informed his governor: "I can hardly forebear concluding that a great assembly is in its dotage." The passage of another five years had not helped. No one any longer called the body "King Congress." Finally, in that heady postwar climate, Congress often could not assemble the necessary number of representatives to form a quorum. Thus enfeebled, the central government was fast deteriorating to little more than a debating society at the very moment when shaping the new nation cried for strength and direction.

Having a central capacity to raise money was the only answer to stop the fatal slide. A power without a purse is no power at all. Prodded by Robert Morris and several other Nationalists—men convinced of the imperative of a strong central government—Congress had sought from the states authority to gather its own funds through collecting customs duties. It wanted to levy a 5 percent tax on all goods imported into the United States. Amending the Articles of Confederation, which such a grant of authority would entail, required unanimous approval. Twelve states had quickly accepted the initiative, with only Rhode Island refusing to go along. Until leaders there could be persuaded of the need for the tax, the Confederation Congress would remain broke and impotent.

Meanwhile, inside the army, the mood was souring. The very idea of peace was hard to contemplate by men who had matured in wartime, whose ties to home villages and counties had been weakened by time and distance—not to mention a distaste for those who had prospered while avoiding the risk of military service. What would home be like now? How would returning soldiers be welcomed? What would they do for a living? Unaccustomed thoughts, those, generating an overall sense of uneasiness. That led in turn to a sharpened concern over their constant condition of poverty. It was one thing to have no money in camp, quite another to head into an unknown future with empty pockets. Individuals had much back pay due them—Washington reckoned it as "four, five, perhaps six years" worth in some cases. They had not been paid at all in months. Moreover, in light of the Confederation's fiscal plight, officers were beginning to wonder about a promise made to them a couple of years earlier. At one of the darkest moments of the Revolution, in the "black year" of 1780, Congress had offered a lifetime pension of half-pay to all officers who would stick with the cause to the end of the war, and a bonus of eighty dollars to enlisted men who would remain with the colors. Now, with the end in sight, those who had stayed the course shared a well-founded fear that their loyalty and sacrifice might be rewarded by a repudiation of the promise. The states, newly freed from the fear of a British takeover, were not in the least inclined to support peacetime pensions. The growing apprehension among veterans received a major boost with the announcement of a reduction in the allowance for meals. Coming at just the wrong time, the ration cut served as a daily reminder to the soldiers of their poverty—a plight made all the more inexplicable in light of the obvious abundance in the countryside beyond the army's camps.

Uneasiness solidified into bitterness in the early fall of 1782. The French forces that had marched with the Continentals to Yorktown, and had there fought alongside them to gain together the great victory, returned to the Hudson Highlands on the way to meet their fleet in Boston. During September and October they camped beside their American colleagues. Having all the earmarks of a family reunion, the French visit was a joyous time of shared reminiscences and farewells. Officers entertained their comrades in mutual exchanges of respect and friendship. And that raised the problem. Food was plentiful in the rich countryside along the Hudson. The harvest had been bountiful. French officers set superb tables, laden with good food and fine drink. When the Americans reciprocated, however, they could afford to serve nothing more than "stinking whiskey—and not always that—and a bit of beef with vegetables." They were embarrassed by their obvious poverty in the midst of plenty. It was a galling blow to the pride of proud men, focusing minds on the manifest unjustness of the situation. Until that coalescing moment, Washington had always been able to count on his officers to control mutinous outbursts in the army. From then on, he could never be sure.

Seeing the restless soldiery as a threat to states' rights as peace approached, many leaders in statehouses around the country proposed dismantling the Continental Army, thinking thereby to avoid the obligation of paying the men. An initial step was a consolidation of regiments, set to take effect on the first day of 1783. That move would reduce considerably the number of officers needed, but without providing a way to balance their accounts. Congress did not have the money, and was unwilling to issue certificates attesting to an amount owed or to the promise of a pension. Those cut would depart penniless. Washington feared the results of such an unfeeling separation of so many deserving men. They would be "turned into the world, soured by penury and what they call the ingratitude of the public, involved in debts, without one farthing of money to carry them home, after having spent the flower of their days . . . in establishing the freedom and independence of their country." The general worried that a failure to pay them would set loose "a train of evils." Already, conversations in camp had turned to the consideration of refusing to go home, of remaining under arms until

Congress was forced to find the money. George Washington had hoped to spend the winter at Mount Vernon. Sadly, he canceled those plans. He dared not leave the army in its current state of mind.

When in November the sullen officers considered addressing their feelings in a letter to Congress, Washington encouraged them, hoping it would vent some of the anger. He was also quite chagrined at his own inability to gain relief for his troops. Insistent messages to Congress and the separate states had been virtually dismissed, so far as he could see, through much of 1782. Washington's influence appeared to be waning as the Union itself weakened. The general had been begging the states for money and men for more than seven years, and his already well-worn arguments for continued readiness were no longer compelling with the end of the fighting in sight.

With Maj. Gen. Henry Knox drafting the document, the officers put their frustrations on paper. "We have borne all that men can bear—our property is expended—our private resources are at an end, and our friends are wearied out and disgusted with our incessant applications." Recognizing the political constraints on Congress, the officers agreed to forgo the promised half-pay pension in exchange for a commutation to a lump-sum payment upon severance, or full pay for a limited number of years, but insisted that enlisted soldiers receive the full eighty dollars due them as a discharge bonus. They also sought an advance of at least some of their back pay, with a commitment for the rest. These were minimum requests, the petition stated. Their denial would sorely try the army's patience and could lead to "fatal effects." Despite such scarcely veiled threats, Washington thought the petition was "couched in very respectful terms." Instead of sending the message, the officers selected three of their number as a deputation to carry it to Philadelphia. There they could assure that Congress considered it fully. Major General Alexander McDougall, a battle-tested leader whose speech retained the burr of his native Scotland, headed the group. Accompanied by colonels John Brooks and Matthias Ogden, he left Newburgh in late December 1782.

Not all in Philadelphia were disturbed by the distress of the army. Some saw it as an opportunity. If members of Congress could be frightened enough by the specter of a military uprising, might not that propel them into convincing the states either to pay their assessments or to permit the central government the right to tax? Lending urgency to such thinking, bad news galloped in from Virginia even as McDougall's committee was en route from Newburgh. Although Rhode Island had never agreed to the import tax amendment, Nationalists believed that the tiny state, being the lone holdout, could be shamed into reversing its vote. However, Virginia, the largest state, had just recanted its approval, joining Rhode Island in opposition. The measure was dead. Anti-Nationalists—those putting states' rights foremost and fearing a strong central government— seemed to be gaining the ascendancy across the land. Historian James Thomas Flexner later wrote that Congress "was as helpless as a turtle that had been turned over on its back." Several alarmed Nationalists, summing things up the same way, believed the times called for extreme tactics to reverse the forces tearing at the seams of the Union. For them, the army's petition had arrived at a most propitious moment. With Machiavellian intent, they launched a bizarre scheme risking the very future of the new nation in a desperate effort to save it at birth.

The army's grievances gave rise to three possible approaches to coerce congressmen into addressing the nation's obligation to its soldiers, which in turn meant they would have no option but to adopt a new method for raising revenue. First, the very presence of McDougall's committee and the obvious justice of the military's position might be enough to persuade a majority of members to support the need for Congress to have taxing authority. If not, the temper of the officers in camp might then be turned to use. A public pledge by the officers to remain under arms until they were paid, although verging on mutiny, would get the attention of even the most reluctant representatives. Fear should spawn reason. Finally, if nothing else worked, a handful of Nationalists knew of the existence in the Newburgh encampment of a hotheaded element already leaning toward outright rebellion. That fringe faction might be manipulated into openly attempting a military coup, which would surely stampede the states into ceding a central funding system. Thus began three months of intrigue in the most incredible of scenarios: civilian leaders using the army to manipulate civil authority.

Robert Morris and his assistant, Gouverneur Morris, as well as Alexander Hamilton, James Wilson, and other involved individuals, began conferring with McDougall at once. The deputation from the army was put to work lobbying individual members of Congress, impressing upon them the woeful circumstances in the army and the anger of its officers. They did their work well, for they had only to describe reality. At one meeting in January, Colonel Brooks stated that emotions in camp had overcome reason, blinding many there to the evil consequences of extreme actions. The nation could expect "at least a mutiny," delegates heard, if they ignored the officers' petition. Meanwhile, the small group of radical Nationalists worked through McDougall to mobilize all the officers at Newburgh to begin preparing for steps beyond petitioning. McDougall wrote to Knox of the need for concerted support, and mentioned the possibility of exerting combined pressures on Congress from both the army and a host of public creditors.

Initially, the first stratagem seemed to be working. By the end of January, most in Congress had become convinced that the army's problems must be settled promptly. They directed the superintendent of finances to take care of the salary issues, including back pay. Representatives also vowed to exert every effort to obtain the requisite funds. That augured well for passage of the revenue package. But then several members balked at commutation of the promised pensions into a lump-sum payment. That smacked too much of half-pay, however it was clothed, and certain delegations had strict instructions from their states to resist pensions, period. Without commutation, there would be no lever powerful enough to effect passage of a taxation measure, nor could there be a clear linkage between the army and public creditors. Momentum was lost as well when General Knox failed to respond with further evidence of deteriorating morale at camp, and it slowed still more when some legislators began to suspect that the army was being used to twist arms. Alarmingly, too, word from the peace negotiations in Europe was upbeat; the war could end soon, removing virtually all hope of setting the new nation on a firm financial footing. The conspirators escalated to the second phase, an attempt to get the officers to openly refuse to disband.

Knowing that Washington would have no part of any ploy to coerce Congress, the instigators in Philadelphia aimed at Henry Knox, Washington's trusted chief of artillery. He had recently been open in complaints about Congress, was an avowed Nationalist, was respected by the rest of the officers, and had Washington's confidence. A former bookseller from Boston, easily the most massive general in the army at about three hundred pounds, and a self-taught professional, Knox had been in uniform since the outset of the war. He could influence the army. In early February, Colonel Brooks left the seat of government and traveled to West Point, the key American fortress on the Hudson, which Knox commanded. He carried urgent entreaties to convince the general to join the effort. McDougall, writing under the prearranged code name of "Brutus," followed with explicit descriptions of what the army must be prepared to do at this critical juncture. Gouverneur Morris also contacted Knox. "The Army may now influence the legislatures," he wrote, "and if you will permit me a metaphor from your own profession, after you have carried the post the public creditors will garrison it for you." At a designated moment, according to "Brutus," the officer corps should make an orchestrated public announcement that it would not disband in the event of peace until pay and commutation matters were settled. What the men in the City of Brotherly Love had in mind, the former bookseller saw, amounted to mutiny. Passive, perhaps, but mutiny nonetheless. While he might applaud the goals sought, Knox could not agree with the methods. He would not help. "I consider the reputation of the American Army as one of the most immaculate things on earth," he responded to McDougall. The officers should submit to virtually any wrong "rather than sully it in the least degree." It is not recorded whether either man recognized the irony in the code name they had selected.

As matters turned out, it probably made little difference whether or not Knox was willing. Events overtook plans. Word reached Philadelphia on 12 February of the signing of preliminary articles of peace by American and British emissaries. Nationalists expected each arriving ship to bring word that the long war was at last over, which, under current conditions, could perhaps mean the end of the Republic. Frantic, the conspirators could wait no longer. Even before hearing from Knox, they initiated the third course, a dark alternative of last resort.

Revolutions inevitably cast up revolutionaries, human flotsam whose values have become warped in the intense heat of violent social struggle. Having overthrown one government, they slide easily into contemplation of overthrowing another. Force is their proven method of choice. If society's rules tend to bind, change the society. If rewards seem too few, seize more. Thus it has ever been; thus it was with the American Revolution.

In the Continental camp at Newburgh, such men gravitated to Maj. Gen. Horatio Gates. A hero of the war, and a goat as well, once the candidate in a cabal to replace Washington, a leader of small talent and large ego, generally discredited but still with some political support,

11

he was a somewhat battered enigma in uniform. Not a few officers believed strongly in him; as many others thoroughly detested him. Washington stood in that latter group. By virtue of rank, Gates was second in command at Newburgh.

In Gates's official residence at the Edmondson house, a few miles from Washington's headquarters, a coterie of outraged young officers congregated during the latter part of 1782. They vehemently resented the indifference of Congress and, perhaps more than others, dreaded the prospects of returning home destitute. Caustically critical of Washington's leadership, they believed Gates would speak more compellingly in their behalf. By winter, they had grown anxious for action, had become zealots espousing force. They longed for a charismatic leader who would step forward and inspire the army to rise in rebellion. Major John Armstrong, one of Gates's aides, envisioned Anthony Wayne leading a column of incensed soldiers. He wrote that, with "Mad Anthony at their head, I know not where they would stop." Gates's long-standing dream of replacing Washington matched well the young malcontents' newfound desire for insurrection. The ambitious general and the Young Turks, revolutionaries who had lost their bearings, were a combination formed in infamy. They began planning for a coup d'etat aimed, apparently, at displacing Congress with a military dictatorship. The full details of how they thought that might be done remain shrouded in the folds of history, but parts of the scheme were soon to surface, and it is known that Gates was in touch with ostensibly supportive members of the central government as early as January 1783.

But that support was not what it seemed to be. Gates and his followers were being used. Although they thought they had the initiative, they actually were pawns. Desperate men in Philadelphia were playing a desperate double game. While they wanted to incite an uprising of the army, they did not want it to succeed. The revolt had to be real enough to shake peace-smitten politicians to the core, but at the same time it had to be contained short of chasing Congress out of town at bayonet point. If unchecked, the mutiny might go too far, might itself lead to anarchy, which would be as fatal to the future of the United States as a failure to establish a sound monetary base. The counterpoise would be—could only be—George Washington, whose storied trustworthiness and vast influence could be counted on to keep matters from expanding out of control. He, too, would be used. It was the most dangerous of games, loosing violent forces that could defy containment by anyone, however powerful. As historian Richard H. Kohn later pointed out, "The whole venture cut a fine line between parallel disasters." Taking such a course could lead to catastrophe; *not* taking it could do the same. The plotters chose to gamble on action rather than inaction. Three steps put things in motion: Alexander Hamilton sent Washington what may have been the most crucial letter he ever received; Robert Morris noisily announced his resignation as superintendent of finances in order to dramatize the seriousness of the situation; and a messenger hurried to the Hudson Highlands to give Gates the word to act.

Washington's role, Hamilton knew, was the central one in the entire Byzantine scheme. If the commander in chief failed to move forcefully enough, and quickly, Gates's uprising could flare into a holocaust incapable of being extinguished short of burning itself out. Yet, Washington could not be informed of the plan, for he would never countenance any such action. The twenty-six-year-old congressman, an aide of Washington's from 1777 to 1781, knew him well. Writing confidentially, Hamilton told the general enough to forewarn him, but no more. Enough, the young congressman hoped, to prepare him to react, but not enough to prompt him to preempt. After revisiting the injustices inflicted on the army, and describing the abysmal state of federal finances, Hamilton gingerly broached the good that could come to both the army and the country if the officers continued to exert pressure for the redress of grievances. Washington's challenge, Hamilton wrote pointedly, would be to keep the protest "within the bounds of moderation." His duty as commander in chief would be "to take the direction" of any unrest in camp. There might also arise an opportunity, Hamilton hinted, "to guide the torrent" if affairs took an extreme turn. The former aide then closed by noting that voices in camp had been aimed at reducing the general's standing, warning him to anticipate a diminished degree of influence in case of "any commotions."

Hamilton's words succeeded in alerting Washington. A second confidential letter from another friend in Congress, Joseph Jones, confirmed that there were "dangerous combinations in the army" and that conspirators were using "sinister practices" to damage the Virginian's reputation. Washington quietly launched his own investigation. The results disturbed him immensely. Unrest in camp was indeed worse than he had thought—and it centered in Gates and his followers. Still, there was no intimation of anything beyond an effort to promote a unified front to push Congress into acting.

Washington puzzled agonizingly over his predicament. The army *did* richly merit the mitigation of its suffering. It had indeed been treated shabbily. And he was, after all, its commander. It was also probably correct that only extraordinary measures would obtain results. Did his duty to his followers oblige him to lead an irregular movement aimed at redress? Or was his first duty to Congress? Whatever the agony, the answer was predictable. No matter the provocations, he replied to Hamilton on 4 March, "I shall pursue the same steady line of conduct which has governed me hitherto." Impropriety in any form was incompatible with his character. Washington would not try to guide the torrent.

On Saturday, 8 March, Col. Walter Stewart, an "agent from our friends in Congress and the administration," as Gates described him, reached the Newburgh cantonment. Stewart had previously been one of Gates's aides. A courageous fighter, a veteran of numerous campaigns, and allegedly the handsomest man in the army, he was widely admired. The colonel called first on Washington, as was proper for a returning senior officer, and then huddled with Gates and some of that general's trusted colleagues. Stewart was either a very accomplished actor or he was himself unaware of the double-dealing by the clique in Philadelphia. He assured Gates of support from Morris and others, including public creditors, and told him the moment to move was at hand.

Gates was ready. Before the weekend was out, his followers had flooded the cantonment with rumors that civilian creditors were ready to join them in a common effort to spur Congress, that leaders in government expected the army to stand up for its rights, and that many congressmen would condone such a stance. On Monday, 10 March, an unsigned circular announced a Tuesday-morning meeting of all field-grade officers and company representatives to consider these issues. As soon as the circular was out, Colonel Stewart's office distributed an anonymous address urging officers to come to the meeting prepared to move beyond the "meek language of entreating memorials." The address argued eloquently that it was time to brandish swords not words.

Those were the papers—the inflammatory address and the notice of the unauthorized meeting—that had so astounded General Washington when copies reached his hands on that darkly memorable day. He had served eight turbulent years as commander in chief of the Continental Army, and another eight as president of the United States lay still ahead, but nothing in his lifetime of momentous events could ever quite match that shattering moment at Newburgh near the end of the war. His mind recoiled in shock as he finally grasped the full meaning of Hamilton's veiled warning about the torrent.

CHAPTER 2
A DANGEROUS INSTRUMENT

The commander in chief was never one to be paralyzed by shock, however severe. Putting the offending papers aside, he turned straight to the task of defanging the incipient insurrection. Gaining time was a first requirement, time to let emotions calm and to prepare a counteroffensive. In angry words, he promptly canceled the illegal Tuesday meeting, but replaced it with an approved gathering set for Saturday, 15 March, five days away. He began at once assembling influential subordinates to assure himself of a strong, active backing in the looming confrontation. Henry Knox would certainly be needed; a letter went out ordering him up from West Point. A courier galloped off to inform Congress of the situation. Through the week, Washington consulted with trusted officers while constantly checking the pulse of units in camp. Aiming to soften some of the anti-Congress sentiment, he published in general orders the central government's recent resolve to settle the nagging pay issues. All the while, he painstakingly developed remarks he would deliver to the assemblage of officers on Saturday. Significantly, though, he did so quietly, intentionally fostering the impression that he would not personally attend the meeting, that it would be chaired by the ranking officer present—whom he assumed would be Horatio Gates. That ploy by Washington would tend to give the conspirators added confidence, and to incline them to surface where they would be more vulnerable to a counterstroke.

Gates took the bait. Another anonymous address—written, as was the first, by Maj. John Armstrong, and again copied and distributed by other members of Gates's close staff—implied craftily that Washington himself must be supportive of aims proposed in the earlier paper, otherwise he would not have sanctioned the Saturday meeting. The second address, too, was a summons to arms. On all sides, stress grew daily. Tension stalked the buzzing camp.

The main encampment was at New Windsor, a few miles southwest of Newburgh. There, on a rise near the soldiers' huts, stood a large structure built of logs and rough-hewn planking. Erected only three months earlier to accommodate religious services and social gatherings, it was originally called the Temple, but was also known as the Public Building or the New Building. Inside, it was essentially a single rectangular room, some forty feet wide by seventy long. A small platform at one end served as a stage. By late Saturday morning—ominously, the ides of March—intense officers jammed the hall, packing into every feasible space. Horatio Gates, as chairman, opened the meeting.

Then, to the great surprise of the crowd, General Washington abruptly entered through a small door off the stage and stepped onto the platform. He asked to speak to the officers, a request the dumbfounded Gates was obliged to honor. The general looked out over the solid mass of uniformed men, and for once did not see reflected in their faces that familiar sense of respectful camaraderie. Sullenness and suspicion were there in good measure, and outright anger in some instances. This was not an audience predisposed to be friendly. Washington was about to attempt the speech of his life.

The commander in chief took the offensive at the outset, heatedly denouncing the demagoguery of the anonymous author of the addresses, berating him for appealing to passion rather than reason, and blasting his "insidious purposes." He scornfully derided the writer's logic, showing that neither of the proposed traitorous alternatives could be accomplished, that either assaulting the seat of government or going into exile somewhere in the wilderness would be a "physical impossibility." Then he ripped into the man's character. "My God! What can this writer have in view" by recommending that the military draw its sword against civil authority? That would inevitably bring ruin to both. "Can he be a friend to the Army? Can he be a friend to this country? Rather is he not an insidious foe?" Washington attacked assertions in the addresses claiming that neither he nor the government had the interest of the soldiers at heart. Congress, though slow in deliberation as democratic institutions are wont to be, the general conceded, was fully as supportive of the army as its powers permitted. Moreover, he added, it was simply preposterous for anyone to presume that he, who had "been the common companion and witness of your distresses," could be in any way indifferent to their suffering. Then he closed his formal remarks with these ringing words:

> And let me conjure you, in the name of our common country . . . as you regard the military and national character of America, to express your utmost horror and detestation of the man who wishes . . . to overturn the liberties of our country, and who wickedly attempts to open the flood gates of civil discord and deluge our rising empire in blood. By thus determining and thus acting, you will . . . by the dignity of your conduct, afford occasion for posterity to say, when speaking of the glorious example you have exhibited to mankind, "had this day been wanting, the world had never seen the last stage of perfection to which human nature is capable of attaining."

As the Virginian paused to gauge the effect of his words on the officers, he sensed that he had not wholly reached them. They were quiet now, intent and self-conscious, but somehow still not satisfied with the turn of events or with their commander's assurances. He needed to do more. To show an example of congressional concern with the soldiers' plight, Washington pulled from his pocket a letter from a member of Congress. He would read it, he said. Men shifted impatiently as he fumbled uncomfortably with the letter. Slowly at first, then accelerating, a murmur swept the crowded room. Those in the back stretched to see what was happening. Something was wrong with Washington. His words were halting. He seemed perplexed by the document in his hand. After a pause, he reached into another pocket and brought out a pair of reading glasses. They were new. Only close associates had seen him wear them before, and never in public. Very simply he said, "Gentlemen, you will permit me to put on my spectacles, for I have not only grown gray but almost blind in the service of my country." He then read the letter—but no one heard. That final humble gesture had done what no amount of rhetoric could. Washington's commanding presence, his stirring words, the officers' own rising sense of shame, the weight of a long week of tension, flashbacks to battles shared, visions of fallen friends, thoughts of privations endured—a tumble of emotions and memories had coalesced in that one electric instant to stun the audience. Many were in tears. Washington folded the letter, removed his glasses, and wisely walked quickly out of the hall. That crystallizing scene terminated the coup d'etat.

Horatio Gates sat speechless. Henry Knox jumped to the floor to propose a statement of appreciation for the commander in chief. Then, in prearranged coordination with Brig. Gen. Rufus Putnam and others, he secured approval of resolutions confirming the patriotic and loyal sense of the meeting. Over weak objections by some die-hard hotheads, the officers adopted a memorial to Congress deploring the "infamous propositions" in the anonymous addresses and pledging continued loyalty to the central government. The meeting adjourned with Gates and his group thoroughly deflated and discredited.

In Philadelphia, meanwhile, news of the uproar at Newburgh had caused the last holdouts to approve commutation, specifically calling for five years of full pay for those officers who were eligible for half-pay for life. Enlisted Continentals were to get four months' pay upon separation. Commutation's staunchest former opponent, Eliphalet Dyer of Connecticut, was the one who asked Congress to grant it. Dyer's grudging reversal, James Madison wrote, had been "extorted from him by the critical state of our affairs." As Nationalists had predicted all along, the passing of that pay proposal levered subsequent approval of a taxation measure. The desperate gamble had worked. The specter of the army in open rebellion had proved to be more frightening to Anti-Nationalists than their fear of a central government able to tax. And George Washington had indeed squelched the rebellion before it could gather any momentum. The conspirators' scheme had successfully walked that "fine line between parallel disasters." The government remained woefully weak, but at least it had a chance of surviving.

That chance had come none too soon. Official word of an armistice reached General Washington at the Hasbrouck house only a month after the climactic encounter in the Temple. With a keen sense of the dramatic, he waited a few days to announce it. At noon on 19 April, eight years to the day after the fighting had started at Lexington and Concord, the war's end was "publicly proclaimed." The commander in chief authorized "an extra ration of liquor" for every soldier.

Reflection on the agitation in the army faded rapidly with the advent of the armistice and the apparent resolution of the pay issues. The affair itself became only a footnote to the story of the Revolution, while Washington's reputation, and that of the Continental Army, soared as a result of the positive outcome of events at Newburgh. Nevertheless, the story could as well have ended differently. In the absence of George Washington, it surely would have. A coup d'etat, even an unsuccessful one, would have altered forever the equation of civil-military relations in the United States, with what calamitous results we will never know. Killing the Newburgh Conspiracy in its embryonic stage, before it could spread havoc in an unready infant nation, must rest among the most important of the legacies left by a man who left so many. And he did it personally, up front and alone, by force of presence and strength of character. Captain Samuel Shaw, an aide-de-camp to General Knox at the time, commented later on the tenuousness of the commander in chief's position: "On other occasions, he had been supported by the exertions of an Army and the countenance of friends, but in this he stood single and alone." Thomas Jefferson put Washington's actions in historical perspective, saying that "the moderation and virtue of a single character has probably prevented this revolution from being closed as most others have been by a subversion of that liberty it was intended to establish."

George Washington himself did not have much to say about the incident once it was behind him. He did suspect that certain men in Philadelphia had fomented some part of the trouble, and he so informed them. Always the practical man of action, though, he quickly turned his thoughts forward rather than to dwell on the months of intrigue.

Still, he had the last word. "The Army . . . is a dangerous instrument to play with," he pointedly rebuked Alexander Hamilton.

CHAPTER 3
VISION

Revolutions do not end with peace treaties. They have two parts, requiring two distinct enterprises: tearing down the old, and creating the new. While winning the war is never easy, history records that forging the peace is a much more difficult task to accomplish. Achieving either, however, verges on the impossible without a coalescing vision to provide direction and unity of effort. Just as there must be a clear view of a war's objectives to guide soldiers, so must there be a shared sense of the shape of the future to guide statesmen. Perhaps the primary reason why revolutionaries so seldom follow battlefield victory with successful nation building is their failure to see that peace is more than merely the absence of war. The revolutionaries who won the War of Independence were not unusual in that regard.

In the war itself, Americans had rather quickly enunciated two strategic objectives, and then had wisely retained them as constant beacons through the long, trying years of the armed struggle. Independence was one, of course, and territorial expansion the other.[1]

For much of the first year of the war, Americans saw their fight more as one to assure their rights as Englishmen than as a struggle to become free. That attitude gave way gradually with the spread of battle-

---

1. I have written in some detail elsewhere about the objectives of the American Revolutionary War. See *The Way of the Fox: American Strategy in the War for America, 1775–1783* (Westport, Conn.: Greenwood, 1975), 77–92.

engendered bitterness. When Thomas Paine published *Common Sense* in January 1776, tapping into the rising sentiment for separation from the British Crown, he accelerated the mood mightily by saying in simple yet powerful words what many had come to believe. "One of the strongest natural proofs of the folly of hereditary rights in kings," he boldly stated, "is that nature disapproves it, otherwise she would not frequently turn it into ridicule by giving mankind an *ass for a lion.*" Through the spring months one province after another concluded that independence should be an expressed aim of the war. By July 1776, despite the concern of several members that a break from the mother country would be premature, the Continental Congress had determined to take that step. Once stated, independence became a sustaining and unshakable objective. Conciliation was thereafter no longer conceivable.

While independence was announced with much fanfare, expansion— territorial aggrandizement—was never officially proclaimed as a goal of the war. But it was an objective from the outset. The drive for empire preceded the desire for independence. A full year before deciding to separate from Great Britain, Congress ordered Continental forces in northern New York to invade Canada, an aggressive American effort to annex by force its neighbor to the north—an effort, by the way, fated to endure for some four decades. Representatives also cast about promptly for means to grab control of the Floridas, Nova Scotia, English-controlled islands, and the vast wilderness to the west. They envisioned a future country stretching from the Gulf of Mexico to the Arctic wastes, and from the Atlantic to at least the Mississippi. Henry Knox, visiting Albany in the first year of the war, and noting its strategic location with respect to Canada and the West, predicted that the city "must one day be, if not the capital of America, yet nearly to it." Paine's *Common Sense* forthrightly addressed the concept of an American empire, saying the conflict with the king was "not the affair of a city, a county, a province, or a kingdom; but of a continent—of at least one-eighth part of the habitable globe."

In early discussions with European powers, American negotiators were prohibited from compromising certain territorial aspirations. Congress established the minimum gains expected from the war as: Canada, all western lands to the Mississippi, free navigation of that river, a port on the Gulf coast, and fishing rights in the western Atlantic. In becoming an ally of the United States, France formally renounced all former claims on the North American continent. In its futile attempt to form an alliance with the Spanish court, Congress spelled out its irreducible territorial ambitions. Americans would reluctantly accede to Spanish claims to lands south of the 31st Parallel, roughly the northern border of present-day Florida, but only should such a step be necessary to gain a pact with Spain. That grudging position also recognized the reality of possession. Bernardo de Galvez, governor of Louisiana, grabbed English posts along the Mississippi in 1779, took Mobile in 1780, and ejected the British entirely from West Florida with the seizure of Pensacola in 1781. In a moment of weakness brought on by war weariness, congressmen further authorized their negotiator in Madrid, John Jay, to consider giving up insistence on the east bank of the Mississippi River. In Paris, an astounded Benjamin Franklin reacted forcefully. "Poor as we are," he wrote, "I would rather agree with [the Spaniards] to buy at a great price the whole of their right on the Mississippi, than sell a drop of its water. A neighbor might as well ask me to sell my street door." Jay withdrew the offer. The front porch of the United States faced west. Manifest destiny, a term still to be coined, was patently a very real part of the personality of the new nation well before it won its place as a republic.

The motivating vision for which patriots were willing to fight and endure was of a United States both independent of Europe and dominant in North America. Those twin objectives emerged early in the Revolutionary War, were overwhelmingly endorsed by American leaders, and remained steadfast throughout the highs and lows of the conflict. To that sustaining and integrating view must be credited a goodly portion of the reasons for the revolutionaries' ultimate victory. Having won the war, though, they were but half through. It was yet to be seen whether they could fashion a similarly effective vision enabling them to meet the second challenge of their revolution: to create a viable country.

Some of the Founding Fathers were striving to do just that in the fading days of the war. To govern successfully, the new country would need to perform several fundamental functions. Perhaps nowhere have the basic imperatives of government been more succinctly articulated than in the Preamble to the Constitution of the United States: ". . . establish Justice, insure domestic Tranquility, provide for the common defence, promote the general Welfare, and secure the Blessings of Liberty. . . ." Insuring domestic tranquility and providing for the common defense necessarily entail having military forces, and it has been demonstrated over time that accomplishing the other three also calls occasionally for the employment of arms. Certain it is, then, that determining the scale and scope of a nation's military structure is an essential prerequisite to the creation of the nation itself. The vision of the shape of a country's future is depicted largely in the consensus formed over the shape of its army.

A letter from Congressman Alexander Hamilton to General Washington triggered the development of a concept for the military establishment of the United States. In the spring of 1783, with peace virtually assured, although hostilities had not been formally ended in a final treaty, the Confederation Congress began seriously to contemplate its peacetime military responsibilities. It appointed in April a committee "to provide a system . . . for military and naval establishments."[2] Secretary at War Benjamin Lincoln would provide the committee his thoughts, of course, as would others. But the viewpoint everyone would want to know was Washington's. Hamilton, the committee's chairman, wrote at once to the commander in chief, requesting his advice.

The general responded with alacrity, an indication that the subject was not a new one at the Newburgh encampment. He directed several of his senior officers to submit ideas in writing, which they did in just days. Washington sent their papers to Hamilton, along with his own comments, on 2 May 1783. He labeled his report, "Sentiments on a Peace Establishment." It was then, and remains today, a benchmark document in the evolution of the military structure of the United States.

Washington saw clearly that "the defence of the Empire" required a strong and broadly based military organization. The deliberations of Congress were therefore of utmost importance, he believed, because "the immediate safety and future tranquility of this extensive Continent depend in a great measure upon the peace Establishment now in contemplation."

He wrote in full awareness of the growing pressures to disband the Continental Army. A peacetime army was itself a source of fear to many,

2. Four of the five committee members would later be instrumental in writing the United States Constitution: James Madison, James Wilson, Oliver Ellsworth, and Alexander Hamilton.

especially the Anti-Nationalists. Not a few also held that the buffer afforded by the Atlantic made a centrally controlled military force unnecessary in any event. Addressing both the fear and the perception, Washington warned, "Altho' a *large* standing Army in time of Peace hath ever been considered dangerous to the liberties of a country, yet a few Troops, under certain circumstances, are not only safe, but indispensably necessary." He understood his task well: to spell out in compelling logic not only how many troops were needed, but why.

The commander in chief's report could be held up even today at the Army War College as a model of clear reasoning to determine the configuration of the nation's military forces. It contained a statement of the threat to the new country, an assessment of the security situation, an analysis of national military missions, and a description of strategic imperatives—and flowing from all that came the derivation of a defense establishment.

Threats there were, and imminent. For obvious starters, British forces remained in Canada and in posts around the Great Lakes. Spaniards controlled Florida, an ominous fact in that Madrid had steadfastly refused to recognize the United States even though both had simultaneously fought the British. Numerous warlike Indian tribes roamed the interior, evoking ancient fears of an ancient foe. And, especially worrisome to a people who had seen much war spill over from European hostilities, and who had just waged a conflict against a monarch, were the "ambitions" of European rulers.

Obvious also were the inherent strengths and weaknesses of the United States. The Atlantic Ocean provided a great shield from Europe, to be sure, while the vastness of the North American continent itself would give serious pause to any erstwhile military adventurer. On the other hand, vulnerabilities abounded. America's long sea coast could hardly be defended anywhere, much less everywhere. Similarly, the frontiers were simply too extensive to secure completely. The Hudson River, an Achilles' heel, afforded an inviting way for an enemy to cut the country in half. Aside from those geographic considerations, economic realities precluded any hope of matching European states in arms, especially in quality and size of navies.

Washington saw three straightforward national aims to be attained by the military establishment: defend the new country's territory and citizens, protect commerce and trade, and promote the opening of the West.

To achieve national aims is the purpose of national strategy. The general's proposed concept began with deterrence. Preparation for war, he always held, was the surest way to provide for peace. Accordingly, the military establishment should be powerful enough—and obviously so—to "awe the Indians" and to impress Europeans with America's serious intent to fight for its interests at home and abroad. However, should deterrence fail, the army had to be capable of defending the country. Certain vital positions and resources would have to be guarded constantly. Beyond that, there should be armed units on hand throughout the land, prepared to respond at once to invasion at any point, with others ready to be mobilized and marched rapidly to the scene of battle. Significantly, along with deterrence and defense, Washington added an offensive component to his overall view. The vast area west of the Appalachian barrier, won from France just two decades earlier and more recently wrested from England, would have to be consolidated. Military forces should march at once to take possession of territory along the Ohio River from Pittsburgh to the Mississippi, and of the forested wilderness northward all the way to Detroit. Only by such a deployment, he reasoned, could the United States preempt encroachment and promote settlement.

Converting his concept to a working military strategy, the commander in chief described a need to establish a network of fortifications and posts. They would comprise the first line of defense. Then it would be necessary to connect the network by road and water, thus permitting rapid movement of men and materiel from central locations to threatened areas, especially in the western forests washed by the Ohio River and its tributaries. In the East, he fastened his priority on the fortress at West Point. Just as that Hudson River stronghold had been considered "the key of America" during the war, so would it remain the center of gravity in any new conflict. Its capture by an enemy would have "the most ruinous Consequences," he proclaimed, putting at risk the very "preservation of the Union." It must absolutely be retained and kept strong. Meanwhile, the second tier of defense would be formed by mobilized forces, fighting units brought to arms rapidly and effectively at the outset of an emergency. To sustain operations required a system of supply depots, while meeting future requirements entailed setting up installations for research and development, places where weaponry could be produced on short notice. In sum, four pillars comprised his strategic concept for the defense of the continent: forces in being for immediate reaction, others having an efficient mobilization capability, a system permitting rapid movement to threatened areas, and a sustaining base.

The peace establishment George Washington envisioned was predicated on accomplishing that strategy. He divided his proposed structure into four major categories. "A regular and standing force" was the first. Regulars would defend the fortress at West Point, guard supply depots, and stabilize frontiers. "A well organized militia," uniformly structured in all the states, would then provide for local defense and mobilization. Third, weapons and equipment left over from the war should be gathered and preserved in a system of storage sites. There ought also to be an appropriate number of laboratories and foundries to manufacture weapons. Finally, there must be one or more military academies for the development of leaders. The general cautiously broached a fifth area for consideration: naval forces and a number of coastal defenses. The new country needed a navy to protect commerce and to support land operations along the seaboard, while the fortifications would aid in the general defense as well as provide protection for shipyards and port facilities. Pleading that naval matters were not in his area of responsibility, though, he declined to define those requirements any further.

To man forts and secure frontiers, Washington calculated that a minimum of 2,631 regulars must be kept in uniform, more if a single regiment should prove inadequate to patrol the southwestern frontier. Sensing that some in Congress would choke on that large a number, he argued that "it is better to reduce our force hereafter, by degrees, than to have it to increase after some unfortunate disasters."

These full-time soldiers would be "Continental Troops; looking up to Congress for their orders, their pay, and supplies of every kind." With the problems of command fresh in his mind, the general went into pages of detail concerning unit organization, operations, length of enlistments, rank, rotation, stationing, rations, etc. For instance, perhaps reflecting on recent disciplinary problems, he urged that rum—virtually a staple for soldiers of the day—be eliminated from the daily ration. And, thinking surely of some of the bumbling senior leaders he had been burdened with, he suggested that promotions be made with an eye toward competence rather than pure seniority—a much-needed reform whose time would not come until the twentieth century.

Most gingerly, for it constituted a political minefield, the Virginian approached the subject of the militia. During the Revolution, militia forces had proven both indispensable and intolerable. Washington's experiences had convinced him that, while no one seemed able to get along with militiamen, the nation could not get along without them. The entire system was in dire need of far-reaching reform. All citizens should have the responsibility to bear arms in the defense of the country, he said, but none should be able to do so on their own terms. There should be regulations prescribing a uniform system of training, organization, equipment, and mobilization. And the regulations should be strictly enforced. Moreover, the new nation should raise a "Continental Militia," a sort of Minuteman organization in every state able to respond rapidly anywhere the United States might be attacked, winning time for other forces to mobilize. These elite units would be made up of men between eighteen and twenty-five years old, carefully equipped and trained, "the Van and flower of the American Forces, ever ready and zealous to be employed" in battle. To provide the right backdrop for such a force, the country had to set a climate "making it universally reputable to bear Arms and disgraceful to decline having a share in the performance of Military duties."

Taking the long view, the commander in chief emphatically spoke of the need to perpetuate the development of leaders who were abreast of the demands of the profession of arms, especially in the more technical fields of artillery and engineers. The Herculean demands of building the Continental Army after the outbreak of war had convinced him that "an institution calculated to keep alive and diffuse the knowledge of the Military Art" was indispensable during times of peace to provide a steady flow of qualified leaders for war. Thus, he felt a compelling need for immediately founding an academy to achieve this crucial purpose.

Ever aware of fiscal and political limitations, Washington had wielded a practical pen. He admitted later that his recommendations "glided almost insensibly into what I thought *would,* rather than what I conceived *ought* to be a proper peace Establishment for this Country." His attempt to envision the future, then, represented what he thought to be within reach, not all that the new nation actually needed. He was a staunch Nationalist, but one rooted in reality.

Still, Washington had poured himself into the report. Lengthy and detailed, largely technical, often narrowly focused, it nonetheless conveyed much of the spirit of the man. Ranging from the somewhat whimsical (after soldiers had "frolicked a while among their friends" they would be ready to reenlist) to the slightly historical ("we might have recourse to the Histories of Greece and Rome in their most virtuous and Patriotic ages"), it ran a gamut of styles. But at bottom, it was a forthright effort to help define the new nation by giving shape and substance to its security needs. With his usual understatement, the general closed with, "Happy shall I be, if any thing I have suggested may be found of use in forming an Establishment which will maintain the lasting Peace, Happiness and Independence of the United States."

There was potential aplenty for his "Sentiments" to be useful indeed in shaping the country's course. His forecast of threats and strategic requirements would play out with surprising accuracy over the next thirty years, until well after James Madison's presidency in the War of 1812. And his prescription for preparedness would prove to be remarkably enduring, every bit as valid in 1883 or 1983 as it was in the year it was written. An effective active army backed up by ready reserve components; naval forces to secure freedom of the seas; defenses for the American homeland itself; a logistical complex to foster mobilization and deployment; a defense industry capable of rapid expansion; and a system of professional education for the development of leaders. Without question, the Father of our Country, his laurels already won in war, saw clearly what was entailed in winning the peace.

The question at the end of the Revolutionary War, therefore, was whether George Washington's personal vision could be translated into an American vision. Would his fellow revolutionaries rise above parochial concerns to seize the opportunity their wartime victory had given them? Could they forge the peace? Could they, too, glimpse the future?

The ageless words of King Solomon, addressing this central requirement of those who would govern, speak uncompromisingly from the pages of the Old Testament: "Where there is no vision, the people perish."

CHAPTER 4
DISINTEGRATION

Victory should spark elation. One would just naturally assume that buoyed spirits would have set an ebullient tone to the meetings of Congress as members went about their work of shifting from war to peace. But that was not the case. A Rip van Winkle, having fallen asleep right after watching the signing of the Declaration of Independence and then awakening seven years later to peer back into the windows of Philadelphia's State House, could have been excused for being confused over which side had won the recent war. The mood was angry and suspicious; the members partisan, divisive. Sectional jealousies and philosophical differences quickly overwhelmed the savoring of success.

Problems cascaded into Philadelphia. Some were of long standing, having been merely subdued by the far greater crisis of invasion. Others were new, born of opportunities suddenly opened to a new nation finding itself in charge of much of the continent. Centrifugal forces, countered ever since 1775 by the need to hang together, reasserted their former power to pull the alliance apart. The vacuum of the West created tensions and strains without precedent. Financial footing, always a cause for concern in a country rich in resources but poor in manufacturing structure, remained elusive. The form of government itself had to be sorted out—how much would be needed to assure the blessings of liberty without trampling those very liberties? And, seeming to touch on all other problems in that grim spring of 1783 was the question of the new nation's military establishment. It was a two-part issue: closing out the Continental Army and setting up the peacetime force.

30

DISINTEGRATION

Everyone knew that the Continental Army would be disbanded. It had been constituted for the war, and the war's end would be its end. On that there was no debate at all. But how? And when?

The soldiers wanted to go home. With the fighting over, they saw little reason to remain in camp waiting for a definitive treaty to arrive. But first they expected the pay due them; they did not want to go home as paupers. Furthermore, enlisted men were beginning to raise the issue of equity, asking why they were only to receive four months' pay while officers were to be given five years' worth. Congress also wanted the army dispersed. In camp and idle, armed men were a threat to the civil government, as the incident at Newburgh had so vividly illustrated. But until British troops actually sailed away, following receipt of the final peace accords, there lingered some possibility that fighting could flare again. Negotiations could always unravel, and erasing the American army entirely might entice London to military adventurism of some sort. Moreover, and ominously, Congress could not afford to keep its word to settle accounts with the men upon discharge. Promising was one thing; providing was another. The superintendent of finances did not even have enough cash to print certificates of promise for them.

Underscoring the urgency of the situation, word reached Philadelphia of rapidly deteriorating morale and discipline in the army. Washington reported in April that it was probably not in his power or that of Congress to hold the men much longer. Guards had to be increased to prevent rioting; large numbers of the men sulked and became insubordinate. Knowing that discharging the Continentals without paying them could well worsen the brittle circumstances, Congress settled on a devious solution. It voted in May to send most of the men home on furlough pending the arrival of a final treaty. The soldiers would in essence be away on unpaid leave, subject to being recalled immediately in an emergency. They would be discharged once the treaty arrived, with accounts to be settled thereafter. That solution took care of the remote threat of a resurgence in the fighting. It also took care of the embarrassing inability to provide the promised severance pay, for the departing troops were not technically being mustered out. However, such an obvious subterfuge was easily seen through. Around campfires, soldiers recognized that Congress was reneging on its recent commitment to them. They were furious. Officers submitted another memorial requesting a better understanding of their plight. A group of sergeants petitioned Congress, demanding reconsideration. Some of the Newburgh conspirators

31

considered resurrecting their attempt to mobilize the seething resentment. But Washington, with immense sadness, supported Congress, telling his soldiers they would have to trust in the ultimate sense of justice of the country and the government. No hostile movement could gain momentum in the face of the commander in chief's opposition. The exodus began, but in great bitterness. A farewell dinner, with Washington slated to be the honored guest, was canceled by the angered officers. There was no parting ceremony. Washington told Congress that one could not be held "under such peculiar circumstances." The Continental Army simply faded away.

By the middle of June, many of the campsites were already empty. Those soldiers remaining were consolidated mostly at West Point, where their numbers continued to dwindle through the summer and fall, aiming for a residue at the end of 1783 of about six hundred men to be consolidated into a single regiment under the command of General Knox. Each departing man was required to cut and stack two cords of firewood before he could leave, a last contribution to the defense of his country. Then, furlough in pocket, he headed home. Homecoming was not always, or even usually, happy. The postwar setting had grown nasty. Economic dislocation and the disruption caused by hostilities had led to a very troubled social environment in which the destitute veterans were not especially welcomed. Few were treated as returning heroes, some were even mobbed. But they blended into the population quickly enough—and quietly. The demobilization was completed with virtually no lasting repercussions save a simmering resentment in the breasts of many old soldiers against their "ungrateful countrymen." History has chosen to focus on the wartime record of the Continental Army, forgetting for the most part the painful final entry on its slate of sacrifices—and ignoring the abysmal way so many of those who had fought the war were treated once it was won. An anonymous soldier of another time scratched these lines on a guardshack wall:

> God and the soldier we all adore—
> In time of war, and not before.
> When the war is over and all things righted,
> God is forgotten, and the soldier slighted.

That disillusioned sentry could just as well have been writing for the men of the Continental Army as they concluded their uniformed service and melted back into the American countryside.

Having found a formula for removing its wartime armed forces, Congress turned to the still more controversial task of designing a peacetime structure. The starting point for discussion would be the report of Alexander Hamilton's committee. He and the other members had done their work thoroughly, and had solid recommendations to make. But they hesitated, sensing that the timing was not right, that their report would find a less than enthusiastic reception among the majority of their colleagues. And they were right. Events of the past several months had brought new faces to Philadelphia and a new balance of beliefs.

States, increasingly jealous of one another and still more so of the federal government, sent representatives charged to prevent any further accrual of central power. Massachusetts, for instance, replaced its entire delegation in June because the former one had voted with Nationalists on the issue of severance pay for discharged Continentals. The suspicious state then set up a committee to keep an eye on the new delegates lest they, too, become tainted. Eliphalet Dyer, who had shifted his position in March to help resolve the deadlock over military pay, found that his moral courage had cost him his political career in Connecticut. Anti-Nationalists were clearly gaining control.

That May, a well-intended but poorly timed initiative had boomeranged to elevate the intensity of antimilitary sentiments. Henry Knox and a group of fellow leaders established the Society of the Cincinnati, a fraternal organization designed to foster camaraderie among former officers. The name evoked the classical ideal set by Lucius Quinctius Cincinnatus, the Roman citizen-soldier who had modestly returned to the simple life of a farmer after leading his country's forces to victory. Washington happily accepted the presidency of the newly formed club, considering it also as a way to assist impoverished officers for whom the government had not provided. But others viewed the organization in an altogether different light. Already inclined to be distrustful of army officers, Anti-Nationalists perceived the society, especially its membership provisions, as an outright attempt to perpetuate an aristocracy. What Washington saw as fraternalism, they saw as an ominous source of political power. A wave of protest swept the land. Coming on the heels of the Newburgh Conspiracy, the imbroglio over the society magnified fears of a standing army in a democracy. Washington, helpless to counter the uproar, was much embarrassed by the self-inflicted controversy. The politician in him knew that the furor would be damaging to the effort to gain approval of a viable peace establishment.

Assessing the prevailing mood, Hamilton's committee pondered what to do. No one saw a good course. James Madison argued that delaying the submission of the report was the only practical option, but even so, he admitted, that course was fraught with grave risk. If a military structure were not voted on before the conclusion of a final treaty with Great Britain, Congress would likely adjourn with nothing at all on the books. And that would be worse than a watered-down version. Already, a disagreement between New York and Massachusetts over western lands had highlighted the urgency to come to grips soon with the vexing issue. Reluctant to raise the issue for fear of being rebuffed, but still more afraid to wait any longer, Hamilton submitted his report on 18 June 1783. That launched a prolonged debate over the shape of America's future military establishment, an often heated argument fated to consume an entire year.

Hamilton's report, cogent and comprehensive, would form the basis of Nationalist military policy until the ratification of the Constitution five years to the month later. He appended the reports of Washington and three other senior Continental general officers: the secretary at war, Benjamin Lincoln; the inspector general, Baron von Steuben; and the chief engineer, Louis DuPortail.[1] Not surprisingly, for they had each held positions of responsibility in building and employing the American army, all four were in general agreement on basic principles—and Hamilton's committee concurred. A peacetime force based on the report Hamilton turned in would have looked very much like the one described by Washington in his "Sentiments on a Peace Establishment." Actually, Hamilton took a somewhat more forceful position than Washington, calling for a larger standing army and placing less reliance on the militia. Whether he was entering the debate at a higher level expecting to bargain downward or whether he was taking a position of principle is unclear.

Before Hamilton could begin to address what kind of a military establishment Congress ought to adopt, though, he had to answer a far

---

1. Interestingly, underscoring the emphasis Washington placed on founding a military academy to produce homegrown professional military leaders to preclude having to rely on foreigners, two of the four had been recruited abroad. Steuben was especially adamant on the need for such an institution.

more fundamental question: did the Articles of Confederation give Congress the authority to create in peacetime any armed force at all? The Articles, framed in war for an alliance between the thirteen states, spoke in specific terms only of wartime. In a lengthy lead-in, Hamilton devoted himself compellingly to the proposition that it would be folly to interpret the Articles as requiring the United States to "wait for an actual commencement of hostilities before they would be authorized to prepare for defence, to raise a single regiment or to build a single ship." Since there was authority to wage war, he argued, there must be a commensurate authority, albeit derived, to maintain a peacetime establishment. Otherwise, he pointed out, "the United States would be obliged to *begin to create* at the very moment they would have occasion *to employ* a fleet and army." Hamilton's logic was too obvious to refute. He succeeded in setting the terms of the debate. Nevertheless, emotion remained more powerful than logic for some in Congress. Thus, while the argument in the months ahead would revolve primarily around the shape and size of military forces, the matter of basic authority would lurk just beneath the surface, remaining a sticky and unresolved point of contention.

Before representatives could so much as read the report, however, they were rudely reminded of their failure to provide for the army. Some eighty recruits of the Pennsylvania line, angered by the lack of support, marched in mutiny from Lancaster to Philadelphia to seek their pay at its source. Entering the city, they gathered additional numbers to their ranks, mostly new men as well. The entire body of troops then surrounded the State House. Emboldened by "spiritous drink from the tipling houses adjoining," as James Madison recorded, they shouted for redress—and gave Congress twenty minutes to meet their demands, or else. When that time limit passed without violence, members mustered the courage to walk out through the threatening mob, suffering only insults and a severe loss of dignity. Pennsylvania officials, worried about upcoming elections, refused to call out the militia to provide security, leaving the congressmen to care for themselves. Although Washington promptly sent a contingent of Continentals under Maj. Gen. Robert Howe to quell the mutiny, the Confederation Congress decided to quit the City of Brotherly Love. It would never return. The representatives set up operations in Princeton, New Jersey.

There, they began right away to bicker over a fresh issue: where to locate a national capital. Having long recognized that they comprised a government of few powers, they were now painfully aware that they were also without a home. For weeks, though, nothing much happened— regarding selection of a permanent seat of government or action on any other issue of importance. The rapid displacement from Philadelphia was one reason; difficulty maintaining a quorum was another. Some representatives had been recalled, some chose not to go immediately to Princeton, and others had quit in disgust over the constant haggling. Hamilton's report languished.

Hoping to spur consideration of the report, Nationalists in late July suggested inviting George Washington to Princeton to discuss military matters. That sparked a minor controversy. Ever suspicious, Anti-Nationalists saw (and not wholly inaccurately) that move as an attempt by Nationalists to use "the sunshine of the General's name" to ram their program through. They insisted that no mention of the purpose of the visit be put in the resolution inviting him. Then, in early August when Congress set about selecting a committee to confer with Washington, some members surfaced again the constitutional issue of whether Congress had authority to raise a peacetime armed force. Emotions ran so strong that lawmakers were unable to agree on whether even to "consider the question of a peace establishment." But other pressures forced a decision. The issue could not be dodged. If British forces vacated the western forts before American troops could get there, Indians would occupy or destroy them. That simply was not tolerable. Americans of every political persuasion believed the forts should be held, especially Forts Oswego, Niagara, Detroit, and Michilimackinac. In mid-August, delegates learned that New York, frustrated by Congress' inaction, was poised to open its own negotiations with the western Indians. That possibility struck at a real nerve, one more sensitive at the moment than the theoretical—and perhaps chimerical—question of authority to raise forces in peacetime. Several states (and not a few of their leading citizens) had a major stake in the opening of the West, and they did not want New York getting a jump on them. Massachusetts, whose claims to western lands overlapped New York's, was particularly indignant. Delegates had no recourse but to address a peace establishment. On 25 August, Washington rode into Princeton to a tumultuous reception by the townspeople.

Setting up his headquarters in a farmhouse near town, on a height dubbed Rocky Hill, the general began at once meeting with the congressional committee. But the business moved slowly. Washington had not much to add beyond those recommendations already on the table. Clarifying some details, stating slight opposition to an occasional point in Hamilton's proposal, explaining his own rationale—such discussions consumed scant time. The general did seize the opportunity to urge Congress to honor its pledges to pay the discharged soldiers, including grants of land in the western territories. That, in turn, led to discussions on opening the West, a subject always close to the Virginian's heart. Settlers needed protection, Indians would have to be pacified, boundaries had to be marked, squatters should be removed, territorial governments must be constituted. All of that, he reminded the committee, required troops. Regulars, preferably, but at least a revamped militia force.

The committee submitted the commander in chief's insights on 10 September. At about that same time, General Steuben, who had been sent to Canada on a fact-finding mission, reported a startling development. British forces occupying the forts around the Great Lakes showed no intention of leaving for at least a year, maybe longer. Though on one hand obliged to be furious that the redcoats were not turning over the newly acquired American lands, congressmen actually felt relief. The main motivation for raising an armed force just then had been the requirement to occupy those forts rather than to forfeit them to the tribes in the area. Steuben's news removed the urgency to act immediately. Hamilton's report was placed on the schedule for debate—but for some six weeks later.

Meanwhile, after learning that British general Sir Guy Carleton was making preparations to evacuate his forces from the bastion in New York City, Congress directed the discharge of all those Continentals who had been furloughed. No funds were available to pay them. Putting his personal chagrin aside, Washington issued farewell orders, urging his former comrades-in-arms to comport themselves as good citizens, despite their disappointments, and to trust in the good intentions of the government. Dispersed as they were around the country, the men were in no position to do otherwise. Several officers not yet mustered out did respond in pointed coolness to their commanding general, but the matter ended there.

On 23 October, Congress finally met to consider a peace establishment. Much had happened since Hamilton and his committee had started work on the subject six months earlier, all of which had weakened Nationalist chances of obtaining the kind of force they envisioned. Foreseeing the outcome, in fact, many had already left Congress, to be replaced generally by Anti-Nationalists. Those new members were opposed to a strong central government and sought to avoid a standing army of any size. They were determined—and they controlled Congress. Typical of them was Elbridge Gerry, who had been among the new delegation sent by angry leaders in Massachusetts. Writing to John Adams, he exclaimed "how ridiculous" it would be "to exchange a British Administration, for one that would be equally tyrannical, perhaps much more so!" After two days' debate, all that the members could manage to agree on was that "some garrisons" must be manned in time of peace.

A week later, a messenger brought the long-anticipated definitive treaty—the Treaty of Paris—signed by Benjamin Franklin, Thomas Jefferson, and John Jay in a small hotel in the French capital on 3 September 1783. The war was over! Congress reacted the way Madison and others had predicted. It immediately stopped work, leaving undone every pressing decision, including pay for soldiers and the composition of the peace establishment. Announcing that it would convene next in Annapolis, Maryland, Congress adjourned. Members quickly departed Princeton. A flabbergasted Washington wrote that their flight came "unexpectedly and surprisingly to me."

The war was not quite over for George Washington. He had one symbolic and intensely personal act to perform before he could return for good to Mount Vernon. The last piece of American land in the original thirteen colonies still held by foreign troops was New York City. It was also the first place the British had wrested from Washington. Having bettered him in battle there in 1776, the king's forces had maintained a lodgment in the city ever since. Returning in triumph on the heels of the departing British would conclude the war for the general. Sending his baggage to Mount Vernon, he rode to West Point, where he joined the shrunken Continental Army to await the sailing of New York's occupiers.

On 25 November 1783, as the last redcoats were rowing out to ships in the harbor, Washington led a victory procession into the city. The thrill of the moment could not be diminished by the stark scenes bearing testimony to an occupation of seven years, or by charred ruins from the great fire that had destroyed so much of the city early in that occupation. Following several days of ceremony and tying up loose ends, and after English sails had disappeared from the harbor, Washington arranged a final farewell with his officers. In Fraunces Tavern, at noon on 4 December, the remnants of the Continental Army's leadership assembled for one last meeting with the commander who had led them for so long. The group was small, only four of seventy-three generals who had served with him, and a similar smattering of other ranks. Washington himself was all but overcome with emotion, and soon so were the others. A toast, tears all around, embraces—and he was gone.

Congress had reconvened in Annapolis, though still homeless and without a quorum. Washington traveled there to formally resign the commission that body had given him on a long-ago June day when the Continental Army had existed only on paper—and the United States itself had been hardly more than a concept. While the commander in chief made his way to Annapolis, slowed by the desire of every citizen along the way to see and hear and touch him, the delegates fretted over the proper way to conduct the meeting. They eventually agreed to a plan devised largely by Thomas Jefferson, who had returned from Paris in time to resume his seat as a representative from Virginia. Washington would enter "the Hall of Congress" and take a seat facing the members, it was decreed. When recognized by the president of Congress, he would rise and bow in salute, demonstrating military deference to civilian leadership. The members would acknowledge his salute by tipping their hats, not by returning the bow. Then the general would tender his commission with a short address, followed by an acceptance speech from the president. It went as planned. Two days before Christmas, the tall Virginian strode to his chair facing a body of about twenty representatives, virtually the entire government of the new nation. The president at the time happened to be Thomas Mifflin, a former major general in Washington's forces—and one of the leaders of the cabal to replace him back in the winter of 1777–78. The ceremony was brief and emotionally jarring. Tears sprang to the eyes of participants as Washington ended his remarks: "Having now finished the work assigned me, I retire from the great theater of action, and, bidding an affectionate farewell to this august body under whose orders I have so long acted, I here offer my commission, and take my leave of all the employments of public life." Then he was away, galloping free for his home on the Potomac, a private citizen for the first time in nearly nine years. The rather powerless body of men he had left behind in Annapolis was now totally responsible for the current and future security of the United States.

For quite some time the representatives did little to discharge that responsibility. No one had much stomach for opening an issue sure to be intractable. But it would not go away. Early in 1784, New York officially demanded to know what Congress was going to do about the forts in the western part of the state, threatening again to make its own accommodations with the Indians. In March, Congress accepted Virginia's cession (for the second time) of its claims to lands north and west of the Ohio River, with the obvious expectation that the Confederation government would provide for their governance. The issue had to be faced. Clearly, as all well understood, the West had to be attended to—and to do so meant raising armed forces. Even those who were unalterably opposed to a standing army recognized that simple imperative. Which posed the dilemma: how could the new nation do what it had to do and yet avoid raising an army? How could Anti-Nationalists remain true to their principles and yet still meet the obvious needs for defense? A committee, composed mostly of solid Anti-Nationalists, was appointed to try to find answers. It reported back in early April. It attempted to draw a line separating the overall defense establishment addressed by Hamilton's committee a year earlier from the narrow matter of finding troops to occupy forts in the North and West and to guard the country's stores of military materiel. Some garrisons, yes, but there should be absolutely "no standing army." The committee suggested using General Knox's troops at West Point, as well as a few Continentals then at Fort Pitt—the storied western bastion guarding the gateway to the West, the spot where the Monongahela and the Allegheny flow together to form the Ohio. Still, this could only be a stopgap measure. For the future, the committee cautioned, a real force would have to be constituted, one of at least a thousand men enlisted for three years.

A thousand men? Three years? However it was cloaked, that sounded like a standing army! Factions lined up at once. Arguments boiled, nearly precipitating duels. Positions hardened, despite frantic behind-the-scenes maneuvering to find a way to reach a compromise.

In the meantime, Nationalists elsewhere had remained rather quiet, having for the most part exhausted themselves in the vain attempt to buck the nationwide tide of antimilitary sentiment. General von Steuben, though, took one last stab by trying to go over the heads of congressmen directly to the citizens. In a letter addressed to the "Inhabitants of the United States," he laid out in words blunt and unpolitic the need for a "Military Establishment for the United States." He ripped into the cherished militia forces, showing mathematically that reliance on the "Militia draughts recommended by Congress" would prove to be prohibitively expensive as well as impractical. On the other hand, he had a solution that he believed would be quite effective, an establishment organized as a legion, which he painstakingly described. Closing with the recognition that his recommendation would be attacked as a standing army, the adoptive American addressed the issue head-on. "Yes Fellow Citizens I admit it—it is a Standing Army, but composed of your brothers and sons. Can you require or conceive a better security—are they not your natural guardians?" He found expected support among Nationalists, Washington included, but it appears that Congress simply shrugged off the effort. Nothing at all came of the baron's attempt in 1784, but his idea of a legion would bear splendid fruit just a decade later.

On 25 May, with ten days to go to adjournment, Congress began debate on the committee report. There was some hope that the vehemence of previous discussions would nudge members toward a less unbending stance. The second day, though, Elbridge Gerry took the floor to harangue the assemblage with a thumping sermon on the evils of a standing army. Any movement toward compromise was thereby ended, as his tirade solidified all the New England states. They would not accept permitting Congress to call a force into being. The central and southern states, on the other hand, were willing to accept a federal force, although they had qualms about its funding. Standing apart from either group, New York would hear of nothing less than an agreement granting it sole control of forts in its own western reaches. No one would give ground. Vote after vote ended the same way; no faction could muster a majority.

Finally, on 2 June 1784, Congress acted. It terminated the service of all remaining regulars save eighty—twenty-five at Fort Pitt and fifty-five at West Point—to guard the nation's war reserves. None were allocated to secure the third major depository, located at Springfield, Massachusetts. By that date the only person working in the Department of War was the chief clerk, Joseph Carleton. All the others had resigned, and Congress had left the positions vacant. A handful of logistical officers stayed on, devoted mostly to trying to find buyers for excess equipment left over from the Revolution. Henry Knox, the senior officer still in uniform, dutifully discharged the last vestiges of the Continental Army, and then resigned his own commission to return to civil life.

Eighty men. A handful of officers. A clerk. Stacks of used equipment. An era had ended in disintegration.

The next day, Congress *recommended* that four states—New York, Pennsylvania, Connecticut, and New Jersey—raise a total of seven hundred men for a year to tend to the country's interests in the West. It directed the nonexistent secretary at war to see to the details, and ordered three hundred of the men yet to be raised to accompany negotiators being sent out to meet with the western tribes. Then it adjourned.

A new era had begun in disarray.

PART 2
THE HUMILIATION
OF WEAKNESS

By 1787 many Americans viewed the army and the defective policy which had created it as the very symbol of the inadequacy of government under the Articles of Confederation.

—Historian Richard H. Kohn, in *Eagle and Sword.*

CHAPTER 5
CONFEDERATION AND PERPETUAL UNION

The Continental Congress went out of business on 1 March 1781. The next day the same members met in the same place, but as "The United States in Congress Assembled," operating under a charter grandly designated as the "Articles of Confederation and perpetual Union between the [thirteen] states."

Technically, it was the Second Continental Congress that had ceased to function. The First had met at Carpenter's Hall in Philadelphia from 5 September to 26 October 1774. Delegates had assembled there to discuss American grievances with London's fiscal and coercive policies, and to consider joint action to obtain redress. They had exaggerated somewhat in styling their meeting "continental," for only twelve colonies had sent representatives, with Georgia, Canada, the Floridas, and Nova Scotia being the most evident absentees. Nevertheless, they fired a warning shot in the form of a statement of the rights of Americans, and they proclaimed a joint boycott of trade with England to last until those rights were honored. Members announced they would meet again in Philadelphia the following spring to contemplate whatever response the king and Parliament might have made to their demands.

Men from the same twelve colonies (Georgia would join four months later, the thirteenth and last colony to do so) convened on 10 May, sitting this time in the Pennsylvania State House. But their world and its problems were no longer the same. Fighting had flared between redcoats and Minutemen on 19 April, three weeks earlier. When British forces marched from Boston into the countryside to capture supplies stored at Concord, they ran into a buzz saw of spontaneous resistance. Armed citizens from all around New England had rushed to the scene, where a clamorous concentration of Yankees faced the shaken English troops, who were ensconced behind barricades in the city of Boston. Blood had been spilled—lots of it. An undeclared state of war existed. The Second Continental Congress found that its first order of business was to address the explosive and unforeseen resort to arms.

What should the assembly do? In fact, what *could* it do? The representatives had been sent to Philadelphia to ponder taxes and the like, not to confront the specter of rebellion. They had no legal basis to address war. For that matter, their very meeting was itself an extralegal act, if not outright illegal. But such distinctions did not deter them—they boldly took up the issue of war without any apparent deep concern over seeking authority to do so. Their options were three, and clear: disassociate their work in Philadelphia from the activities of rebels outside Boston, provide the insurrection moral support only, or embrace the rebellion wholeheartedly. There was a little hesitation, but not much. They chose the third course.

Deciding to wage war against the mother country in the name of all the colonies was one thing. The next question was how. In addition to lacking legal authority, Congress had neither money nor forces nor arms nor anything else essential to implement its decision. What it did have was *moral* authority—and the impetus of the war fever sweeping the land.

Congress seized the flapping reins of revolution. It acted with a celerity that would be remarkable in any governing body at any time, but that even in retrospect appears simply incredible for one starting from a dead stop and having no operating procedures at all. In six blurring weeks, the Second Continental Congress put the colonies in a state of military readiness, sought allies, adopted the armed units around Boston as the Continental Army, selected senior officers, appointed Congressman George Washington as commander in chief, wrote rules for the army, set strategic priorities, raised and sent to New England units from other states, decided on the approach to take toward London, and voted a line of credit to finance the conflict. That amazing performance—achieved in an era when messages were transmitted at the speed of horse or sail—has never been topped in more than two centuries of subsequent American history.

CONFEDERATION AND PERPETUAL UNION

As 1775 rolled into 1776 with the war showing no signs of reaching an early end, and with the initial glow of enthusiasm dulled by the bloody and expensive realities of battle, America's ability to wage a sustained military effort revealed its first major fault. The country had no central executive power. The various colonies were conducting the war. They provided men and materiel and money, along with instructions on their use. Congress was cast in a coordinating role. For all its power of moral suasion, the assembly in Philadelphia had no constituted authority whatsoever. Some historians have described the organization as a council of ambassadors from the several states, a description growing increasingly apt as Congress lost the services of such strong leaders as Washington, Jefferson, Franklin, and Adams. The passage of time and the erosion of fervor in the states were uncovering the potentially terminal consequences of the patriots' half-united condition. Some had seen the difficulty from the first. Benjamin Franklin, for one, had long urged a fuller form of union. He had plied his colleagues with copies of a constitution he had written, called the "Articles of Confederation and Perpetual Union." Congress considered his plan in January 1776, but set it aside. Union and independence were too closely linked in the minds of Americans, and the decision for independence had not yet crystallized. But as events of that year led inexorably toward a break from allegiance to the Crown, so too did they tug states toward forming a firmer linkage.

Richard Henry Lee of Virginia stood up in the chamber on 7 June 1776 to move for consideration of declaring independence. He called also for a formal joining of the thirteen states. The time for both steps was right. Congress appointed a committee of one delegate from each state to prepare a draft constitution. Meanwhile, a second committee, headed by Thomas Jefferson, was put to work drafting a statement declaring independence. John Dickinson, a lawyer and militia leader from Pennsylvania (with ties also to Delaware), led the group preparing the charter of union. He was a good choice, a respected theoretician who had previously drafted many of Congress' significant papers. Writing the bulk of the document himself, Dickinson patterned his effort on Benjamin Franklin's earlier version, to include taking its title. He also used as a model the procedures worked out over time in meetings of the Continental Congress. His draft was submitted to Congress on 12 July, ten days after that body had voted for independence, and a week after Dickinson himself had left. He had refused to sign the declaration, believing that the country must have a central government before it would be able to handle independence.

Designed largely to meet wartime exigencies, Dickinson's draft gave Congress substantial powers, but with one serious limitation: it denied the central government the authority to raise money. Congress would have remained dependent upon the states for funding. Nevertheless, rapid passage seemed assured because of the virtual unanimity over the need to present a united front in the war effort.

But the document contained an unanticipated seed of self-destruction. The two aims of the Revolution—independence and territorial expansion—came into direct confrontation in one of Dickinson's provisions. He and his committee had proposed that Congress should have the power to set the western boundaries of the states, to handle land grants beyond those boundaries, and to decide upon the establishment of any new states to be carved out of new lands. However, the opening of an American empire in the West would trample on aspirations several states held for an empire there of their own. Various members had other disagreements with one provision or another, but the issue concerning the West proved to be the toughest to solve. Because unanimous approval was needed for implementation, representatives prepared an amended version and presented it in late August. That new effort, too, failed to satisfy everyone, forcing still more delay. Then British victories in New York and New Jersey prompted Congress to flee Philadelphia in September for safer lodgings in Baltimore, further postponing attempts to find compromise language until the spring of 1777.

With Congress by then back in Philadelphia, members approached the matter again. But state jealousies eroded slowly. Representatives wrestled with the constitution, endlessly it sometimes seemed, making a series of hard-fought changes, most tending to reinforce the relative strength of the states. They removed the provision allowing the central government to set western boundaries. Summer passed. The British seized Philadelphia that fall, putting Congress to flight once more and causing further delay in the agonizing attempt to forge acceptable provisions. However, the low ebb of the nation's fortunes, presenting a real threat of defeat, made the delegates more flexible. Progress became imperative. After coming to rest in York, Pennsylvania, they concluded their work, agreeing to the Articles of Confederation on 15

November 1777. Nearly a year and a half had been lost since Dickinson had submitted his draft. Delegates sent the document to the states for ratification, with high hopes of gaining acceptance by the following spring. In a forwarding letter, they admitted that the Articles were imperfect, and warned that every state would find something in them it did not like. But parochial concerns, they pleaded, should be set aside for the greater benefit of the country. Their hopes were in vain.

Most states concurred that year, though not without some arm-twisting by proponents. Representatives from eight of them ceremoniously signed the Articles on 8 July 1778. But Maryland, New Jersey, and Delaware held out through the summer, raising again the issue of western boundaries. Those three, having no lands of their own in the West, but with influential citizens who harbored ambitions there, insisted that Congress should be given the authority to establish the limits of states beyond the frontier. Leaders from around the country urgently appealed to the "patriotism and good sense" of the three dissenting states, gaining grudging acceptance that winter from Delaware and New Jersey. Maryland remained unmoved.

Sensing that Maryland would never bend, Virginia's delegation proposed in the spring of 1779 that the union proceed with just twelve states. While there was some support for that stance, the general feeling was that an incomplete union would be more dangerous than the ad hoc arrangements that had served the thirteen states for some four years. Furthermore, Virginia's envied status as the state with the most valid claims to the largest part of the West left suspicions smoldering in several places. There the matter simmered for nearly another year. Finally, in February 1780, in an effort to move toward accommodation and to cement the union, New York offered to give up some of its shakier claims to western lands. That small crack created movement. A special committee appointed to search for solutions recommended in July that Congress ask all states with claims to make "a liberal surrender" of them. Desperate in that grimmest of years, the "black year" of the Revolution, Congress did so in September. Virginia, pushed by Thomas Jefferson, agreed on the second day of 1781 to cede its territory north and west of the Ohio River. Connecticut followed suit. With that the impasse was over. In February, Maryland authorized its delegation to sign. On 2 March 1781 the Articles of Confederation became effective. It had been a long and painful birth.

Philadelphia was the scene of a rousing celebration after criers announced the news. Bells rang, cannon boomed, leading citizens drank a toast with the president of Congress, fireworks lit the evening sky. The next day's *Pennsylvania Packet* reported that "every manifestation of joy [was] shown on the occasion." The paper also recorded that "The *Ariel* frigate, commanded by the gallant Paul Jones, fired a *feu-de-joye,* and was beautifully decorated with a variety of streamers in the day, and ornamented with a brilliant appearance of lights in the night." By adopting the Articles of Confederation, the writer continued, "has the union, began by necessity, been indissolubly cemented."

For the remainder of the war and beyond, the nation—now a formal confederation called the United States of America—would be headed by the United States in Congress Assembled. Although the Confederation Congress is often referred to in common usage by the same title as its predecessor, the Continental Congress, they were distinctly different entities. The distinction is important. The Articles of Confederation were in fact a written constitution promulgated and agreed to by all thirteen states. The Continental Congress, on the other hand, had been constituted only in the minds of men, ratified only in popular acceptance. It had been held together by the glue of necessity, by the recognition among revolutionaries of the stark choice between hanging together or hanging separately—and by the indomitable will of a handful of patriots who persevered through all adversity.

The Continental Congress had proven to be an effective instrument to launch rebellion and to set directions, but it had turned out to be woefully inept as a structure for a wartime government. It contained two embedded flaws, either of which would have been fatal to any such ambition: in addition to its inability to tax, it had no executive power. Unfortunately, the Articles of Confederation inherited those same two mortal defects. Men saw the shortcomings at the time, but were powerless to make repairs. As soon as the document had been ratified, a committee composed of James Varnum, James Duane, and James Madison, three ardent Nationalists, set to work to prepare a plan to provide Congress the power it would need to implement the Articles. The three reported that an amendment was needed to allow Congress to use the army and navy to enforce its decisions on the states. Being in the process of overthrowing one government that had tried just that, the states were in no mood to agree. Fear of "executism" was too strong. The report was suppressed.

Although evidence abounded to warn Americans of the dangers flowing from such critical omissions, a compelling case to that effect was never made during the writing and ratification process. While many—principally Nationalists—had found the argument convincing all along, and never missed a chance to say so, others—Anti-Nationalists for the most part—chose simply to ignore the facts, preferring to accept the risks inherent in a weak confederation rather than to face what they considered to be the graver dangers of a strong central government. Most Americans, though, probably failed to fully discern that the Revolution had been kept afloat in large measure by fiscal legerdemain and foreign loans, and that George Washington had been, in effect if not in law, the wartime executive for military affairs. Indeed, while no one in or near the Confederation Congress in the last two or three years of the war could have avoided learning of the Articles' fiscal shortcomings, members themselves might very well have missed recognizing the general's unique role. His constant deference to Congress, coupled with the fading of the fighting after the Battle of Yorktown in 1781 and the constant turnover among delegates, masked not only the fact but the significance as well.

At first, in the heady days of 1775, Congress had attempted to run the war. But members, serving on a multitude of committees, soon became overloaded. As Washington proved to be both trustworthy and competent, delegates tended more and more to rely on his judgment. They even once granted him emergency powers afterward called "dictatorial," a remarkable step for a body of men known to possess an almost congenital horror of a "man on horseback." To be sure, some worried that Washington was growing too powerful, that the child was outstripping the parent, and they took pains from time to time to raise the point. On such instances, the commander in chief normally ignored the barbs. Occasionally, though, he lost his patience. Many in Congress "seem not to have any conception of the difficulty and perplexity attending those who are to execute," he snapped after one particularly galling episode of interference. "In a word," he added, unable to conceal his irritation, "when they are at a distance, they think it is but to say Presto begone, and everything is done." The ultimate result of the so-called Conway Cabal, an abortive attempt by some congressmen and others to replace Washington with Horatio Gates, underscores his singular status. The affair itself actually strengthened the Virginian, for it obliged the revolutionaries to recognize that he was as close to irreplaceable as a human being could be. In a very real way, George Washington was the Revolution.

Congress established four executive departments in early 1781: war, marine, finance, and foreign affairs. That was an overdue move to make the government more efficient, but it did not diminish the commander in chief's clout. For one thing, it occurred as the war was entering its final phase, the wait for peace. For another, the individuals involved were Washington's supporters. Robert Morris, who became the superintendent of finances, handled marine (naval) matters as an added duty. The war office remained vacant until October, when Congress appointed fat, gouty, lethargic Maj. Gen. Benjamin Lincoln. An administrator, he was not expected to present a challenge to Washington. Nor did he. Furthermore, as Congress weakened progressively over the years, it became less and less inclined to dispute the executive leadership of the commander in chief on matters military.

The United States in Congress Assembled sat in constituted authority during the final three years of the Revolution. It received the grand news from Yorktown—with members literally passing the hat among themselves to get money to pay the expenses of the bearer of those tidings. It wrangled long over the shape of the peacetime military, and presided over the dissolution of the Continental Army. It pondered the pitfalls and opportunities of the West, and worried always over ways to raise money. It handled the diplomatic tasks associated with sealing the peace with England. At the beginning of the summer of 1784 it faced a new role, one for which it possessed neither adequate machinery nor pertinent experience: steering the country through what everyone knew would be a most critical period, its initial peacetime years.

Having already been found wanting, and no longer bolstered by the binding cement of war or the reinforcing steel of General Washington, the union based on the Articles of Confederation should realistically have been expected to encounter traumatic times. For the Confederation, the phrase "Perpetual Union" rang with a hollow sound.

CHAPTER 6
THE BASTARD CHILD

The army spawned by the Confederation in the summer of 1784 was fated to have a less than glorious life. Historian Richard Kohn described it as "the bastard child of quarrelsome, uncertain congressional parents." Its bloodlines were indeed suspect. States did not control it, and soldiers were recruited for duty outside their own areas—so it was certainly not a militia force. Enlistments were for short terms, and the states furnished soldiers only if they chose—so it was certainly not a regular force. Few members of Congress rode away from Annapolis pleased with the "poor expedient" they had constructed as a compromise solution to answer the security needs of the new nation.

Among those few was Elbridge Gerry. Back in Boston, he gloated over his successful efforts to block the raising of a standing army. If the government truly required a force to guard depots and for service on the frontier, he proclaimed, its size "ought to be limited by an express article of the Confederation." Massachusetts legislators supported him, and further instructed their delegates to the Confederation Congress to "prevent the raising of a standing army of any number, on any pretense whatever, in time of peace."

Meanwhile, the envisioned 700-man force began to form, after a fashion. Pennsylvania, more immediately concerned than others by the Indian menace, attempted right away to raise its quota of 260 men, and eventually did. New Jersey started that summer as well, but was unable to meet its goal of 110 soldiers. Connecticut, with an allocation of 165 men, could not even begin enlisting them for several months because its legislature had adjourned before learning of Congress' request. New York, angered that Congress had not authorized the use of state troops, refused to provide any at all. Since Pennsylvania had the largest quota, it had the privilege of naming the commanding officer of the regiment. It designated Josiah Harmar, a battle-tested and respected thirty-one-year-old veteran of the Revolution, and the trusted personal secretary of Thomas Mifflin, the president of Congress. Harmar received an imposing commission as "Lt. Col. Commandant of the United States Infantry Regt. and also Commander of the Army." Trouble was, he was out of the country, having been sent to England to deliver the ratified copy of the peace treaty. The naming of other officers had to be delayed until his return. All in all, it was a most inauspicious start. The better part of 1784 was gone by the time just a fraction of the regiment could take to the field. And a fraction it would remain.

In its 3 June resolution creating what it termed "the Peace Establishment," Congress had been very specific about the regiment's intended purpose. The unit was "immediately and indispensably necessary for taking possession of the western posts, as soon as evacuated by the troops of his britannic Majesty, for the protection of the northwestern frontiers, and for guarding the public stores." Immediately and indispensably necessary. Strong words, those. And widely accepted as true. By mid-1784 the northwestern frontier had begun to loom as the country's most pressing problem. Potential danger lurked elsewhere, certainly—along the southwestern frontier, for instance, where Spaniards and Indians opposed United States expansion. But those other areas were for the moment relatively quiet. Active preparations for their security could be postponed, trusting to luck that they would remain calm. Not so in the troubled land beyond the Alleghenies.

But along with problems beckoned opportunity. Even in the midst of the Revolutionary War, the immensely fertile lands in the West had continued to exert an almost hypnotic pull on Americans. War's end sharply increased that pull. Settlers, many of them former soldiers with land grants, streamed through passes in the mountains. Fortune hunters coveted the forest and its furs—a beaver pelt was the most valuable commodity on the continent. Adrenaline ran in the veins of land speculators. Owners turned their attention to properties long ignored. Congress itself saw fiscal salvation in selling tracts in its vast new national domain. Since Congress had never acted on Virginia's 1781 cession of western territories, the state again offered them up in March 1784. Selling those fertile lands was a way for the debt-torn central government to make money. Maybe the only way. Delegates did not delay this time. On 23 April they passed an ordinance providing for eventual statehood for lands in the Ohio Valley. An appreciable number of congressmen sought personal wealth as well. Many became involved in land speculation. Owners, settlers, merchants, officials, speculators—though all saw a region rich with promise, they found it also racked with turmoil. Squatters occupied innumerable sites; land claims overlapped confusingly; British officials agitated to maintain a large unoccupied buffer between the Ohio River and Canada; Spanish officials sought to block American use of the Mississippi River; rambunctious Kentuckians rumbled about independence even as they demanded protection; Indians remained sullen if not outright hostile. Still and all, promise outweighed problems.

George Washington's personal activities in the months after he hung up his uniform provide a glimpse of the West's magnetic influence on the times. Within weeks of returning to Mount Vernon he had begun to try to update and sort out his tangled interests on the frontier. They had suffered grievously from neglect during the long years of the Revolution. The manager of a mill Washington owned in western Pennsylvania was much in arrears with the general's share of income; thirty thousand acres with a fifteen-mile frontage on the Ohio River might bring in a handsome rent; the legal titles to his western holdings needed clarification in light of new laws; tenants of some tracts had refused to pay rents; rival claimants in certain areas had put some of his land up for sale; and so it went. The whole mess, he saw, could only be straightened out on the ground and in person. Washington set out in September on a 640-mile inspection tour. The trip brought back memories—and opened windows on the future.

The site of old Fort Necessity—where a young Washington had first tasted military defeat, and which was now his property—he reckoned would be "a very good stand for a tavern." No sentimentality there. The mill, which he found had grown dilapidated without proper care from its overseer, held less promise for future profit. Washington tried to sell it and its related property, but could find a buyer for only one cow. A band of Scotch-Irish squatters occupied one of his tracts, a twenty-eight-hundred-acre piece along a stream emptying into the Ohio River.

Negotiations with them proved fruitless. They had muscled in some ten years earlier, having forcibly displaced a former tenant. They would neither move nor pay rent—and the Virginian had no way to enforce his rights, except to sue them in a regional court. He eventually did, but with scant hope of success. He also attempted to visit his acreage fronting the Ohio, a long journey farther downriver. After making arrangements to borrow a boat and an escort of a handful of soldiers from Fort Pitt, he had to cancel his plans. Restless Indians in the area made so distant a trip by so small a group too hazardous. Having been stricken with the land speculation bug ever since his youthful forays beyond the mountains of Virginia, Washington came to a very reluctant decision. Since he would be unable to oversee his lands himself, as the chaotic situation so obviously demanded, he would have to consider selling them—particularly those in western Pennsylvania, where settlers were clustered relatively thickly but lived pretty much at the edge of law.

Nevertheless, the trip left him stimulated and forward looking. He returned to Mount Vernon with three related thoughts churning in his mind: the opening of the West, driven by the spontaneous migration of people, was proceeding much more rapidly than anyone had anticipated; that migration called for supporting highways and waterways; and if not handled properly the western settlers could coalesce into a nation apart.

Colonists of old, hacking out an existence on the uncivilized frontier of the Atlantic seaboard, had evolved into a people quite distinct from their English relatives. In just the same way, settlers in the West could develop an identity different from their countrymen in the thirteen states. Over the mountains, they were cut off from the rest of America. If left isolated, Washington worried, they might decide to break away to carve out their own independent republic. That was not mere hypothetical musing, for it was not at all certain at the time that the thirteen original states would themselves successfully resist the tug of separatist tendencies, bound as they were only in a "firm league of friendship" by the Articles of Confederation. In fact, one could readily hear talk of the forming of a new state around the forks of the Ohio, where settlers who had considered themselves Virginians had become Pennsylvania citizens by virtue of an agreement between the two states in 1779. They would have named it Westsylvania. A similar scheme by speculators, before the Revolution spiked their plans, would have created a state there called Vandalia. Settlers in what is now a part of Kentucky petitioned Congress in 1775 to be admitted as Transylvania, the fourteenth colony. Farther south, in the western reaches of North Carolina, secessionists proclaimed the independent state of Franklin, but could not make it stick. Nowhere in the western lands did full allegiance to the United States exist. The people inhabiting those wild regions were inclined to be less than admiring of the ways of the East anyway, evidenced by the very fact of their migration. Mercantile interests of the seaboard and pioneer values beyond the mountains were in many ways incompatible, while matters of life and death differed greatly depending on which side of the slopes one lived. Crediting his own firsthand observations, Washington cautioned that the westerners "stand as it were upon a pivot." They could turn either way, he added, with the "touch of a feather."

The Virginia planter did note one element working temporarily to limit separatist pressures in the West. Trade. Settlers in the landlocked interior needed access to markets. The two obvious routes to the outside were the Great Lakes-St. Lawrence waterway to the Atlantic and the Ohio-Mississippi river passage to the Gulf of Mexico. However, British in the north and Spanish in the south blocked those two exits, ironically helping the United States to consolidate its hold on its western territories. Washington believed that the United States must hasten to take advantage of the time it had thus been granted by the obtuseness of those two European powers. Before making "any stir about the navigation of the Mississippi," he said, the country should turn to "the arts of peace." He defined those arts as facilitating east-west communications by "clearing rivers, building bridges, and establishing conveniences for traveling, etc." In short, forge land and water links between the eastern seaboard and the Ohio Valley. Bind the people of the frontier to those in the East. Keep them Americans all. Rely on joint commercial interests to counter the inevitable cultural divide of the Appalachians.[1]

1. In 1784, young Andrew Jackson was seventeen years old, and bore a still vivid scar from a British saber slash received three years earlier when he was a Revolutionary War soldier. He was soon to move over the mountains to become one of those "different" westerners. His name was destined one day to define an age and a political power Washington had so uncomfortably sensed.

His remarkable breadth of vision, demonstrated so often in wartime, remained continental in scope.

But not even the former commander in chief could escape parochialism altogether. In putting his vision into practical plans he reverted to being a Virginian. One proposal was to cut a route from the Maryland and Virginia tidewater westward to the Monongahela River south of Pittsburgh. A network of roads, portages, and waterways would originate with a canal at the rapids of the Potomac River, not far from Mount Vernon. Another concept, a rival route in New York, recommended following the Hudson and Mohawk rivers. Thomas Jefferson urged Washington to throw the weight of his prestige behind the Virginia effort quickly before the northerners got the jump on them. For the time being the British refusal to evacuate their garrison at Fort Oswego on Lake Erie stymied progress on the Hudson-Mohawk line, but that could change suddenly. Washington agreed with Jefferson, and turned his awesome energy to canal building.

Lieutenant Colonel Josiah Harmar did not have the luxury of contemplating such grand visions. Upon returning to America that summer, he immersed himself in the extraordinarily detailed and complex business of putting together the new nation's first army. And it was not going well. To begin with, he was not quite sure who he worked for. Both the Confederation Congress and the Executive Council of Pennsylvania issued him instructions, so he dutifully reported to both. Recruiting was complicated by uncertainties over whether the states or Congress would pay the costs of enlisting the men, while the quality of those accepted to the colors was sacrificed to the urgency of filling the ranks in time to march west that year. Perhaps half the recruits were of foreign birth, with most being Irish—American citizens were not attracted by the pay of six and two-thirds dollars a month. By late fall, although Harmar counted fewer than three hundred men under arms, not half as many as he had hoped for, he could wait no longer. The unready regiment set out for Fort Pitt, on a march that quickly turned into fiasco. Desertion thinned rosters at once, with some sixty runaways reported to be "lurking" around Philadelphia alone. Indiscipline along the way, and still more desertions, further marred the new army's reputation. Drunkenness and public rioting earned several of the miscreants a severe flogging, to no discernible improvement in overall behavior. Residents of the bustling frontier village of

Pittsburgh, grown up around Fort Pitt, watched with some curiosity the unimpressive arrival of the woebegone column of soldiers sent out by the central government to awe the Indians. The bedraggled troops looked somewhat less than awesome to the wilderness-toughened westerners.

With a new bride by his side, Commandant Harmar followed his troops to the Ohio Valley for what would turn out to be seven years of command there. Soldiers spent the winter strengthening Fort McIntosh, some forty miles downriver from Fort Pitt, and assisting Indian negotiators. Survival, though, was the little army's primary occupation. Rations were short, the weather harsh, pay late or missing, and drunkenness rife. Training and discipline stood likewise in short supply. Officers and soldiers alike drank so heavily that Harmar had to place strict controls on the issuance of liquor. Death was ever present, but from accident, disease, and murder, not from battle. The arrival of spring brought the soldiers some relief from the privations of winter—and happy anticipation of the approaching end of their one-year enlistment.

With nothing much to show for its earlier attempt, Congress, sitting in New York City, turned again in April 1785 to the challenge of forming an army. All previous reasons for raising a fighting force were still there, only now more compellingly so. Problems were the more pressing for being a year older. Moreover, Congress had yet another reason to have need of an army. The protection of settlers and surveyors. The land ordinance passed that year established procedures for surveying and settling the West, neither of which could be accomplished without security. In the light of such pressures, the debate this time around turned on how, not whether, to raise an army. Indicative of this altered mood, delegates broadened the stated purpose of the regiment to include defending legal settlers "from the depredations of the Indians" and preventing "unwarranted intrusions" of squatters.

This time Congress started at the top. Having earlier strengthened the powers of the secretary at war, it appointed Henry Knox to the vacant position. That was a good move, and one sure to inject some sorely needed energy into the overall effort. Then members decided to extend the length of enlistments from one year to three. The previous year's sobering results with short-term enlistments made that an unavoidable change. Besides, reality had somewhat stilled talk of the dangers posed by a standing army. It was hard for anyone to find much to fear in Harmar's ragtag regiment. As an expedient to curtail debate, and in hopes that many of the regiment's 1784 men would opt to stay on in the new force, Congress called on the same four states to provide troops. The regiment would remain organized into eight companies of infantry and two of artillery.

Difficulties surfaced at once. While New York and Connecticut promptly began enlisting soldiers, the legislatures of Pennsylvania and New Jersey had adjourned, requiring a delay in their recruiting until the fall. The new men would not be available until long after the prime campaigning weather of 1785 had passed. Worse, chagrined Pennsylvania officials, having counted on keeping a good number of their current soldiers under arms, learned that few intended to stay. They rushed as many of them as possible to the most distant posts, hoping that the prospects of a long journey home would encourage some to reenlist. With Knox's weight thrown into the balance, the four states eventually filled most of their quotas, partly by seeking enlistments outside their own borders and partly by not being overly concerned with the caliber of recruits. One officer complained that the men were "the offscourings of large towns and cities—enervated by idleness, debaucheries and every species of vice. . . ." By the middle of 1786, more than two years after Congress had said such a force was "immediately and indispensably necessary," Harmar finally had a nearly full regiment— in quantity if not in quality.

As it was, it was none too soon. In 1785, despite the disruption of rebuilding the regiment—sending one army home while recruiting and deploying another—Harmar had begun to extend operations deeper into the Ohio Valley. A stockaded enclosure, named Fort Harmar, rose late that year where the Muskingum flows into the Ohio. It was the Confederation's first permanent presence in the territory it had resolved to control. With more troops on hand in 1786, the regiment penetrated still farther into hostile country by building a series of posts along the Ohio River and on its tributaries. Not powerful enough to face the Indian nations in battle, the regiment was taking a serious risk each time it diluted its strength by starting a new fort. Knox directed Harmar to pursue a conciliatory policy, telling the tribes that the army would keep white settlers south of the Ohio River in return for peace. That put the soldiers squarely in the business of dispossessing squatters, an unpleasant enough task under any circumstances, but especially galling when it was recalled that the hated British regulars had been doing just that before the outbreak of the Revolution. Nor was the little army up to the task. Scattered in pennypackets along a thousand miles of river and pioneer path, greatly outnumbered by would-be settlers, and having no authority to do much more than destroy the cabins of intruding farmers, the soldiers soon found themselves waging a losing battle. Settlements evacuated and burned one year were merely reoccupied and rebuilt the next. Harmar was trying to dam a stream with a sieve. Fed by land lust, immigration from abroad, and high taxes in established regions, the flow of settlers became a torrent and then a flood. How many people went west in those early years will never be known, but a count made by an officer at Fort Harmar between 10 October 1786 and 12 May 1787 provides a glimpse. His tally of those passing his wilderness outpost in that period was "177 boats containing 2,689 souls, 1,333 horses, 766 cattle, 102 wagons and one phaeton; besides a number which passed in the night unobserved." The population of Kentucky alone exploded from a few hundred in 1779 to around thirty thousand by the end of 1785. The U.S. Army was unable to so much as count the people heading west, never mind control or protect them. By 1787, Knox was warning Congress that further attempts to remove the encroaching westerners would likely be futile, saying that their numbers would permit them to "defy the power of the United States."

Overstretched and outmanned, Harmar's regiment provided a presence but hardly a power. Indians stalked and sniped and stole about as they wished. The army had but small impact, and won scant respect. It even failed in its mission to provide security to surveyors when survey crews lost confidence in their protectors and refused to continue working. "Those men who are to be purchased from the prisons . . . and brothels of the nation at two dollars per month, will never answer our purpose for fighting of Indians," a well-known land developer, John Symmes, later said of them.

The soldiers found themselves increasingly squeezed between bristling tribes to the north of the Ohio River and unappreciative Kentuckians on the south bank. Treaties signed after the peace pipe was smoked in both 1784 and 1785 failed to stop atrocities or slow migration. Fur traders and British army officers kept the Indians on the edge of war with the settlers, while frontiersmen grew ever more impatient with the timid policies of Congress and the embarrassing impotence of its army. In 1786, for instance, a large band of Kentucky settlers twice raided northward into Indian lands, and British authorities convened a conference of tribes at Detroit to incite them to retaliate against American encroachments. Frontiersmen were not alone in frustration with the Confederation's weakness. Several states began talking about taking unilateral action to protect their citizens and interests over the mountains. Knox, trying desperately to avert war in the West, kept a tight leash on Harmar. He emphatically directed the commanding officer to follow federal orders only, not those of any governor. Moreover, American units could initiate no offensive action whatsoever without the secretary's express approval. Knox's deep concern was valid. Affairs were steadily worsening. Harmar needed more troops and better support for them, and soon. Unless Congress acted to strengthen its army, Knox warned, the West could explode. Worse, he added, frontiersmen, angered by what they perceived to be the indifference of their eastern countrymen, might become tempted to seek security through an association with another government. Or, as Washington had feared, they might decide to take off on their own by declaring themselves independent.

Inside the army, morale was anything but high. If not engaged in ejecting squatter families, soldiers could normally be found huddling for protection in their dreary posts. Leadership was abysmal. From all accounts, few officers were effective. Many appeared to be indifferent to the privations of their men, while some were flatly brutal. Drill—that time-tested method for developing discipline, motivation, teamwork, and battle skills—seems never to have been seriously considered. In the fastness of the western forests, officers apparently viewed training requirements as being more or less limited to individual musketry, sentry duty, and survival skills. Always poorly fed and clothed, the troops were paid hardly at all. Seeking funds, the regiment's paymaster personally visited the seat of government on more than one occasion, only to be put off each time. Congress was broke. At a low point in 1786, Harmar himself bought food for the men to ward off starvation. In another striking example, Knox could not at one key juncture obtain enough money—he needed only a thousand dollars—to send the regiment a crucial shipment of lead and powder. Deaths from disease cut into the army's numbers, as did several executions for various offenses. Not until 1787, though, did a member of the regiment die by Indian action. Wyandot warriors captured that hapless soldier under the eyes of his friends at Fort Harmar and dragged him off to be killed at leisure. Later, they gleefully displayed his scalp on a pole, taunting the soldiers, who were forbidden to retaliate. The brooding servicemen were "rather prisoners in that country, than in possession of it," noted one observer pungently.

For all manner of reasons, the Confederation was unable to project effective military power into the West. Political pressures to limit central strength. State rivalries. Fiscal impotence. The overwhelming flow of settlers. Diplomatic inability to close down the British posts on the Great Lakes. The preference of many for militia. Inefficient internal administration of the military. Slack training and discipline. Fear of a standing army. Those were causes, painfully obvious to some Americans but generally invisible to most. The single symptom seen by all was the pitifully weak regiment sent to the valley of the Ohio. The bastard child had not done well. "By 1787," wrote historian Kohn, "many Americans viewed the army and the defective policy which had created it as the very symbol of the inadequacy of government under the Articles of Confederation."

CHAPTER 7
A ROPE OF SAND

Inept the army may have been, and a symbol of the weakness of the Confederation, but it nevertheless represented an attempt by the government to wield power. It served as a fig leaf to cover the country's nakedness of strength and will. In other areas and other ways the humiliation was virtually complete. The "new constellation among the world's nations" did not enjoy full respect at home, much less abroad. In foreign capitals the conventional expectation—in some of them it was gleeful anticipation—was that the United States would rather soon shatter into several pieces. Even those who thought a republic could survive had severe doubts about the capacity of one to function in a land so large, for the nation occupied an expanse of territory greater than that of France, Prussia, Great Britain, and Spain combined. Trends and events in America reinforced the doubts of foreign observers. To be a nation in more than name required diplomatic respect, political cohesiveness, internal security, economic soundness, and the power to protect interests. The United States, bound by the Articles of Confederation, boasted none of that. John Adams was not merely being colorful when he described the Articles as "a rope of sand."

Consider the necessity of protecting interests. America was a trading nation, a legacy of its colonial heritage. Ships sailed from ports in all the states, carrying the produce of an agrarian economy and returning with products from around the globe. American goods were in worldwide demand. Frenchmen craved tobacco, for instance, and elderly Chinese men thought ginseng restored virility; American ships were eager to supply such wants, expecting to return home laden with French brandy or tea from the Orient. The national interest clearly called for a naval force of some kind. But at war's end, every vessel in the Continental navy had been sold off—save one, the frigate *Alliance*. It alone was expected to show the flag and protect trade. However, Congress was unable to sustain even a one-ship fleet. In August 1785, *Alliance,* too, was sold. America's navy ceased to exist. But not the need for one. Challenges arose right away after the signing of the peace treaty, ranging from the Mediterranean to the Caribbean.

For centuries, the Barbary pirates had plundered European shipping in the Mediterranean Sea. Based on fortified enclaves along the North African coast, the states of Morocco, Algiers, Tripoli, and Tunis had developed flourishing piratical enterprises, concentrating on kidnapping for slavery and ransom. All were Muslim countries, a remote part of the Ottoman Empire, and under rather loose control from Constantinople. They sold captured Christians into slavery—a highly lucrative business, for the Christian slave population on the Barbary Coast numbered in the tens of thousands. Attractive women were particularly sought for consignment to harems. Ships' officers and wealthy passengers were held for ransom. European nations responded by sending occasional punitive expeditions, but more often by simply bribing the rapacious potentates of the various states. American ships had formerly been protected by flying the British flag, but after the Revolution that immunity was gone. Pirates swarmed. American crews and passengers were put on the auction block. Countering that threat became yet another headache for the Congress.

Morocco had abolished Christian slavery in 1777, perhaps believing that doing so would lead to more profitable links with other countries by making it more conscionable for them to engage in trade and to pay tribute. The sultan sent word through American representatives in Paris that he was interested in establishing relations with the United States. Benjamin Franklin forwarded the request to Congress, favorably recommending it. Years passed with no action. Finally, in 1784, Moroccans seized the American ship *Betsey* and demanded negotiations. Under those conditions, "negotiations" could only be viewed as a discussion over the terms of tribute, even though *Betsey* and her crew were released. Shortly after the capture of *Betsey,* Algerian corsairs seized two other American vessels, *Maria* and *Dauphin,* taking a total of twenty-one crew members.

Thomas Jefferson, then in Paris, argued against paying ransom or tribute, insisting that force should be applied to stop the piracy and free the American hostages. But Congress had no navy to send. It sent negotiators to Morocco and Algiers. Jefferson's assistant, Thomas Barclay, went to Morocco, while Revolutionary War veteran John Lamb journeyed to Algiers. Lamb had no luck at all. The dey of Algiers wanted ransom, not trade, but the price he set was more than Congress could scrape up. The negotiations fizzled out—and the hapless crewmen became slaves. Barclay's effort was more successful. Armed with a draft agreement, he met with the sultan in Marrakesh, where he concluded a treaty in June 1786. He greased the deal by giving a sizable bribe to the Moroccan ruler, a reference point perhaps for Jefferson's aversion to paying off the Barbary states when he later became president. "Millions for defense," he would proclaim in 1805, "but not one cent for tribute." By then, of course, the United States had military teeth. The president could say that and make it stick. The Confederation, though, had neither the money nor the guns to deal with the remaining Barbary states. Corsairs continued to attack American merchant vessels. The Stars and Stripes afforded no protection. Ships and citizens at sea were on their own.

Still worse, for the magnitude of its economic impact, was the loss of traditional trading partners in the Western Hemisphere itself, the region where American trade was the most extensive. No longer a part of the British Empire, the United States did not have automatic access to the Crown's ports and markets. Without modification, Great Britain's Navigation Acts would be seriously detrimental to American merchants—and London refused to modify them. That refusal essentially closed the West Indies to American shipping, causing a traumatic disruption in commercial patterns between the Atlantic seaboard and Caribbean islands. The disruption had to be endured because the Confederation did not have the ability to open those ports by threatening a retaliatory tariff on British exports. Some states attempted unilateral action, but usually with more harm to their neighbors than help to themselves. Many shippers found ways to circumvent the laws, while the eagerness of other states—notably the Dutch—to expand trade helped buffer the loss of established arrangements. Nevertheless, the over-all result was to throw commercial affairs into considerable disarray. That situation was not improved when France began insisting on the repayment of wartime loans. The Dutch offered in 1786 to buy up the United States debt to France, but the damage had already been done. The skewed trading arrangements had sent commercial activi-ties into a downward spiral.

While foreign shippers had optimistically pushed more and more goods to the new republic, exports from the United States had dwindled. The imbalance caused American prices to plummet. That fall flattened the already fragile postwar economy; depression blanketed the land. Descent into depression, always painful, hurt all the more because the fall was so far and so quick. Having been generally denied ac-cess to European products during the war, Americans had gone on a buying spree when peace was announced. Warehouses soon bulged with goods to meet the pent-up demand, especially luxuries from England. Inflation soared. Merchants purchased on credit, which English busi-nessmen were eager to extend. Optimistic consumers, enticed by the good terms being offered, also bought on credit. For a year or so, the country indulged in a gigantic shopping frenzy. The moment of reckoning came, however, when the value of American goods crashed. Boom became bust. The economy staggered drunkenly as creditors called in their loans. Debtors could not pay. Jails began to fill with bankrupt citizens, especially with hard-hit small farmers and small businessmen.

Congress directed John Adams in London to seek a commercial treaty with Great Britain before the precarious situation became irretriev-able. But His Majesty's ministers were no more responsive to that issue than they were to the repeated demands to remove their soldiers from the northwestern parts of the United States.

Money supply was another part of the difficult economic equation. The colonies, with no mint of their own, had always found cash to be in short supply. They had grown accustomed to dealing in what-ever national specie could be had, with Spanish coins often in greater circulation than British. Indeed, American money itself later came to be patterned after Spanish denominations largely for that reason. At war's end, however, more hard currency was available in the United States than ever before in the history of the colonies, a phenomenon caused by the large expenditures of the various armies. That windfall helped fuel the postwar buying surge, but with the result that the record stores of specie fled rapidly to Europe, largely to England. The continued one-way flow of goods prevented replacement of the currency, leading to a dearth of ready cash. Specie-prosperous merchants had begun the buying spree; credit-supported individuals sustained it. As a result, commerce again became largely a barter proposition. That put an unusually heavy burden on the small farmer. No matter how hard he worked, there was often simply no money to be found to pay off his loans or to pay taxes. Not a few lost their farms and ended up in jail. The manifest unfairness of it all led legislatures to declare certain debts uncollectible, further scrambling the already chaotic fiscal environment. Moreover, within two years of peace, seven states had adopted some form of paper money. Fiscal chaos soon followed. Congress, unable under the Articles to take centralized action, could only watch as the states galloped off in thirteen different directions and the economy tumbled. Reliant on others for its own funding, the central government muddled along helplessly. Not only insolvent, it was locked into a dramatically worsening situation. In 1786 its entire income amounted to less than a third of the *annual interest* it owed on the national debt. Ever more desperate, Congress sold land in the West—discounted to about ten cents on the dollar.

Experiences on the diplomatic front were as embarrassing as those in the economic arena. England did not even bother to establish a mission in the United States, so contemptuous were the British of the Confederation Congress. Ministers would deal only with the separate states, holding that the central government was unreliable. Furthermore, London sent secret—and later not so secret—instructions telling the governor-general in Canada to retain possession of the fortifications and trading establishments south of the Great Lakes. In the face of American complaints, British officials justified those actions by saying that states had reneged on treaty obligations to make restitution to Loyalists. While that claim was specious, it did contain a trace of truth. Congress had fulfilled its part of the treaty by recommending that the states comply, but they had chosen not to listen. This was doubly embarrassing, because the central government was helpless to do anything about it. Some legislatures added insult to injury by passing laws blocking the collection of British debts—an actual violation of the treaty that Congress was powerless to stop. England also made little effort to hide discussions with Ethan Allen and others over attaching Vermont to Canada. Both New York and New Hampshire claimed the granite hills and flinty people lying between them. The Vermonters, wanting no part of either neighbor, had declared independence and applied to Congress for statehood. Not wanting to antagonize anyone, though, that body was reluctant to accept Vermont's application or to side with one state or the other. At the same time, it was unable to prevent English meddling.

Spaniards, meanwhile, were stirring up trouble in the Southwest. Owning Florida and much of the Mississippi River, with forts on the west bank as far north as St. Louis and on the east to the modern-day location of Memphis, Spain had a choke hold on all commerce passing through the Gulf of Mexico. In 1784, with covetous designs on the area that later became the states of Kentucky and Tennessee, Madrid closed the Mississippi to Americans. Cut off from river trade and tied very loosely to a weak government east of the Appalachians, the western settlers might well switch allegiance for the obvious economic gains. Or so ministers in Madrid calculated. It was not a far-fetched scheme. The westerners did in truth harbor ideas of independence, and some of their leaders (James Wilkinson and Daniel Boone being two of the better known) were entertaining thoughts of selling their loyalty to the Spanish. Moreover, some influential men in the Northeast, not empathetic with the West, were not so sure that opening the Mississippi was in the northerners' best interests. Influential political leader Rufus King wrote Elbridge Gerry to say that if the West had the use of the Mississippi he would consider every settler heading there "as forever lost to the Confederacy." Madrid was aware of such divisions among Americans.

In 1785, Spain sent Don Diego de Gardoqui to New York City to forge with the United States a treaty aimed at receiving formal recognition of Spanish ownership of the Mississippi. America's negotiator was John Jay, the secretary of foreign affairs.[1] Jay had instructions

---

1. Gardoqui had in previous negotiations sized up Jay and his wife. He anticipated a relatively easy conquest. She was susceptible to subtle bribery, and she could sway her husband. Gardoqui told his government that presenting "a few timely gifts," giving elegant dinners, and "above all to entertain with good wine" would win the day.

to insist on the right of Americans to navigate the length of the river. When he discovered that Gardoqui would not bend on that point but would on others, Jay accepted an agreement establishing commercial links and guaranteeing the southern and southwestern borders of the United States, but at the price of forgoing American use of the Mississippi for twenty-five years. Not bargaining from a position of strength, which would have permitted him to insist on more, Jay believed gaining security in the Southwest was the best he could get, and was worth a twenty-five-year wait for the use of the river. Furthermore, the closure of that waterway would oblige settlers to look more to the United States for commerce, a position not inconsistent with the thinking of Washington and others. But it was a position rooted in weakness, nonetheless. If the United States had not been so nearly prostrate at the time, the compromise would very likely not have seemed at all favorable. As it was, when the details of the arrangement became public, westerners became apoplectic. The five southern states exploded. Virginian James Madison, normally mild mannered in debate, thundered, "The use of the Mississippi is given by nature to our western country, and no power on earth can take it from them." The southerners angrily prevented the treaty from being approved, ironically handing Gardoqui a clear diplomatic victory—for nothing had changed except that westerners had become more unhappy than ever with their central government, and that southerners were upset at northerners, who had for the most part backed the treaty's provisions. Another wedge had been driven between the sections of the United States. Odds for fragmentation of North from South or East from West had been boosted. And Spain was thereby in a better bargaining position to seek the allegiance of the discontented.

When Washington had hung up his uniform at the end of the Revolutionary War, he had settled into retirement with a stoic anticipation that the Republic would find its rightful way after some inevitable disruption and experimentation. In preparing to leave the service, he had written and circulated to the states a fervent plea for them to select a path of selflessness, to provide the central government the powers needed to shape a lasting union. That plea, the Virginian vowed, would be his first and last attempt to give his countrymen political advice. Known popularly as "Washington's Legacy," the document received wide readership and acclaim. And it was promptly ignored. That was to be expected, the general sighed ruefully. Americans would in due course reach a common point of understanding on the need to move beyond sectionalism, he believed, but through a process of political maturing that could not be hurried. He was sure that "the good sense of the people" would eventually overcome parochial prejudice. He retained his confidence for about two years.

By the middle of 1786 Washington's equanimity had vanished. Watching developments from Mount Vernon, he saw a gathering storm. "We have probably had too good an opinion of human nature in forming our confederation," he lamented. Believing there was "more wickedness than ignorance" in the conduct of many of the state legislatures, he warned that if self-interest continued to prevail the result would be "another convulsion." Writing with unusual emotion, he confided to John Jay: "I think often of our situation and view it with concern. From the high ground we stood upon, from the plain path which invited our footsteps, to be so fallen! so lost!" Embarrassments on every front galled the proud patriot mightily. He witnessed daily the evils of economic dislocation. That Congress still could not raise its own money by taxation troubled him. It got by, hand to mouth, surviving on loans from abroad, mostly from the Dutch. He railed at the evidence of disunion when New York violated the Articles of Confederation to negotiate directly with Indian tribes, with Congress unable to intervene. In fact, as Washington sourly noted, that body was a "shadow without substance." It seldom had enough representatives to do anything at all, even if it had possessed the requisite authority. The continuing morass of affairs in the West frustrated him. And of special pain was the fact that his soldiers were as yet uncared for.

Perhaps no man in the nation had more of an emotional stake in the ultimate success of the Republic than did George Washington. Not only had he led the country through eight torturous years to victory, to become the very icon of the nation's existence, but he had acquired a moral obligation to the men of the Continental Army—a debt of the soul, a debt of such depth that it could be truly comprehended only by one who has commanded soldiers in battle. He had acquiesced in the shabby treatment of those who had fought by his side. Congress and the states, helped financially by Dutch investors, had by late 1786 made a good dent in the debt owed the soldiers by providing them certificates of pay and grants of land. Still, they suffered more than most Americans during the depression—often being forced to sell their certificates and grants at highly depreciated terms—which served to remind their former commander in chief that he had disbanded them destitute. He had done so in the belief that their initial distress would be more than adequately compensated for by virtue of their owning citizenship in a new and thriving democracy, that their future life would be better for their current sacrifice. But the Republic was not thriving. It was tottering. Voices in increasing volume predicted its demise. Many saw the emergence of perhaps three distinct nations determined by geography and special interests. Several individuals began looking wistfully over their shoulders at the old monarchical form of government. Some made quiet overtures to see if some European prince might not be available. Others mentioned making Washington a king. He would have no part of such talk. "What astonishing changes a few years are capable of producing," he reacted. "What a triumph for our enemies to verify their predictions! What a triumph for the advocates of despotism to find that we are incapable of governing ourselves, and that systems founded on the basis of equal liberty are merely ideal and fallacious!"

Faction was the word then in use for political parochialism, for the tendency to break off into groups seeking gain at the cost of the whole, for pursuing self-interest over the common good. Foreign observers predicted an early breakup of the United States. Typical was the comment of Josiah Tucker, dean of Gloucester Cathedral in England. "A disunited people till the end of time," said Tucker, "suspicious and distrustful of each other, they will be divided and subdivided into little commonwealths or principalities, according to natural boundaries." Faction in any form was anathema to Washington. He fought anything contributing to the disintegration rather than the integration of the union. That attitude brought him into philosophical opposition to the first veterans' organization in America, the Society of the Cincinnati. Although he had accepted its presidency, and even though he believed it to be a worthy club, he came to understand that large numbers of his countrymen were infuriated by a group that limited access to Continental Army officers and their heirs. Denied entry themselves, protesters attributed evil intent to the society. Whatever the validity of that perception, it was very real. And it was just one more factor tearing at the fabric of the country. Washington fashioned changes in the charter aimed at removing the causes of distrust, and vigorously pushed them through at the Cincinnati's first national meeting in 1784. The furor eventually faded.

Faction also arose in state versus state competition. In his attempts to weld together a plan to open a route to the West, Washington was obliged to obtain cooperation from Virginia and Maryland on joint usage of the Potomac River. The protracted discussions, and the sectional jealousies they revealed, highlighted for him the extreme difficulties inherent in trying to achieve improvements in interstate commerce under the Articles of Confederation. When talks reached a point in the spring of 1785 where success stood in the balance, he brought the negotiators to Mount Vernon. Under pressure from the great man himself, they overrode parochialism to reach agreement, to include writing rules for sharing all the waters of Chesapeake Bay. They also established a schedule for future meetings. Known as the Mount Vernon Conference, that meeting led to much more than a two-state pact on the mutual use of waterways. When Maryland's legislature considered the agreement for ratification, it decided to ask Pennsylvania and Delaware, two other states closely involved in matters concerning the navigation of the Chesapeake, to attend the next round of talks. Urged on by James Madison, Virginia responded to that broadening of the talks by suggesting a convention of all thirteen states to consider "a uniform system in their commercial regulations." Early in 1786, Virginia sent invitations to a national meeting in Annapolis in the first week of September. A major step had been taken in the direction of reinforcing unity. Musing over the possibilities, George Washington regretted that "more objects were not embraced by the meeting" than interstate commerce, but at the same time he felt instinctively that the nation was not yet ready to alter the "rope of sand." Despite all the turmoil, centrifugal forces still held sway in too many locales. Nevertheless, he lobbied hard with correspondents and visitors in support of the Annapolis Convention.

George Mann's tavern, a spacious three-story structure in Annapolis, was the site of the convention. At the opening session on 11 September, only twelve representatives from five states were in attendance. Four other states had named delegates, but none of them showed up. Washington had been right; the mood in the country did not yet support a move for more centralized power, even in the limited area of trade. The delegates selected John Dickinson, the principal author of the original, undiluted Articles of Confederation, to serve as chairman. More than that they could not do, with so few states represented and with instructions from those at such variance. Yet the men at Mann's tavern did not want to lose the opportunity presented by their very gathering. They were activists. Seven of the twelve had borne arms in the Revolution. Ten had served in Congress. All were Nationalists; Anti-Nationalists had forfeited a voice by staying away. The twelve agreed that something positive must come out of the convention. They also readily agreed that trade problems were but a symptom, not a cause. Commercial weakness was merely one piece of the larger mosaic of political crisis. The root cause of the nation's unremitting series of humiliations was the abject weakness of the Articles of Confederation. The cure was to amend that document. Accordingly, the delegates decided to write a report of their deliberations that would recommend convening another meeting in which representatives would come explicitly empowered to strengthen the Articles.

Alexander Hamilton drafted a forcefully stated report to that effect. His colleagues toned his fiery words down a bit, and after two days of discussion voted approval. The report, calling for a meeting to be held the following May in Philadelphia, underscored the need for representatives to arrive armed with a broad mandate to repair the flawed Articles. It was to be held for "the sole and express purpose of revising the Articles of Confederation." The fundamental question that Americans had to answer was whether the United States would be one nation or an alliance of thirteen. A local newspaper, praising the call for a convention, wrote that prospects were good for the emergence of a federal union established on principles sure to rescue the separate states not only "from their present Difficulties, but from that insolent Hauteur and contemptuous Neglect, which they have experienced as a Nation." Having done all they could, delegates closed the Annapolis Convention on the afternoon of its fourth day. Dickinson personally carried a copy of the report to Congress. As the men rode away they were not optimistic. They knew what an uphill battle it would be to convince the states to respond favorably.

But unexpected help was brewing at that very moment in the western counties of Massachusetts.

CHAPTER 8
CAPTAIN DANIEL SHAYS

Daniel Shays was an unlikely figure to play a key role in shaping the government of the United States. A man of limited ability and ambition, poorly educated, a subsistence farmer in western Massachusetts, he was not the type to seek power or high position. There was nothing flashy about him. Yet, in one six-month span he burst into national prominence—and infamy—and moved America.

His origins were humble. The date of his birth is unknown, but it was around 1747. Shays lived most of the first three decades of his life in obscurity, surfacing in 1775 as one of the gaggle of angry New Englanders who took up arms to resist British forces around Boston. Evidently respected by his peers, he was elected to a second lieutenancy in a Massachusetts regiment. He promptly gained recognition for courage under fire at the Battle of Bunker Hill, and subsequently saw action at Ticonderoga, Saratoga, and Stony Point. Winning a reputation for leadership as well as for bravery, he earned promotion to the grade of captain. He was a caring commander, considerate of his subordinates and in turn admired by them. The Marquis de Lafayette, the young French nobleman serving as a general in the Continental Army, awarded him a sword for exemplary service. That exceptional accolade seems to have been the high point of Captain Shays's military career. He resigned his commission on 14 October 1780, under circumstances never fully explained, and settled near the town of Pelham in western Massachusetts.

Places like Pelham were hit especially hard by the economic chaos of the mid-1780s. All across central and western Massachusetts, farmers and townsfolk compiled long lists of grievances. A shortage of currency. Unequal taxation. Inadequate representation. The requirement to pay debts in specie. Excessive legal fees. Suppressed prices for produce. A heavy burden of debt. And on top of all that, a lack of empathy by leaders. The state was dominated by eastern merchants, who appeared to be indifferent to the plight of residents in the western counties. Many of those westerners came increasingly to view the state government as being a cause of their travail, and to believe the courts were manifestly unjust. Perhaps significantly, a good proportion of the disaffected citizens were recently returned Continental Army soldiers who found the current situation particularly intolerable. Still resenting their maltreatment during and at the conclusion of the war, the veterans contemplated with increasing bitterness the relative wealth of merchants and speculators, not a few of whom had gotten rich on the sacrifices of soldiers. Those former Continentals were struggling like everyone else to make a living, but also to effect their reentry into civilian life. It was not easy. Daniel Shays had to sell the sword Lafayette had given him.

In the summer of 1786, irate citizens all over the western two-thirds of the state met in a series of assemblies to discuss their complaints and to let state officials know of their unhappiness. Then, spurred on by a surge in seizures of property for overdue debts and taxes, fed-up farmers and their supporters rose in rebellion. The American Revolution had itself given them a process and a language to deal with an iniquitous government. Essentially a debtors' revolt, it was a spontaneous uprising and, at first, leaderless.

Courts were scheduled to sit in late August in judgment of debtors, which under the circumstances meant they would render judgments against them. A throng of fifteen hundred men, shouldering muskets and pitchforks, took over the county courthouse at Northampton to prevent that court from sitting. Other mobs did the same thing in other towns in succeeding days. Legal processes were disrupted in at least five counties. If the courts can't sit, they can't take away our property, seemed to be the reasoning. A newspaper described one of the confrontations: Some four hundred men, portrayed as ragged, disreputable, and drunken, surrounded the building where the court was attempting to do business. A ringleader shouted to bystanders, "I am going to give the court four hours to agree to our terms, and, if they do not, I and my party will force them to it." The reporter added that the court decamped at once to avoid encountering "any coercive measures." Mostly hardscrabble farmers, calling themselves "regulators" and wearing a hemlock twig in their caps as a mark of self-set authority, the rebels ranged far, leaving cowering judges and sheriffs wherever they went.

Governor James Bowdoin saw his state splintering. Residents of the eastern reaches had been agitating for secession in order to form their own state of Maine. Now this violent rebellion in the western counties pulled from another direction. Incensed by the "despicable, degenerate mob," he reacted immediately to suppress the incipient insurrection by sending the state supreme court to crack down on perpetrators. Meeting on 19 September in Worcester, only forty miles from Boston, the court managed to indict several of the "regulators" from that region. The court then moved on to Springfield, fifty-five miles farther west, with obvious intentions of doing the same thing in Hampshire County. That town, on the banks of the Connecticut River and in the center of the rugged western half of the state, lay in the heart of rebel strength. Having seen what had happened at Worcester, the insurrectionists vowed to prevent further indictments.

Led by Capt. Daniel Shays, about five or six hundred men marched defiantly to Springfield, their ranks swelling as others joined en route. Directed by the governor to protect the supreme court, the local militia leader, Maj. Gen. William Shephard, assembled a military force about as numerous as the rabble mustered by Shays. Accounts of the strength of the opponents vary widely, but numbers were irrelevant. The critical factor was that men on both sides were local inhabitants; militiamen and rebels were of common stock. Some were related, while quite a few had served together in the recent war. The two milling groups faced one another warily on 26 September. Shephard was in a tight spot. Knowing that most of his men were in sympathy with the Shaysites, he was not sure if they would obey orders to act against them. And he was not at all convinced that the situation itself was so serious as to call for the shedding of blood. Probably aware of Shephard's dilemma, Shays called his bluff. Rebels chased the court out of town— while the militia only watched. Satisfied with their handiwork, Captain Shays and his men dispersed.

Although other men also led rebellious bands, Shays's successful facedown of militia forces catapulted him into prominence. A short time later a circular letter, bearing his name and calling for general resistance to the Massachusetts government, sealed the captain's position as the nominal leader of the revolt. It has been forever after known to history as Shays's Rebellion. Certainly among the least charismatic of rebel captains of any age, and as reluctant a revolutionary as one could imagine, he was unalterably cast as the leader by events at Springfield.

Springfield was not just another county seat. It was the site of one of the nation's major weapons depositories. Huge Henry Knox, the secretary at war, happened to have been personally on the scene to witness the failure of the militia to protect the court. The experience seared him. Although Shays and his men had made no move toward the federal arsenal, the secretary had been horrified by the very thought. The arsenal, established there at the urging of Knox himself, contained maybe fifteen thousand muskets, numerous artillery pieces, a foundry for casting cannon, and a large stockpile of gunpowder. If the rebels should capture those stores, the insurrection would be immeasurably strengthened. And there was not a single federal soldier assigned to guard the facility. Knox began quickly to try to drum up adequate security.

The secretary turned first to Governor Bowdoin, asking him to order militia units to watch over the arsenal. Militia leaders, though, thought securing a federal installation was beyond the authority of state troops. Besides, they were not a bit happy about being drawn into an argument with their hemlock-wearing neighbors. Knox next asked Congress to raise federal forces for the task. Shocked by the eruption in Massachusetts and the inability of local officials to cope with it, and concerned that rebellion might prove contagious and spread to other states, Congress was ready. Sitting in New York City, it was close enough to the scene of action to sense clearly the deep anxiety stirred up by the rebellion. Representatives promptly voted to sharply increase the size of the federal army, nearly tripling it to 2,040 men, with all new soldiers to be enlisted in New England. Still, they were reluctant to admit that regulars were needed for internal security, for possible use against American citizens. To cloak its real purpose, Congress announced that the new men were being raised for service against Indians. As it turned out, delegates did not need to be so devious. The mood across the country was shifting in light of the emergency; taking a tough stand on this issue was politically acceptable. Be that as it may, Congress had insufficient funds to support the additional troops anyway, and very few were ever recruited. There was not time. Some members may have remembered Alexander Hamilton's earlier admonition that, without an army in being, Congress would be obliged to begin finding a force at the outset of a crisis, at the very moment when employment was called for. Voting to raise the soldiers was the one bold peacetime step ever taken by the Confederation Congress in military matters, but its own weakness precluded it from being able to follow through. Massachusetts would have to deal with the revolt alone, hopefully securing the weapons at Springfield in the process.

The violent affront to domestic tranquility shocked not only Congress, but the entire country. Reports from the scene rapidly ranged up and down the length of the states. Magnified by rumor and fear, those reports were uniformly apocalyptic in nature. David Humphreys, a former aide of Washington's, wrote from Connecticut, "Everything is in a state of confusion in Massachusetts." He added that New Hampshire suffered "tumults" and Rhode Island was "in a state of frenzy and division on account of their paper money." Noah Webster, who was in Massachusetts that fall lecturing on behalf of his crusade to adopt a purely American version of the English language, was moved by the turmoil to suggest that America should abandon its brief experiment with a representative democracy. "I would infinitely prefer a limited monarchy," he wrote, "for I would sooner be the subject of the caprice of one man, than to the ignorance and passions of the multitude." Henry Knox consistently penned highly incendiary letters: the rebels amounted to about 20 percent of several counties; they were "desperate and unprincipled men"; they were urging the overthrow of all property; they felt both their poverty and their force, and they were determined "to make use of the latter in order to remedy the former." Henry "Light-Horse Harry" Lee revealed talk in Congress about asking George Washington to rush to Massachusetts to bring his "unbounded influence" to bear. The general's "appearance among the seditious might bring them back to peace and reconciliation." Washington wisely declined that suggestion. "Influence," he responded, "is no government." Still, the former commander in chief was aghast. "What, gracious God, is man!" he wrote, "that there should be such inconsistency and perfidiousness in his conduct?" In deep distress at the violence and the painfully obvious inability of government to act, he moaned, "I am mortified beyond expression when I view the clouds that have spread over the brightest morn that ever dawned upon any country." He was also attuned to the practical aspects of the circumstances. "Commotions of this sort, like snow-balls, gather strength as they roll, if there is no opposition in the way to divide and crumble them." Virtually every American of any influence, Nationalist and Anti-Nationalist alike, shared a similar concern over the peril to freedom posed by Shays's Rebellion.[1] Daniel Shays and his insurgents had mobilized public opinion, crystallizing emotions in a way nothing else had been able to do. The years of weakness and humiliation had filled people to the very bursting point with a gnawing fear of pending disaster. Shays provided the exploding pinprick.

Thoroughly galvanized by the aggressiveness of Shays's insurgents, and alarmed by the state of anarchy existing west of Worcester, the Massachusetts government followed a course both conciliatory and coercive. It passed laws addressing some of the grievances of western citizens, and extended a pardon to all who would lay down their arms and take an oath of allegiance. At the same time, though, it threatened those in rebellion by adopting measures suspending certain rights. Those coercive measures merely added to the fury of the malcontents. They increased their activities as fall turned into winter, effectively preventing the reestablishment of government in the western reaches of the state.

Once again Shays marched on Springfield, this time showing up the day after Christmas to break up the work of the court trying to meet there. Governor Bowdoin could take no more. He ordered the call-up of over four thousand militiamen for thirty days to deal with the insurgents once and for all.

To assure loyalty, the men would come only from the eastern parts of the state. To assure toughness in the employment of force, they would be commanded by Maj. Gen. Benjamin Lincoln. Lincoln was to re-

1. One notable exception was Thomas Jefferson. In Paris, he was insulated by the Atlantic from the wave of fright sweeping the United States. He ventured the idea that "a little rebellion now and then is a good thing." He would remain at his ambassadorial post long enough to witness the beginnings of the French Revolution.

store civil authority, at the point of a bayonet if necessary. He was to prepare "to march a respectable force through the western counties." That presented no problem for Lincoln, a staunch Nationalist. The money shortage did, however. The state, like the federal government, had no funds to back up its resort to arms. But indignant Massachusetts officials were resolved to put an end to the rampage. At their request, private citizens stepped forward to donate around twenty thousand dollars to fund the mobilization. Lincoln, a former federal officer, would thus lead state troops paid for by private subscription.

Faced with the reality of an escalation in the conflict, Captain Shays realized that he needed more firepower. He set his eyes on the federal arsenal at Springfield.

Wearing his threadbare old buff and blue uniform, and at the head of some fifteen hundred men, Shays approached the town a third time. He intended to help himself to the guns and powder there. Henry Knox's greatest fear had been realized. With heavy and effective weapons, and plenty of veterans trained in their use, Shays's troops would be formidable, especially in defending their own homes and fields.

The only force standing in the way was a body of Major General Shephard's militia from Hampshire County. On 25 January 1787 the two leaders faced each other again in a wintry version of the encounter four months earlier. This time, though, Shephard was better prepared. He had himself taken cannon from the armory, which he had pulled into line alongside his nine hundred soldiers. And his own backbone had been stiffened by the continuing strife in his state and by the resolve of the governor to use arms if necessary. Still, he could not be sure of his men's willingness to do battle with their rebellious neighbors. Confidently aware that at every previous encounter between militia and rebels the militia had backed down, Shays formed his men and began to move toward Shephard's lines. The general shouted a warning to halt, but the rebel ranks continued. Commanding a force badly outnumbered and perhaps unreliable, Shephard decided to open the fight at long range with artillery, of which Shays had none. The general ordered his gunners to fire warning shots over the heads of the oncoming men. The fieldpieces, last fired in anger at British and Hessian soldiers, ruptured the winter calm in a blast of flame and sound, bouncing echoes across frozen fields in the Connecticut River valley and shrouding the gun crews in a pungent white cloud. The smoke cleared to reveal

Shays and his troops still advancing. Shephard then ordered the fieldpieces to be aimed and fired directly into the midst of the rebels. Again the guns roared. Men fell mangled. Four crumpled forms lay dead or dying when the smoke dissipated. The survivors, unprepared to stand up to artillery, broke and ran. The only battle of the rebellion was over. For all of their numbers and anger, the Shaysites had never developed the discipline and will necessary to make a fighting force effective.

Shays's retreat from Springfield was the beginning of the end of his revolt. Lincoln and a mobile militia column reached the scene two days later. He dispersed rebels lingering in the area, and, despite the onset of a blizzard, plunged straight into the snowy fastness after Shays. With his state threatened by mob action, Lincoln showed none of the lethargy that had marked him during much of the Revolutionary War. He maneuvered his command shrewdly and aggressively. Making a swift night march, he surprised Shays's band in Petersham early on 4 February, overcoming them almost without a shot, capturing 150 and scattering the rest. Before the militia's thirty days expired, Lincoln had disrupted all the uncoordinated groups of insurrectionists and had chased the leaders over the borders into neighboring states. Meanwhile, Knox kept searching for federal troops to man the arsenal. By the end of February he had hustled 125 newly recruited men from Connecticut to Springfield. With the rebels scattered and the arsenal secured, the situation in Massachusetts was under control for the first time in six months.

Since other states would not take action to extradite rebels from sanctuaries on their territory, and the federal government could not, quiet did not return to the border regions right away. Replacing the thirty-day militiamen with others, the state garrisoned Berkshire and Hampshire counties until April. Officials jailed all rebels at first, but soon released them—except for several of the leaders, who were sentenced to death. But even they were eventually pardoned. The rebellion simply evaporated. Shaysites had gained many of the reforms they had sought, which is all they had wanted to begin with, so there seemed little reason to resist further the state's newfound sense of firmness.

While the rebellion folded meekly as spring came to Massachusetts, it had a powerful and lasting impact on the United States. More than any other event since the adoption of the Articles of Confederation, it moved the nation toward the writing of a new constitution. It had raised specters of civil war, of anarchy, of mob rule. To the humiliation of weakness had been added the full recognition of its twin: the peril of weakness. The lack of central power actually imperiled democracy by placing a republican form of government at risk.

When delegates left the Annapolis Convention back in September 1786, they had predicted a rousing fight to win acceptance of the need to send representatives to a national convention with instructions to strengthen the Articles of Confederation. They reached their homes at about the same time as the early reports of rioting and rebellion rolled out of western Massachusetts. Understanding full well what Washington had meant when he spoke of a snowballing effect, and wearied to death of the constant cascade of crises flowing from weakness, the diverse elements of American citizenry merged in a unity of will not seen in more than a decade, not since patriots had mutually pledged their lives, their fortunes, and their sacred honor in declaring independence in 1776. Over the winter, majorities in the legislatures of twelve states concurred in the imperative for change and named delegates to go to Philadelphia in May, thereby assuring broad support. On 21 February 1787, Congress endorsed the convention, thereby making it legal. George Washington broke his self-imposed retreat from public life to announce that he would attend the convention as a delegate from Virginia, thereby lending it that bright aura of promise that only his personal involvement could have done.

The catalyst had been Daniel Shays. For the rest of his life, Shays denied that he had been anything more than an angry individual who had simply stepped forward in the absence of a real leader. He was probably speaking the truth. In the retrospective glare of history, we can say that the results of Shays's Rebellion were, ironically, positive. Daniel Shays, as it turned out, achieved good by becoming a rebel. It is also good that he was an ineffective one. Fortunately for Massachusetts, the insurrection had no focusing purpose. It was essentially aimless. The leaders and their mobs wanted to prevent the work of government, which they deemed to be hostile to their rights and interests, but they had no plan beyond that. They were unprepared to substitute another form of government, to declare themselves independent, or to seek to spread their rebellion to discontented elements in nearby states. Light-Horse Harry Lee later summed up the potential danger when he wrote, "Nothing was wanting to bring about a revolution but a great man to head the insurgents."

After Shays was granted amnesty in 1788 he moved to New York, settling eventually in the small town of Sparta, where he lived in obscurity until his death in 1825. His tombstone could have read, "Here lies Captain Daniel Shays, a Patriot. As a Continental Army officer he helped win the war, and as the leader of Shays's Rebellion he helped shape the peace."

PART 3
THE COMMON DEFENCE

We the People of the United States, in Order to form a more perfect Union, establish Justice, insure domestic Tranquility, provide for the common defence, promote the general Welfare, and secure the Blessings of Liberty to ourselves and our Posterity, do ordain and establish this Constitution for the United States of America.

—The Preamble to the Constitution of the United States of America.

CHAPTER 9
THE BRITISH LEGACY

The Constitution of the United States was written by fifty-five men—and one ghost. Those fifty-six began converging on the Pennsylvania State House in Philadelphia in the spring of 1787, where they were to labor—or lurk, in the case of the ghost—until the middle of September.

Attendance fell short of anticipation. In all, seventy-four delegates had been appointed by twelve states—only reluctant Rhode Island had declined to take part, holding that the very purpose of the convention was not in its best interests. The nineteen missing individuals had various excuses for not showing up, with many simply wanting to avoid linkage to an exercise they considered to be either futile or evil. Patrick Henry was one who chose not to come. The well-known Virginia patriot, of "give me liberty or give me death" fame, turned out to be more Virginian than American. Petulantly saying he "smelt a rat," meaning an effort to strengthen federal power at state expense, he remained at home to look after state business.

For those who did attend, May of that year was not a good month to travel. Stormy weather, with drenching rains, turned the best roads bad, the rest into quagmires. With several having hundreds of miles to traverse, delegates straggled slowly into Philadelphia. George Washington's problems in getting there were typical. Although he had planned to depart Mount Vernon on the eighth, so as to arrive well before the opening session, set for the fourteenth, heavy rain and high waters along the way kept him on muddy roads until the thirteenth, a

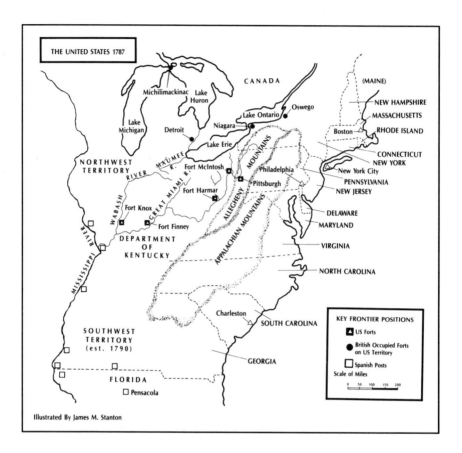

THE UNITED STATES 1787

Illustrated By James M. Stanton

Sunday. He need not have pushed so hard. Only two states—his own Virginia and host Pennsylvania—had delegates there in time. Indeed, not until the twenty-fifth of that sodden month were enough states represented to reach the quorum needed to officially open the proceedings. And even then, a Friday marked by cold rain and lightning, just twenty-one individuals took seats to conduct the first order of business: electing George Washington to serve as chairman. The last of the fifty-five delegates would not arrive until August.

The weather had broken enough on the day Washington reached Philadelphia for exuberant citizens to welcome him. Thrilled that the Grand Convention was to be held in their city, and all the more so that Washington himself was participating, cheering crowds thronged his route from the ferry landing at the Schuylkill River. Cannon salutes echoed off buildings while the town's bells rang out a raucous welcome. The City Troop, resplendently uniformed and handsomely mounted, proudly escorted the famous visitor to Benjamin Franklin's residence. At that time Dr. Franklin was eighty-one years old, the president of Pennsylvania, a delegate to the convention—and the only man in America whose prestige could come close to matching Washington's. Looking forward to his role as host to the convention, Franklin had set aside a complete cask of the finest porter. We may assume it was opened on this occasion.

Franklin and Washington may have been the best known of all the delegates, but among the others were many of the most distinguished Americans of the time. Thomas Jefferson, whose duties in Europe kept him away, exclaimed upon seeing the list of names that the convention was "an assembly of demi-gods." Over three-quarters of them had served in Congress, and most had held positions of influence in state or federal government, or both. Eight had signed the Declaration of Independence. A large proportion had been involved in the process of preparing state constitutions. Thirty had seen active military duty, of whom seventeen had been officers in the Continental Army, with the other thirteen being veterans of militia service. Surprisingly enough, many were quite young for such significant work. Jonathan Dayton of New Jersey was only twenty-six, Charles Pinckney of South Carolina just three years older. Alexander Hamilton, who may have done more than anyone except James Madison to make the convention possible, was a seasoned thirty. At thirty-three, Edmund Randolph was already governor of Virginia.

But for all their differences of age or experience or section, the fifty-five shared three common characteristics destined to shape their deliberations in the weeks ahead. First, evident in their very presence at this convention, was the realization that flaws marred the current form of government. They had all suffered the humiliation of weakness. Changes were necessary, they agreed, but just what those changes ought to be was another matter. Second, every delegate was a patriot, a participant in some way in the winning of independence from Great Britain. That war had been quite probably the defining event in the adult lives of all of them. Third, their cultural heritage was British. By measures of language, history, political philosophy, family, religion—all those molding elements that determine a people—they were inextricably linked to the former mother country. Life for 150 years in the New World may have put a unique twist to their Britishness, but environment alone could not eradicate the essence of their heritage. Englishmen they were, of a different sort to be sure, but certainly not French or German or Spanish, or even Irish.

The range of issues the members set out to contemplate was as broad as government itself: finance, commerce, sovereignty, justice, and security prominent among them. Fundamentals forging the fate of the United States of America. It may well be, though, as many historians have since concluded, that in no way did the convention end up having a more profound impact on the nation-to-be than it did in the field of security, in providing for domestic tranquility and the common defense. It was this issue that made the convention possible in the first place, and it certainly sparked the most passionate debates. Emotions on the subject ran so deep, were so gut-wrenching, because of an irreconcilable conflict between what members knew must be, yet were by heritage reluctant to accept. They were constrained, knowingly or subconsciously, by the fact that their cultural roots were planted so deeply in English soil. The motivating revelations of recent experiences clashed with their restraining body of inherited knowledge. One part of them said an army was essential for security; another said that an army would itself be a threat to security. That clash created a dilemma for virtually every member of the convention, a dilemma directly resulting from the military legacy passed down to them by Great Britain.

No two delegates so represented the opposing sides of the argument as did Alexander Hamilton and Elbridge Gerry. Epitomizing those espousing the need for a regular army, Hamilton was on a collision course with Gerry, who fervently believed that a standing army would be a curse to destroy democracy in the fledgling country. Both men had publicly and forcefully staked out their positions long before, in the waning years of the Revolutionary War.

Hamilton's rise to fame had been nothing if not meteoric. Growing up on the island of St. Croix, Alexander was virtually orphaned at the age of eleven when his mother died, his father having deserted the family some years earlier. Aunts sent the sixteen year old to New York for an education; from that point on, he was on his own. Entering King's College (now Columbia University) in 1773, he soon fell in with the radical movement and became an active opponent of British coercion. Speaking out in gatherings and in pamphlets, the youth attracted attention for the power and maturity of his views, showing an inner force not at all foretold by his short stature and slight build. When war broke out, he quickly became a captain in the Continental Army, commanding, at nineteen, a company of artillery. Though he may not yet have known the need to shave regularly, he led his artillerymen well in several battles, gaining experience under pressure and enlarging his reputation. Early in 1777, General Washington selected him to be an aide-de-camp, a position making him a personal confidant of the commander in chief. Brilliant and talented, energetic and ambitious, he quickly won the general's complete trust and admiration. Service in that capacity for more than four years—years as formative for young Hamilton as they were fraught with danger for the young nation—comprised his education in the complexities and imperatives of "providing for the common defense." Marriage to Elizabeth Schuyler in December 1780 linked him to one of the wealthiest and most powerful families in New York—and eventually brought him eight children. Upon leaving Washington's headquarters in 1781, Hamilton took command of a battalion in Lafayette's division and distinguished himself in a valiant attack on a British strongpoint during the Battle of Yorktown. Though still an officer in the Continental Army, he represented New York in the Continental Congress in 1782 and 1783, where he found himself opposed by a tall, angular representative from Massachusetts, Elbridge Gerry.

Like almost everything about the two antagonists, Gerry's path to prominence had been quite different. Born in 1744 into a well-to-do family in Marblehead, Massachusetts, Gerry graduated from Harvard at the age of eighteen and entered the family shipping business. Within a decade he had become wealthy and decided to enter politics in his colony. Caught up in the swelling resistance to British rule, he became a follower of Sam Adams, the Massachusetts rabble-rouser who played a key roll in sparking rebellion. Gerry was an active agitator and propagandist in many of the events around Boston in the fateful three years leading up to the day of Lexington and Concord. Following the example of his mentor, Sam Adams, Gerry focused his efforts on revolutionary organization, content to leave the actual fighting to others. Building on his business experience, he labored to bring some order to the chaotic supply situation in the months between the outbreak of war and his election to the Continental Congress in January 1776. There he supported and signed the Declaration of Independence. Always a fractious sort, Gerry's tenure in Congress was marked by dissent and disagreement. He did not like George Washington's way of waging the war, and attempted to have him replaced. Nor did he like the idea of an alliance with France, or very much else for that matter. In fact, he became so upset with his colleagues that he resigned in a huff, claiming that the lawmakers were infringing on the personal rights of individuals and the sovereign rights of states. Significantly, though, he signed the Articles of Confederation before departing. For a time he turned to privateering, the sending to sea of armed vessels to prey on shipping for profit and patriotism. Returning to Congress toward the end of the war, he found there yet another object for his disdain: Colonel Alexander Hamilton.

From the outset, the two congressmen fought. Hamilton was a Nationalist through and through; Gerry was as staunchly Anti-Nationalist. Hamilton, the Continental Army veteran, thought a regular army was absolutely essential to the safety of the nation; Gerry, whose hatred for uniforms could be traced to redcoats in the Boston Massacre of 1770, thought a standing army was absolutely inimical to the safety of the nation. Hamilton, a close observer inside the army during the dark days of the war, believed the weakness of the central government was the reason the Revolution had nearly been lost; Gerry, a signer of both the Declaration of Independence and the Articles of Confederation, believed the central government already had too few restraints on its power. Hamilton wanted to place the future security of the new nation in the hands of a defense establishment with muscle; Gerry wanted to rely on the militia and three thousand miles of ocean.

Gerry won that first round. Hamilton had been unable to convince war-weary congressmen to embrace a concept of preparedness. He left in disgust to practice law in New York. Gerry, meanwhile, worked to abolish the remnants of the Continental Army and to assure that the emerging peace establishment would not include a standing army. In a passionate and climactic address on the floor of Congress, he swung enough votes to his view to eliminate almost all of the central government's defense capability. More than any other single person, Gerry was responsible for the fact that the army of the United States had shriveled to a grand total of eighty soldiers by 2 June 1784.

In the summer of 1787, the former foes met again, in the very room where Gerry had stood for independence on that long-ago July day. This time, however, the issue of a national defense establishment was not predominantly theoretical. It had been three humiliating years since the Continental Army had been disbanded, three years of painful practical experience for the delegates to ponder. Gerry's own opposition could itself no longer be so implacably unbending. Chastened by Shays's frightening example in his own state, even that strident Anti-Nationalist had to admit to the need for some kind of a ready military force. This round would go to Hamilton, although that was by no means a foretold outcome as the convention got under way in the cold and rain. The bad weather of May gave no hint of what the summer would actually bring. It was to be a torrid season in the Pennsylvania capital, hot and humid and miserable—the worst since 1750, old-timers said.

When time came to sign the new Constitution in September, Alexander Hamilton would be the only New Yorker to put his name on it. Elbridge Gerry would be the only New Englander to refuse to do so. Instead, he would conclude his work at the convention by protesting what he perceived to be the folly of his countrymen.

When Gerry walked out of the Pennsylvania State House on that September day to come, insightful members might have sensed a phantom striding out with him, the ghost all would recognize as having been present during every single session since that rainy opening day back in May. Both Gerry and the ghost would be heard from again.

CHAPTER 10
THE GHOST OF CROMWELL

The ghost participating in the Constitutional Convention was Oliver Cromwell's. The Great Protector, the man on horseback, the military dictator, the general who had turned his army first on the throne and then on Parliament. Cromwell. The very name was the personification of the evil potential in a soldier grown too powerful. Oliver Cromwell. Nothing more need be uttered to conjure up the danger inherent in a standing army. An English-speaking person could hardly have grown to adulthood in the eighteenth century and not have heard the haunting story of Oliver Cromwell.

So far as can be determined from all the notes made during the convention, the delegates in debate very carefully avoided referring to anyone by name. They wanted to shape a government that would rise above and last beyond individuals. But historic figures were fair game. Cromwell led the list of men whose names surfaced most often in those notes. His was a prominent presence the framers could hardly ignore.

Cromwell was the central figure—and the symbol—of the most intensely disturbing era in English history. Lasting for more than six decades, from around 1625 to about 1690, the period was marked by civil war, rebellion, insurrection, religious persecution, social upheaval, wars abroad, executions, massacres, economic distress, and political chaos. Not to be outdone by all of that manmade strife, Mother Nature chose that same period to scourge the people with two crushing disasters: the Black Plague that devastated London, and a raging fire that destroyed much of that same hapless city.

Americans, knowing the enduring scars left by our own Civil War, can quite well appreciate how searing to the English psyche would be their country's much longer and more bitter time of troubles. It is not at all surprising that men of English heritage, steeped in history as were all educated individuals of their time, and assembling less than a century later to write a constitution for a new government, would have been molded both emotionally and mentally by that traumatic era.

Coming to the throne in 1625, Charles I began at once to clash with Parliament. When members refused to vote the combative new monarch enough money to conduct his wars with Spain and France, Charles resorted to bullying Parliament and to relying on forced loans. When his soldiers returned from war, the king decided not to disband them, but rather to billet them with citizens, with the greater numbers of armed men seemingly being placed in the homes of those who had most resisted the loans. The seeds of implacable resistance to a standing army were sown by that decision. Some time later, momentarily gaining the upper hand in the seesawing power struggle, Parliament forced Charles to accept a Petition of Right that included prohibitions on billeting soldiers in private houses and restrictions on the peacetime grant of military commissions. The ever-simmering dispute escalated until a crisis caused by a revolt in Scotland brought about a complete rupture. Civil war flamed in 1642. By 1644 the most outstanding battle leader on either side was Oliver Cromwell, who skillfully commanded a trained and effective force known as the "Ironsides." In another year he became the lieutenant general of all Parliamentary forces, which had been reorganized to resemble the "Ironsides" and were known as the New Model Army. Cromwell's brilliant victories ended the war in 1646. The king was captured.

That should have been the end of it, but Parliament then tried to disband its army without pay, leading to a split among the victors. Cromwell, several members of Parliament, and most of the army rebelled. A long period of confusion, including a second civil war, ended with the New Model Army dominant. Military leaders quickly consolidated power, purging Parliament of all but those supporting the army. They beheaded Charles I.[1]

---

1. Killing the king was a chilling and unforgettable event. Englishmen would forever afterwards remember that the army had done it. While there would

With real power residing in Cromwell and his army, but with a residue—the "Rump"—of Parliament theoretically having legislative authority, a republic was established. Called the Commonwealth, the new government operated under a council of state, the title and office of king having been abolished. The House of Lords had also been disestablished. Many Catholics remained in revolt, especially in Ireland and Scotland. Cromwell personally led an invading army across the sea to Ireland, where he brutally suppressed the rebellion, leaving a legacy of hatred enduring to this day. When Charles II landed in Scotland, raising a force of Royalist supporters, Cromwell rapidly attacked them, destroying the Scottish army and chasing Charles back to France. War broke out with the Dutch, but at home Cromwell was secure. His New Model Army, about seventy thousand strong, was by any measure a standing army. Composed of loyal veterans, it was disciplined and trained—and well paid. One of the ways Cromwell found sufficient money to meet his military payroll was to sell Royalist estates. Inevitably, his high-handed methods led to friction with the Rump Parliament. Cromwell turned it out in April 1653 and set up a new one. In December of that year, Cromwellian supporters in Parliament resigned, transferring their powers to the general. Four days later, Cromwell established the Protectorate, giving himself the title, "Lord Protector of the Commonwealth of England, Scotland, and Ireland." Having been ruler in all but name, he finally had corrected that omission. He would later reject a suggestion that he assume the title of king—"Lord Protector" entailed power enough. At least, it entailed enough for so long as he controlled the army. The written constitution setting up the Protectorate mandated a standing army of thirty thousand soldiers. Cromwell had come to power on the shoulders of a professional force; he had consolidated that power with a large and reliable body of regulars; he then perpetuated his power with a constitutionally established standing army.

Actually, the issue of a large standing army in *peacetime* was moot, for England remained almost constantly at war during Cromwell's decade

---

be a Royal Navy once more, and one day a Royal Air Force, there would never again be a Royal Army. An English army, or a British army, but not a royal one.

of dictatorship. Repeated cycles of conflict with the Dutch, the Spanish, and the French filled the years. Nevertheless, the English people got a thorough taste of government by a man on horseback. And they did not like it.

The depth of that dislike surfaced immediately after Cromwell's death in 1658. His son, Richard Cromwell, succeeded him as lord protector, but soon became embroiled in an argument between the army and Parliament. An almost comic-opera scenario ensued. In April 1659, Richard dissolved Parliament. A rump session then convinced him to resign as lord protector. Next, the army threw out the Rump Parliament and installed a military committee to govern. Visceral resistance to that military coup returned Parliament to office. Finally, the commander in chief in Scotland, Gen. George Monk, marched his troops to London, where he took charge. Monk convened a new Parliament, which opened negotiations with Charles II, still in exile. Tired of experiments with other forms of government, the English were ready to return to monarchy. If it was an evil, it was at least one they understood. Charles and Parliament reached agreement quickly. Proclaimed king in May 1660, he returned to London that same month, a little over eleven years after the execution of his father, and just twenty months after Oliver Cromwell's death. Royalists dug up Oliver Cromwell's body, ripped it asunder, and scattered the pieces across the English countryside.

The Restoration did not mean the end of strife. Charles II, hardly a beloved favorite, had been by no means a universal choice. Old animosities and arguments lurked just beneath the surface, stilled for the moment only by a general relief over the end of dictatorship. Both sides reached immediate agreement to disband the New Model Army. A wiser Parliament this time found money to provide separation pay for the soldiers. Charles gained authority to retain about five thousand men under arms. Commanded by the trusted General Monk, they were ostensibly for the king's personal protection and to garrison various fortresses. The unrelenting contest between Parliament and Crown for control of the army was only at the halfway point.

England soon found itself at war once again with Holland and France, even as violent uprisings rocked the kingdom. The king just could not leave well enough alone. Whether at war or in peace, Charles's constant stirring of religious unrest at home kept his subjects in turmoil.

Nor did his Byzantine dealings with foreign courts diminish Parliament's growing level of suspicion. Especially galling was the king's warm relationship with Louis XIV, who surreptitiously gave Charles fiscal support to help pay his army, thereby providing him a measure of independence from Parliament. Domestic backing dwindled steadily in the face of the evident and increasing ties to France, England's ancient enemy of choice. Political parties began coalescing, with the labels "Whig" and "Tory" appearing, initially as terms of disapproval. Tories generally came to be those who supported the Crown, whereas Whigs were those usually behind Parliament. Political disarray, domestic violence, religious intolerance, yet another war with Holland—all this and more continually heightened tensions between Charles II and his subjects, with issues concerning the military establishment often being at the center of controversy. The reign of Charles II, though a quarter of a century long, was a turbulent one.

When James II succeeded his brother in 1685, he found his throne to be resting on a keg filled with a highly volatile mixture, a black powder made up of religious bigotry, court intrigue, and factions at war's edge with one another. He was not astute enough to avoid lighting the fuse. Within months, a pretender to the Crown launched a military campaign to unseat the new king. Loyal regiments quickly disposed of that threat and others, defeating rebel forces in the field and executing their leaders. Pressing his advantage, James attempted to punish some of the sources of rebellion and to change many of the existing rules regarding the expression of religious beliefs. Both Whigs and Tories united against him, for reasons founded in religious prejudice, but also claiming that he was illegally retaining under arms those regiments raised to combat the earlier effort to depose him. In June 1687, several prominent Englishmen wrote to William of Orange, the Dutch grandson of Charles I, asking him to come to England to save the country. William, who was married to Mary—his cousin and also a grandchild of Charles I—was interested. He saw it as a way to strengthen his hand against Louis XIV of France. Accepting the invitation, William landed with an invasion force in November. Several key leaders promptly joined him, leaving James no reasonable chance to resist successfully. He escaped to France. William entered London in near-bloodless triumph in December. Leaders of the successful overthrow set up a provisional government—not overlooking to pay off the remnants of James's army before it was disbanded.

The "Glorious Revolution," made possible by a foreigner at the head of an invading army, had finally put Parliament in control. England would need a new king, monarchy still being the preferred form of government, and an army, because war with France was all but inevitable. Louis XIV was sure to try to put James back in power. Nevertheless, after their recent bitter experiences with the last two kings, the members were absolutely set on making sure that the army could never again be used to coerce Parliament. With that imperative in mind, they opened negotiations with William and Mary, dual descendants in the royal line. The resulting contract, put on parchment, gave the Crown jointly to the two of them, while establishing written rules regarding armed forces that reach even to this day into most English-speaking countries.

In return for the throne, William and Mary had to agree to the Declaration of Rights. That document and other laws passed at about the same time formalized the raising and maintaining of military units. To begin with, "the raising or keeping of a standing army within the kingdom in time of peace, unless it be with the consent of Parliament, is against the law." The right of citizens to bear arms was assured. Soldiers were banned from polling places and from the House of Commons. Any army raised would automatically be disbanded unless Parliament renewed its authorization annually. Money to support the army would be Parliament's responsibility. In such provisions was the answer to Parliament's long-standing dilemma—how to raise an army necessary for security without at the same time creating a threat to security.[2]

The concepts embedded in those measures also provided precedent for men sitting in Philadelphia a century later. Fear of a standing army . . . no similar concern over a navy . . . funding centered in the legislative body . . . command of forces entrusted to the executive . . . prohibitions against military involvement in internal affairs . . . short-term authorizations for the use of force. It was not by coincidence that

---

2. Time would prove the acts effective—not until twentieth century air attacks by Germans would the English homeland know battle again.

the emerging Constitution would reflect many of the concepts developed at such terrible cost in the mother country, for that cost had not been paid only there. English colonies along the Atlantic seaboard had shared in the trauma of the era. Indeed, to a significant degree, they had been shaped by it.

Between the coronation of Charles I in 1625 and the advent of William and Mary sixty-five years later, English lodgments in the New World had gone from a few wilderness settlements struggling for survival to an unbroken stretch of thirteen thriving colonies. While many adventurers and not a few criminals were among the earlier arrivals, the major impetus prompting settlers to risk the hazardous ocean crossing was escape from the societal chaos so prevalent in Europe. Endemic warfare, religious persecution, incessant internal crises—these helped mightily to people colonial America. However, the wrenching experience of quitting familiar homes and lands for a new beginning on a new continent would leave colonists unalterably biased against the causes of the intolerable conditions in their former lives. Probably more often than not, the most prominent symbol of that upheaval was the sword—soldiers enforcing unpopular decrees, suppressing religious freedom, marauding in the countryside, impressing young men for one war or another. Unhappily, refugees from repression found that flight to America was not far enough; the wars of Europe spilled over into the colonies, obviously influencing their security needs, but also changing their very composition. Conflict with Holland eventually converted Dutch settlements along the Hudson River into the colony of New York, but lands to the north along the St. Lawrence River evolved into an ever-menacing threat from the French, while Spanish bases in Florida and along the Gulf Coast added a potentially vulnerable flank to the south. Moreover, soldiers were occasionally used against the colonists themselves—for instance, in stamping out Bacon's Rebellion in Virginia and suppressing Leisler's Uprising in New York, both after the death of Cromwell. Many colonial governors were former army officers who ruled, it was noted, with a hand resting heavily on the hilt of a saber. All told, Americans of the late seventeenth century understood fully the philosophy behind the Declaration of Rights imposed upon William and Mary. Indeed, they probably approved of provisions limiting royal military power even more overwhelmingly than did their countrymen in England.

Another century of experience served only to solidify in American minds an enduring distrust of regular forces. For many in the thirteen colonies, it became an unyielding article of faith that a standing army was entirely incompatible with republican principles. Pamphleteers in England hammered on the theme, providing a theoretical underpinning for their receptive cousins in the colonies. Actual encounters with regulars and a nearly continuous state of warfare added reality to theory. France and Great Britain[3] fought a series of wars beginning after the "Glorious Revolution" of 1688 and lasting more than a century. Until the Treaty of Paris recognized the independence of the United States in 1783, an objective of all those conflicts was to gain dominance in North America. Evidence of how the colonists viewed those Old World dynastic struggles is seen in the names they gave them. They retitled the War of the League of Augsburg "King William's War." Mary escaped being linked to the fighting, but not because of her gender, for the War of the Spanish Succession became "Queen Anne's War." Colonists used "King George's War" as the label for the War of the Austrian Succession. The pattern broke with the Seven Years' War, which on this side of the Atlantic was known as the French and Indian War. Fittingly enough, for that one began in America, having been started on the western frontier by a brash young Virginian named George Washington. Patriots called the final conflict of the series the Revolutionary War or the War of Independence, whereas Englishmen referred to it as the War for America. The first four of those conflicts brought large numbers of redcoats to North America, generally elevating the disdain colonists held for them, and at the same time increasing the chances for friction between civilians and soldiers. The fifth and final clash, of course, brought more regulars than all the others combined—and as enemies, not friends.

Troubles between British regulars and American citizens began right after the French and Indian War ended in 1763. Great Britain, having ejected France from Canada and Spain from Florida, was finally triumphant in virtually all of North America east of the Mississippi River. London decided to station some of its army in America to keep the

---

3. The kingdoms of England and Scotland were officially combined in 1707 under the name Great Britain.

peace on its new frontiers. Colonists raised the point that the king had not seen fit to do so when French troops had been there to pose a real threat, and they questioned the need now. They also suspiciously thought the number of redcoats excessive for the task. The soldiers quickly proved their worth, however, in suppressing a bloody Indian uprising known as Pontiac's War. They remained. To avoid another flare-up, English officials drew a boundary along the Appalachians beyond which white settlers could not go. That arrangement infuriated both settlers and land speculators. They refused to comply with the new arrangements, forcing the army to remove squatters and burn their farms. Whatever residual goodwill may have lingered for the king's soldiers dissipated at that point.

The British treasury had been emptied by the expenses of the Seven Years' War. Ministers, searching for every possible way to raise revenue, thought it only equitable for the colonies to help pay the costs of maintaining an active force in America to defend them. Colonists thought otherwise. They had not wanted the army in the first place, and they emphatically did not want to be taxed to support it. "Taxation without representation," they cried, and resisted all efforts to levy taxes. Civil unrest followed. London responded by reinforcing its fleet and army in America. In 1768, believing that colonists had become more of a danger to peace than Indians, king and cabinet evacuated posts in the interior and consolidated regiments along the Atlantic seaboard. With the arrival of troops came the Mutiny Act—a law requiring civilians to quarter soldiers and to provide certain support for them. Tensions grew. Resistance led to rioting, which led inexorably to bloodshed.

Hotheads like Samuel Adams in Massachusetts and Patrick Henry in Virginia fanned emotions into flame. Episodes of violence increased across the land. On 5 March 1770, a taunting mob confronted and cornered a squad of British soldiers in Boston. The soldiers, a part of the garrison of four regiments sent to the city to enforce taxation attempts, became frightened. They fired into the jeering crowd, killing five men— making them martyrs. Elbridge Gerry and leaders of his passionate persuasion commemorated the so-called Boston Massacre on its anniversary every year thereafter to remind the public of the threat to freedom entailed in a regular force. A standing army, they preached, was a standing invitation for a man on horseback to overthrow the constituted government.

Things did not get any better in Boston. After that port's infamous "tea party" in December 1773, London placed the recalcitrant colonials under martial law and appointed Gen. Thomas Gage, the commander of all British units in America, to serve also as governor of Massachusetts. That was galling to the pride of the people of Massachusetts and an unendurable affront to the concept of civilian supremacy. Gage shifted his headquarters from New York City to Boston in May 1774. The Revolutionary War exploded less than a year later.

There can be no doubt that bitter experiences in the dozen years before the outbreak of the War of Independence elevated in American hearts the already high level of fear and loathing for a standing army in peacetime. Events of those years placed an indelible exclamation mark to existing antimilitary sentiments. The very words of the Declaration of Independence trumpet the depth of that feeling. About a third of the document is devoted to a denunciation of the militarism of George III. The Declaration fairly shouts out that the monarch "has kept among us, in times of peace, Standing Armies, without the consent of our legislatures. He has affected to render the Military independent of and superior to the Civil Power."

It is all but sure that the citizens of the United States, as they headed into the final quarter of the eighteenth century, had come to dread a standing army every bit as fervently as did their British brethren. Probably more so. To men sitting in the Constitutional Convention, the ghost of Oliver Cromwell brought long shivers—and an abiding determination never to permit its reincarnation.

CHAPTER 11
A JEALOUS EYE

The fifty-five framers of the Constitution, like human beings of any time or place, were prisoners of their culture and their experience. As Americans, they had been shaped by their English heritage to distrust a standing army, an inherent distrust that had been sharpened to outright distaste by recent encounters with redcoats, both before and during the Revolution. Having learned from history as well as life to abhor the forces of the Crown, Americans intuitively applied those lessons to their own troops as well. A standing army, even though composed of one's friends and neighbors, was an instrument not to be trusted. It was a danger to those who loved liberty. It bespoke tyranny. Samuel Adams, reflecting in 1776 on the necessity of fielding a large and well-trained army of Continentals, reminded his countrymen of the dark side to a standing army. "Such a Power should be watched with a jealous Eye," he wrote. If the Colonists' deep-seated beliefs had needed articulating, there had been more than enough to talk about in the later years of the War of Independence. By their very actions, Continental soldiers gave ample reinforcement to the fears of a standing army in the United States.

When undisciplined recruits drove Congress from Philadelphia to refuge in Princeton in the summer of 1783, it was but the last of several such affronts to civilian control of the military. The first serious incident aimed at civil leadership had occurred on New Year's Day 1781 after men in the Pennsylvania line decided to force Congress to meet its commitments to them.

But that was not the first mutiny to occur in the Continental Army. Embittered by the failure of their country to feed or clothe or pay them, troops had from time to time risen in concert to protest in the only way they knew how—by quitting. Forceful and prompt action by officers, often assisted by other units, had usually ended those episodes. In May 1780, for instance, two regiments of the Connecticut line stationed at West Point gathered at dusk to announce their intention to leave for home because of the lack of food and pay. They bayoneted their colonel when he tried to talk them out of going. Other officers quickly placed the Pennsylvania line astride the Connecticut soldiers' route. Sobered by the thought of having to fight their way out, the malcontents returned. But they continued milling around late into the night, grumbling about their shabby treatment. One wrote that they clustered in angry groups, "venting our spleen at our country and government, then at our officers, and then at ourselves for our imbecility in staying there and starving in detail for an ungrateful people who did not care what became of us."

Thoughts of marching home in protest of maltreatment shifted easily in the minds of disgruntled soldiers to considerations of marching against the source of the maltreatment itself. Seeking improvement in that way seemed not altogether inappropriate to men who had enlisted in a movement predicated on the proposition that using arms against an unjust government was proper. And that is just what the soldiers of the Pennsylvania line chose to do on the first day of January 1781: march on Congress.

Having themselves stood in the way of the Connecticut line several months earlier, the Pennsylvanians were not about to be deflected by others. Shouldering muskets, dragging six pieces of artillery, and fortified with rum, they set off for Philadelphia. When officers attempted to halt them, they plunged straight on, killing two captains and wounding others. Brigadier General Anthony Wayne, a Pennsylvanian himself, caught up to the column and followed it cautiously into New Jersey, looking for an opening to talk some sense into the men.

Word of the mutineers' intent traveled the wintry roads rapidly to Philadelphia. The approach of that determined and obviously angry body of soldiers frightened Congress. Delegates hastily selected a committee to ride out to intercept the hostile column before it could reach the seat of government. The mutineers halted at Princeton, where they began to bargain with the congressional representatives.

Meanwhile, General Washington was readying a force to pursue and punish the mutinous band. To disregard such indiscipline in the Continental Army was unthinkable, especially an act of violence aimed at Congress. He intended to take tough measures to preclude future eruptions of that sort. To do less would risk the spread of rebellion in the ranks. A thousand men, well fed and wearing new shoes, assembled to march from West Point to Princeton to subdue the Pennsylvanians. As it turned out, they were too late. Congress caved in to the pressure, agreeing to meet the demands of the threatening soldiers. For the moment confrontation was averted, but appeasement tends only to unlock doors to further trouble.

As Washington had feared, the mutiny's apparent success inspired others to emulate the Pennsylvanians. On 20 January, New Jersey troops, billeted at Pompton in their home state, started off drunkenly in the direction of Trenton, making demands "similar to those of the Pennsylvania line." Having already decided to suppress any further mutiny immediately and harshly, Washington sent a message to the representative Congress had earlier dispatched to deal with the Pennsylvanians, saying that he would "compel the mutineers to submission" and urging that "no terms be made with them." He selected several hundred New England soldiers for the unpleasant task, and assigned a North Carolinian, Maj. Gen. Robert Howe, to command them. His orders to Howe were blunt:

> The object of your detachment is to compel the mutineers to unconditional submission, and I am to desire you will grant no terms while they are with arms in their hands in a state of resistance. . . . If you succeed in compelling the revolted troops to a surrender you will instantly execute a few of the most active and most incendiary leaders.

When Howe caught up with the mutineers they had already returned to their cantonment in Pompton, having been convinced to do so by an officer who had promised them pardon if they would "conduct themselves in a soldierly manner." The men, though, remained surly and under arms. After a night march through deep snow, Howe surrounded them and called for surrender. The surprised New Jersey soldiers gave up quietly. A military surgeon accompanying Howe, Dr. James Thatcher, recorded what happened next:

> General Howe ordered that three of the ringleaders should be selected for condign punishment. These unfortunate culprits were tried on the spot . . . standing on the snow, and they were sentenced to be immediately shot. Twelve of the most guilty mutineers were next selected to be their executioners. . . . The wretched victims, overwhelmed by the terrors of death, had neither time nor power to implore the mercy and forgiveness of their God. . . . The first that suffered was a sergeant, and an old offender; he was led a few yards' distance and placed on his knees; six of the executioners, at the signal given by an officer, fired, . . . the other six reserving their fire in order to dispatch the victim should the first fire fail; it so happened in this instance; the remaining six fired, and life was instantly extinguished. The second criminal was, by the first fire, sent into eternity in an instant. The third, being less criminal, by the recommendation of his officers, to his unspeakable joy, received a pardon. This tragical scene produced a dreadful shock and a salutary effect on the minds of the guilty soldiers.

Thatcher was right about the impact of the executions. Although there were to be other mutinies, including one directed at the Connecticut legislature, Continentals had heard Washington's clear message: Congress was off limits as a target of military displeasure.

That rule, of course, would apply only as long as the officers remained loyal. It was they who enforced discipline, who kept disgruntled soldiers in line. Which is what had made the 1783 conspiracy at Newburgh so worrisome to both Washington and Congress. If army officers could not be depended upon to support the cause, the cause itself was lost. That fact helps explain the numbing shock Washington and others had felt when they discovered in 1780 that Benedict Arnold, a hero who held high command, had become a traitor in uniform long before he was found out.

Congress had endured disruption from both the fortunes of war and the ignominy of military insult. It had been chased from its place of business by soldiers of both sides, by campaigning British troops and by mutinous Continentals. And it had seen itself menaced by a cabal of officers. Being placed at risk by enemy maneuvers was one thing, being threatened by your own army was quite another. Only the powerful figure of George Washington had prevented those internal incidents from unraveling the fabric of the Continental Army, which elevated the esteem held for him but did not incline Americans to be any better disposed toward a standing army.

In the face of all that, it would have been rather surprising if most delegates to the Constitutional Convention had not had some qualms about a regular military establishment. Their fears were real—and well founded. A standing military force would indeed pose a threat to the very republic it would be created to secure. History assured them of that. But recent events also assured them that the republic could not endure *without* a competent military. That was their dilemma. When all was said, though, it remained obvious that the new nation had no option other than to field a national army. Only one thing was more dangerous to liberty than having an army—and that was not having one.

The great question, then, was how to maintain control over a strong army. How could such a force be kept loyal to the republic? Who would watch it with a jealous eye?

CHAPTER 12
THE COMMANDER IN CHIEF

After living two centuries with the Constitution, Americans today easily accept the concept of the president as the commander in chief of the nation's armed forces. It was not always thus. Delegates to the Constitutional Convention were overwhelmingly certain that there should be an executive in the revised government, but they had considerable trouble coming to grips with the details of the office itself. It was too new a concept. History was of some help, but mostly for its negative examples. Their own experiences beyond state government embraced only European-style monarchy and the executiveless Confederation Congress. Neither was an acceptable model. One had been recently discarded, and the other was about to be. Designing the presidency— for that is actually what they had to do—consumed as much of their intellectual energy during the ensuing months as any other single subject.

The summer's work started slowly. Nine states were represented on 25 May 1787, giving the convention a quorum at last. James Madison of Virginia selected a seat front and center with the self-appointed intention of recording all of the convention's proceedings. A man diminutive of size but brilliant of mind, he has been described as having "the maximum of intellect on the minimum of body." No one would work harder or do more to shape the Constitution that summer. Electing a presiding officer was the first order of business on that stormy Friday. Robert Morris, speaking for the Pennsylvania delegation, nominated George Washington, who was unanimously approved. After settling a handful of administrative details, the convention adjourned for the weekend. Several additional members took their seats on Monday, bringing the total of states represented to eleven; Rhode Island would boycott the entire proceedings, and New Hampshire's representatives would not arrive for weeks yet. The business of the day continued to be deciding upon the rules under which the delegates would operate. Tuesday saw two more members seated—John Dickinson and Elbridge Gerry—and the completion of preliminary arrangements. Among the procedures adopted was the order of voting: it would be done by state, by geographical location from north to south—the same arrangement the Continental Army had used for parades and ceremonies. If any person in the State House had been lulled by the leisurely pace of events up to that juncture, he was drawn up sharply as soon as the last vote on rules was taken and the convention turned to substantive business.

George Washington recognized the first speaker, Edmund Randolph. The young governor of Virginia, handsome, possessed of a strong voice, stood to present a proposal for what amounted to a wholly new form of government. One predicated on consolidation, not confederation. Instead of a confederation based upon the individual states, and beholden to them, Randolph suggested substituting a federation that would not only be superior to the states but would rest directly upon the people of all the states. It would be a central government of and for the individual citizens of the United States. Rather than merely revising the Articles of Confederation, Randolph was essentially recommending that they be superseded. Repair by replacement. His proposal, worked up principally by Madison with the assistance of the rest of the Virginia delegation, including Washington, was a bombshell in the State House.

A government, Randolph said, must be able to defend against foreign invasion. It must have the strength to keep the peace both between states and within them. It had to protect its borders and interests. And it must foster the general welfare of the states. The Articles of Confederation, he reminded the intent men absorbing the import of his words, failed on every one of those counts. Congress could neither prevent a war nor support one. It could not keep the peace. It could not "check the quarrels between states, nor a rebellion in any." Madison, keeping notes, wrote that the speaker "cited many examples," which included Shays's insurrection and the problems of Harmar's regiment. Thinking of the unrest west of the Alleghenies, Randolph added that the government could not even "defend itself against the encroachments from the states." James McHenry of Maryland recorded concisely in his notes that day, "The journals of Congress a history of expedients." To remedy all of those defects required a bold leap; the Articles must be "corrected and enlarged" in a major way, not just tinkered with. The governor then presented a document containing fifteen resolutions, the sum of which would comprise a federal rather than a confederal form of government.[1] The first purpose proclaimed for the new government was to provide for the "common defence."

Charles Pinckney of South Carolina quickly chimed in by similarly proposing a framework of a government having real power at the center. With that double thunderclap to ponder, the convention adjourned, with delegates voting to return the next day to begin discussing Randolph's resolutions—"to take into consideration *the state of the union,*" as New Yorker Robert Yates recorded. The Virginia plan did not explicitly mention an army or navy, although Randolph spoke of military force in his opening remarks, as did Pinckney. In the minds of Madison and most others, the need for regular forces was apparently too evident to require stating. A government capable of meeting the purposes outlined would obviously have military power. Moreover, one of the resolutions called for the establishment of a "National Executive," an office to wield that power.

Beginning that Wednesday and continuing for days thereafter, the convention met in committee of the whole, a device permitting the

---

1. The terms used to describe various forms of government were changing at the time of the Constitutional Convention itself, and have shifted even more with the passage of time. Delegates at first tended to refer to the arrangement under the Articles of Confederation as "federal," and the form broached by Randolph as "national." The previous distinction between Nationalist and Anti-Nationalist was fading, however, because by the summer of 1787 virtually all leaders believed that the nation needed a stronger central government. They only differed on degree and method. Madison later wrote that the Constitution was both national and federal. In the drafting and the ratification of the Constitution, "federal" became the accepted word to express the concept undergirding the document. Accordingly, Federalists were supporters of the Constitution, whereas Anti-Federalists were opposed to it. The text hereafter will use that formulation.

entire body to act as a committee to consider the resolutions without having to make final decisions on them. When finished, the committee of the whole would present a report to the convention—to itself, in effect—which could then be acted upon as a fresh document. In this configuration, a committee chairman replaced the president. That freed Washington to sit on the floor with the Virginia delegation. Members elected to the chair Nathaniel Gorham of Massachusetts, who had just finished a term as president of the Confederation Congress, and who very much favored a stronger government.

On Friday, 1 June, after two days of discussion on other aspects of Randolph's plan, the committee of the whole took up the resolution establishing a national executive. Charles Pinckney rose to say he was much in favor of a vigorous executive, but was afraid that if given too many powers the position could become "a monarchy, of the worst kind, to wit an elective one." James Wilson of Pennsylvania made a motion that the wording of the resolution be changed to stipulate that the executive was a single person, not a committee. Pinckney seconded the motion. Quiet followed. There was no discussion. Perhaps members glanced nervously from the corners of their eyes in Washington's direction. If there were to be a chief executive, they all knew, it would be the former commander in chief. Washington said nothing. The silence grew loud. Madison scribbled on his note pad that "a considerable pause" ensued. The chairman finally asked if the members were ready to vote. Aged Benjamin Franklin, weak of voice and limb but still sprightly of mind, interjected to urge discussion. On a matter of such great importance, he said, it was essential that the delegates speak their minds. That broke the dam. Debate began. On one point or another, delegates would wrestle with the issue all summer. Having the likely first occupant of the office present during those discussions proved to be a bit awkward at times—Madison told Jefferson later that it was in fact "peculiarly embarrassing." But Washington never officially spoke on the subject, and the members forged ahead.

What would this "national executive" be called? Would he be one person or a committee? How long would he serve? What would he be paid? How would he be elected? Could he be removed? Could he succeed himself? Who would take his place if he died in office? What powers would he have? What would be his relationship to the other branches of government? Once begun, the questions rolled forth, gathering momentum as differences of opinion surfaced. For most delegates, contemplating a national legislative body did not require a leap of the imagination. Their congresses, Continental and Confederation, had given them much experience to lean on. But envisioning a national executive was quite another matter. They were building a government for which no close parallel existed, and designing a head for it with no good precedent to consider. In the hindsight of history their debates on this topic seem rather more quaint than on most others, not surprisingly, for there was no obvious or easy handle to grab. Certain issues that appear today to be peripheral were argued exhaustively, whereas others that now seem central passed with hardly a nod. Overall, on this subject, the framers were unsteady in focus. Of some things, nevertheless, they were very sure. They wanted the executive to be strong—but not too strong. They wanted him to control the nation's sword—but on behalf of the republic, not against it. They wanted him to be like— well, like George Washington was in the Revolution. There was the model. They all but said it.

Washington had in superabundance that attribute called, for lack of a more expressive term, presence. Everyone who described his physical appearance, and they were numerous, made note of how strangers stood in awe at just the glimpse of him. A small head on a large, strong body made him appear even bigger than he was, while a natural gracefulness set him apart whether mounted or afoot. When he spoke, which was seldom, it was with sincere diffidence. Although one observer recorded, "His language is manly and expressive," he was not a dynamic or even a good speaker. But when he did have something to say, everyone listened. Austere, slow to smile, firm, reserved, exuding almost glacial dignity, he was not a man one would walk up to and slap on the back. A very impressed Englishman wrote that, had Washington been born in the forest, "he would have been the fiercest man among the savage tribes." And yet he projected a sense of quiet courteousness, of caring concern for others. He infected those around him with a contagious confidence. One historian, describing the Virginian's impact on others at the Constitutional Convention, wrote that his colleagues "sensed that he would never be overbearing, power would not turn his head." His very presence had held the Revolution together for eight trying years; his countrymen fully expected it to do the same thing in the trying early years of the new nation.

As the summer progressed, the shape of the figure of the executive began to look more and more like that of the man presiding over the convention. The job description was tailored by the framers to fit the tall Virginian. Washington's image was what they had in mind as they tried to visualize the executive in action. Pierce Butler of South Carolina later confided, "Many of the members cast their eyes towards General Washington as President, and shaped their ideas of the powers to be given to a President by their opinions of his virtue." Even on small matters—pay, for instance—he inspired comment. Dr. Franklin, believing the chief executive should receive full expenses but no salary, reminded delegates that an example had already been set. They had all seen, he said, "the great and most important of our offices, that of the General of our armies, executed for eight years together without the smallest salary, by a patriot whom I will not offend by any more praise. . . ."

The first item addressed was the matter James Wilson had raised. Should the executive be single or plural, one person or a committee? On this the convention was of two distinct minds. Randolph, regarding a single executive as "the fetus of anarchy," proposed a triumvirate. Pierce Butler thought such an arrangement would paralyze the government in moments of crisis, yet he admitted to being concerned about giving one man such power, asking rhetorically why might not "a Cromwell arise in this country as well as in others?" Benjamin Franklin, too, worried that a person acting alone might prove to be "fond of war." Lest his remark be construed as a veiled criticism of Washington, he quickly added, "The first man put at the helm will be a good one. Nobody knows what sort may come afterwards." George Mason of Virginia spoke in support of establishing a trio of leaders, one each from the northern, middle, and southern states, thereby assuring that the executive office would remain in touch with all the corners of the country. Countervailing arguments, emphasizing simplicity, historical example, and probable effectiveness, sprang from every direction. Elbridge Gerry, of all people, newly attuned to such considerations by the recent trouble in Massachusetts, recognized that an office composed of three members would be "extremely inconvenient in many instances, particularly in military matters, whether relating to the militia, an army, or a navy. It would be a general with three heads." His was the final word. The committee of the whole voted. Backers of a single executive prevailed, seven states to three. Washington sided with the majority of Virginia's representatives in favor of the single executive.

As the days passed, delegates worked their way through all of Randolph's resolutions, albeit a bit randomly, postponing some matters, skipping around, returning repeatedly to issues already voted. The final report did not address straight out the role of the executive in military matters. It simply stated that he would have the "power to carry into execution the national laws" and to appoint officers. But it was evident in discussions and implicit in the language of the developing document that members believed the executive would head the military. George Mason articulated a key reason behind their thinking when he stated, "The purse and the sword ought never to get into the same hands whether Legislative or Executive." Authority to raise money would reside with the legislative branch, all agreed, so the control of military forces would without question fall to the executive. And, in fact, no one appears to have raised a question on the matter, either in or out of session.

But if *what* was not an issue, *how* was. How the executive would exercise such responsibility was the subject of considerable conversation in private gatherings of delegates after the close of daily convention sessions. The mind's eye had trouble separating the image of George Washington, the commander in chief of the Continental Army, from that of the person in the office of the national executive. After all, during the war Washington had been the national executive in virtually every way but name. Trying to envision the position now, delegates gathering in clusters in boardinghouses or around dinner tables kept picturing a general commanding a large and loyal armed force—and who also carried the mace of the chief executive officer of the land. Put that way, the image of George Washington faded out, to be replaced by one of Oliver Cromwell.

One result of those informal meetings showed up as soon as the convention went back into full session and William Paterson of New Jersey introduced an alternative plan of government. The basic argument over the differences in the Virginia and the New Jersey plans was between big states and small ones, a fundamental conflict over representation not to be resolved until later in the summer, when a compromise solution was found. Nevertheless, both Randolph and Paterson envisioned a chief executive who would be in charge of the nation's regular fighting forces. Paterson, though, brought out into the open the question of how that duty would be discharged. The executive, he stated specifically, would "direct all military operations." He then went on to place definite constraints on that power. The executive would under no circumstances "take command of any troops, so as personally to conduct any enterprise as General or in other capacity." In short, the executive would provide civilian control over the military, but would not saddle up to lead in person. He would direct but not command. The mace and the sword would not be combined.

On Saturday, 16 June, the convention went back into committee of the whole to compare the two plans. Alexander Hamilton took the floor on the following Monday and held it all day, speaking for six hours. He vehemently opposed the New Jersey plan, saying it would not provide a powerful enough central government. Desperate times, he said, called for a more determined course. He sketched a concept of a government of far stronger coercive powers than any in the room had dared discuss before. His approach was so dramatic a departure from the Articles of Confederation as to make Randolph's plan seem tame by comparison, which some historians have suggested was Hamilton's intent. The young New Yorker's daylong, virtuoso performance, raising the possibility of yet a third form for a federal government, had its desired effect—it stopped any momentum for Paterson's alternative. When James Madison also tore apart the New Jersey proposal the next day, the delegates voted to focus their energies on Randolph's plan. With further revision, it would become the new form of government.

Although Hamilton had savaged New Jersey's overall approach, he echoed Paterson in proposing that the executive shall "have the direction of war when it is commenced, but he shall not take the actual command in the field of any army" unless authorized by the legislative body. A consensus seemed to be gathering. Delegates wanted the executive to be in control of the army, but they did not want to give him the ability to turn the army against the government. They also sought civilian supremacy over the military, a cardinal principle of the republic. John Adams had spoken for most when he told a senior officer during the Revolution, "We don't choose to trust you generals with too much power for too long a time." Tyranny flowed from unchecked power, delegates knew, which made it difficult to see how the executive could function as a general, or could be permitted to lead in battle.

He must be a civilian, not a soldier. Thus would be minimized the chance of the position giving birth to a despot. Washington may have been the model, but Cromwell's ghost nudged the sculptors' hands. They instinctively feared the very idea of a man on horseback, even one of their own creation.

In personal conversations, members had begun to use the title Washington had carried in the Revolution. When speaking of the function of the executive in directing the military, they referred to him as the commander in chief. Luther Martin of Maryland pointed out the "unreconcilable dilemma" of having a commander in chief who could not command. It was indeed a dilemma. Nor were the members of the convention able to reconcile it. They postponed decision, but never got back to the question again. The series of checks and balances that emerged later, as the military clauses in the Constitution were hammered out, apparently provided the members assurance enough to counter their latent fear of despotism. Perhaps they simply decided to leave it to the first executive to set the precedent. For whatever reason, they left the matter unsettled. The Constitution is silent on how the commander in chief is to execute his duties.[2] As a result, the president possesses unusually broad latitude in military matters. John Adams, who did not serve in the convention because he was representing the United States in London, but who was destined to follow Washington in the presidency, was surprised when he learned what strength the framers had entrusted to the person in the position. The chief executive, Adams later wrote delegate Roger Sherman of Connecticut, has raw power "greater than that of an avoyer, a consul, a podesta, a doge, a stadholder; nay, than a king of Poland; nay, than a king of Sparta." That Adams settled on Sparta as the ultimate example to make his point is illustrative. Sparta, the militaristic city-state of ancient Greece, was the epitome of a military establishment overshadowing the society it sprang from, of an army possessing a state rather than the other way around.

2. A time would come seven years later when Washington would have good cause to reflect on the convention's failure to come to grips with the "unreconcilable dilemma." He would then have occasion to decide whether the commander in chief would personally lead in battle or not.

The concern embedded in Adams's words reflected the quintessential American uneasiness with those who wield the nation's military might. Which could also help explain why delegates to the convention chose not to attempt a more explicit resolution, preferring to leave the details unstated rather than to risk a return to the impotency of the Articles of Confederation.

Gradually a solid majority, all but a die-hard handful led by Elbridge Gerry, concluded that a strong executive was more a protector of liberty than a menace.[3] The checks and balances built into the Constitution, as well as the fact that power flowed from the people not the state, made that so. The strength of the commander in chief would permit him to control the army, while the checks on that power would preclude the president from turning the army against the rest of the government. So long as everything worked right, strength was security. If, on the other hand, democracy went awry, the strength or weakness of the president hardly mattered. As Washington paraphrased Benjamin Franklin, when the "people shall become incapable of governing themselves and fit for a master, it is of little consequence from what quarter it comes."

In late July the convention took a ten-day break, turning all its records over to five of its members—a "Committee of Detail"—to prepare a consolidated version of the positions by then agreed upon. The whole of which, Washington recorded in his diary, would comprise "a Constitution for the United States." The committee did its work well. Assembling on 6 August, delegates found the first draft of the Constitution awaiting them. It gave for the first time a name to the executive: "The President of the United States of America." It then said

3. Two of the three members of New York's delegation—Robert Yates and John Lansing—left in protest over the apparent direction of the convention. They reflected the opinion of the state's governor, George Clinton, who retained strong Anti-Nationalist sentiments. The state thereby lost its vote, for the rules required the presence of at least two members for a state to be able to cast a vote. Alexander Hamilton, the third member, was able to participate in discussions. Frustrated, though, and needing to shore up his political position in New York, he spent much of July and August in that state.

the president "shall be commander in chief of the Army and Navy of the United States, and of the Militia of the several States." In that role, he would appoint and commission "all the Officers of the United States." He also had to take an oath—he was to swear to "execute the office of President of the United States of America."

Debates later in August and in early September led to the final wording of the Constitution of the United States. In one of the more subtle but significant of changes, the delegates broadened the oath of the chief executive. In its final form, it required the president to "preserve, protect and defend the Constitution of the United States." That oath is unique in America. The Constitution itself obliges all executive, legislative, and judicial officials, state and national, to swear simply "to support this Constitution." Only the president is sworn to preserve, protect, and defend it. The three verbs were not chosen without purpose. They are active, and require action. At times military action. And that is what the framers of the Constitution had in mind when they made the president the commander in chief of the nation's armed forces.

CHAPTER 13
TO MAKE WAR

When the convention recessed to give its Committee of Detail time to consolidate the first two months' work, delegates not on the committee tried to escape the sweltering city. George Washington went fishing.

After hitching Washington's horses to Gouverneur Morris's coach, the two men drove out "to the vicinity of Valley Forge to get trout." While Morris happily clambered up and down stream banks, wading into dark swirls despite his wooden leg, the former commander in chief harkened to a distant echo. Turning from the trout streams, he rode alone to the site of the Continental Army's encampment. As he recorded in his diary, he wandered "over the old Cantonement of the American army of the Winter, 1777 and 8," and attempted to visit "all the Works, which were in Ruins." He searched for the regimental streets and the rows of huts where an army had suffered, and had been reborn. They were gone. Crops covered the traces, except in the "woods where the grounds had not been cultivated." But the images remained sharp in his mind. Here he had been when some in the Continental Congress had started the abortive attempt to replace him. Here he had agonized over the sacrifices extracted from men inadequately supported by a weak central government. Here he had watched a German professional soldier transform a rabble of patriots into a regular force able to stand toe-to-toe with the best of British and Hessian units. If Washington had required any emotional reinforcement to bolster his work in the convention, he probably found all he needed in this return to Valley

Forge. Convening in solitude with his memories, he was not a threat to the trout that day.

A few days later, he set out again to fish, this time with a larger party of friends. They went to Trenton. There, at Christmastime in 1776, Washington had surprised and routed a garrison of Hessians, launching a brilliant ten-day campaign that turned the course of the war. Although all he confided to his diary was his success with the fish (better than at Valley Forge, but nothing to brag about), he must have sensed again the tingle of excitement battle brings, and victory brands. Did he see bloodstained snow in the August heat? Did he recall that some of those very streets had been swept clean of enemy resistance by the gallantry and guns of Capt. Alexander Hamilton? Did he reflect that, in the crisis of those dark days, the Continental Congress had seen fit to confer "dictatorial powers" on him because there was no executive in the fledgling country other than the commander in chief?

The two trips must have refreshed Washington of body. They could not have failed to refurbish him of spirit and resolve.

When delegates returned from the long recess to study the first draft of the Constitution prepared by the Committee of Detail, they found clauses regarding the military establishment scattered throughout the document. In addition to items pertinent to the powers of the commander in chief, several more were clustered under the powers of Congress, and a number were sprinkled around in other parts. The members of the committee had remembered only too well the debilitating arguments back at the end of the Revolution over whether the Articles of Confederation permitted or prohibited a peacetime military force. Two of the five, James Wilson and Oliver Ellsworth, had been members of Alexander Hamilton's committee of Congress charged in 1783 with preparing a peacetime military establishment. They could not have forgotten their failure and frustration. The committee was not about to let those old battles revive—the new constitution would specifically authorize a military establishment.

Members debated with some heat a variety of issues from 6 to 14 August before they encountered one involving a serious military relationship. Curiously enough, it was not primarily a military clause. The item in question was a section of the draft that precluded members of Congress from simultaneously holding other offices in the government. Several members were opposed to the restriction for a variety of reasons, one of which was that it would preclude military officers from service in the Senate or the House. Some of the delegates had themselves held military rank while serving in Congress, and saw nothing wrong in the practice.

Gouverneur Morris announced his concern that blocking soldiers from service in Congress would tend to isolate them from the political process. That would be dangerous in a democracy, he thought. Furthermore, it would deprive the country in wartime of the contributions of some of its best leaders. On the first point he was adamant and colorful: "Exclude the officers of the army & navy, and you form a band having a different interest from & opposed to the civil power; you stimulate them to despise & reproach those 'talking Lords who dare not face the foe.' Let this spirit be roused at the end of a war, before your troops shall have laid down their arms, and though Civil authority 'be intrenched in parchment to the teeth' they will cut their way to it." Morris knew from firsthand experience what he was talking about, having been one of the instigators of the Newburgh Conspiracy. Others in the room had also been involved in that ill-advised effort to coerce the Congress. They could not have missed his meaning. For that matter, everyone listening would have recognized the event he was referring to, even if they did not grasp the full extent of the warning. Nor did any need reminding that Parliament's failure to pay Cromwell's New Model Army at war's end had led directly to military dictatorship in England. The point was telling. Turning to his second reason, Morris asked where the country would have been if such a rule had pertained at the outset of the Revolution, thereby rendering the Continental Congress unable to appoint Congressman George Washington to the command of the Continental Army. He then proposed an amendment permitting members of Congress to accept commissions in the army and navy, with the proviso that they then vacate their legislative seats.

Morris was an unabashed supporter of a strong military presence in the government. His own extensive combat experience in the militia early in the Revolution had given him an abiding appreciation of the significance of well-led and fully trained armed units. Later, as a member of the Continental Congress, he had visited George Washington at Valley Forge, an experience that left him a lifelong admirer of the general and a close friend. The two shared common philosophies, and even looked alike. After losing a leg in an accident in 1780, Morris devoted his energy to the war effort by assisting with financial affairs. He has been called the most brilliant man at the convention. He was certainly one of the most active, speaking 173 times and taking a leading role throughout.

Morris's amendment found considerable support, but because of other arguments raised, the issue was set aside without action. Referred later to a committee selected to reconcile all such postponed matters, the provision returned and was approved in a formulation similar to Morris's proposal. The Constitution states, in Article I, Section 6: "No Senator or Representative shall, during the Time for which he was elected, be appointed to any civil Office . . . and no Person holding any office under the United States, shall be a member of either House during his continuance in Office." The word "civil" reveals the intent of the framers. They left the door open for members of Congress to accept military commissions, but at the same time required military officers to resign their commissions before being able to serve in Congress. They thus underscored the separation expected between the two institutions.

Elsewhere, the Constitution is quite specific about the responsibility for waging war. It is a federal burden forbidden to individual states. No state shall "keep Troops, or Ships of War in time of Peace," nor shall one "engage in War, unless actually invaded, or in such imminent Danger as will not readily admit of delay." Even in war, states are prohibited from granting "Letters of Marque and Reprisal," which is to say they were denied authority to engage in the then lucrative business of privateering. On the other hand, the weight of providing for the common defense and insuring domestic tranquility is placed solely on the shoulders of the national government. In fact, still more specifically, the framers vested in the House of Representatives, the institution closest to the citizens of the country, the power to "provide for the common Defence." On insuring domestic tranquility, though, the responsibility extends to the entire country, the United States, not to a single branch of the central government. Article IV, Section 4, proclaims: "The United States shall guarantee to every state in this Union a Republican Form of Government, and shall protect each of them against Invasion." The federal government is thereby charged with fending off both insurgency and foreign attack, with preserving each state's government, and with protecting the territory of each. The same section goes on to stipulate that, when so requested by a state, the strength of the United States shall also protect that state "against domestic Violence." The framers wisely left unstated the designation of forces to be employed, implying that security would ordinarily be effected with federalized militia.

The meat of the nation's war powers are to be found in Article I, Section 8, in the part of the Constitution devoted to the legislative body of the government. Remembering the long struggle in England between the Crown and Parliament over control of the army, and having noted the evils flowing from a military establishment controlled by one or the other, the framers set out to prevent either the legislative or the executive branch of the federal government from acquiring dominance over the military. Since the president would be the commander in chief, Congress should have a tether on his actions. An ideal arrangement would be one preventing either from acting without the support of the other. Making war should require cooperation, which would be attainable in situations involving the nation's true interests, but could not be gained in an effort by one branch or the other to overthrow the government. Having in mind the need for such checks and balances, delegates turned to the consideration of military clauses on 17 August. The Committee of Detail had grouped most of them under a listing of specific powers of the legislature:

- To make rules concerning captures on land and water;
- To subdue a rebellion in any state, on the application of its legislature;
- To make war;
- To raise armies;
- To build and equip fleets;
- To call forth the aid of the militia, in order to execute the laws of the Union, enforce treaties, suppress insurrections, and repel invasions.

The first of those powers passed without discussion. Debate began in earnest on the second as members differed on whether the federal government could act on its own or should have to await a request for help from the state. That brought Elbridge Gerry to his feet. Obliged by Shays's uprising to recognize the need for a stronger government, Gerry had nevertheless not lost any of his distrust of a federal establishment. Nor had he been mellowed by the arrival in Philadelphia of his young bride and new baby. He remained as combative as ever. The Boston battler was emphatically against "letting loose the myrmidons of the United States on a State without its own consent." The states themselves, he argued, would be best able to judge whether or not they needed assistance. "More blood would have been spilt in Massachusetts in the late insurrection," he claimed, "if the General authority had intermeddled." He had conveniently forgotten that it had not been the lack of an invitation that had kept federal forces from intervening in Shays's Rebellion, but rather the lack of troops with which to intervene. Following a great deal more discussion, the clause finally emerged in the Constitution not listed under the military powers of Congress, but in Article IV dealing with state issues, where it assured states of federal protection against domestic violence. It is probably significant that the power to use regular troops internally was given specifically to neither the legislative nor the executive branch. Historian Robert W. Coakley sees that as clear "testimony to the fear of standing armies that pervaded the meeting." However, the power is certainly implied in the president's obligation to "take Care that the Laws be faithfully executed."

Next, the convention took up "To make war." Charles Pinckney objected at once to giving Congress this power, saying the legislature would be too inefficient to direct the activities of war. With the example of the ineffectiveness of the Continental and Confederation Congresses fresh in everyone's mind, his case was easy to make. Proceedings would be too slow. Sessions would be too infrequent. The House of Representatives would "be too numerous for such deliberations." Pierce Butler registered agreement, and offered the thought that the authority should reside with the president. He would "have all the requisite qualities," Butler said, "and will not make war but when the Nation will support it." Gerry, appalled at the very thought, jumped back to his feet to chide the members, saying that he "never expected to hear in a republic a motion to empower the Executive alone to declare war." James Madison, in unusual cooperation with Gerry, moved to replace the word "make" with "declare." They would leave it to the president to repel sudden attacks. Roger Sherman of Connecticut liked the original version, saying that the executive should "be able to repel and not to commence war," and that "declare" was too narrow a word. The debate was slipping into a quagmire over definitions.

Oliver Ellsworth, confusing the situation as much as helping it, turned the argument somewhat philosophical. "There is a material difference between the cases of making *war* and making *peace*. It should be more easy to get out of war, than into it. War also is a simple and overt declaration, peace attended with intricate & secret negociations." The issue was not merely of entering into war, but also of terminating it. All the delegates had seen how abruptly the Revolution had begun—and how difficult and prolonged were the peace negotiations. George Mason of Virginia spoke against giving the "power of war to the Executive," because he was "not safely to be trusted with it." Mason was "for clogging rather than facilitating war; but for facilitating peace." A policy of hard in, easy out. Therefore he preferred "declare" to "make." The terms had to be defined.

War, delegates agreed, entailed three identifiable steps: starting it, fighting it, and ending it. With an understanding that "make war" meant to wage it, which was obviously an executive function, the convention voted eight to one (Massachusetts abstained) to empower Congress to declare war. Pinckney remained unsatisfied. He moved that the entire clause simply be struck. No one supported him. Madison noted that the suggestion died "without call of States." Pierce Butler wanted the entry and exit of war linked. Whoever had the right to take the country to war ought to have the responsibility of getting it out. He moved, therefore, that Congress be given the "power of peace, as they were to have that of war." Gerry seconded him, but the members were not convinced. Peace was too nebulous—was peace the absence or the end of war? Besides, other provisions had already established in the executive branch the authority to conduct foreign policy and to make treaties. Moreover, both logic and common sense urged that waging and terminating war should be linked in the executive branch. Ending a war would surely be based almost entirely on results gained on the battlefield. The measure was voted down unanimously. The clause went into the Constitution giving Congress the power to declare war. Once war was declared, the commander in chief would "make" it, and the president, with the consent of the Senate, would end it. With that, the convention was adjourned for the day.

Several other items were referred to the Committee of Detail on 18 August, including one authorizing the president "to procure and hold for the use of the U.S. landed property for the erection of Forts, Magazines, and other necessary buildings." Someone, Washington perhaps, or one of several others very familiar with his 1783 "Sentiments on a Peace Establishment," realizing that federal forces would require control of posts located inside states, sought to incorporate the right to do so into the Constitution. George Mason moved that the Committee of Detail also take up giving the Congress the power "to regulate the militia." His reason, he said, was that he wanted there to be "no standing army in time of peace, unless it might be for a few garrisons." If the militia were strong and well regulated, which would be impossible to achieve if the thirteen states retained separate control, Mason argued, there would be no need for much of a regular force. The task went to the committee.

Then the convention took up the army clause. Nathaniel Gorham suggested that, before beginning discussions on the clause itself, "raise armies" should be changed to "raise and support armies." Given Congress' recent inability to support Harmar's regiment, the motion won immediate acceptance. That wording also removed any lingering doubt over whether a regular army could be maintained in peacetime. It could. However, the clause left open how big that force could be. At that juncture, Elbridge Gerry gained the floor. How veterans of the 1783 and 1784 debates over establishing an army must have grimaced. They were not to be disappointed with the performance of the unrepentant antimilitary representative from Massachusetts. It was vintage Gerry.

First of all, he huffed, "there was no check here against standing armies in time of peace." The document as now written would permit the Congress "of itself" to maintain an army of whatever size it chose, which would give rise to "great opposition" to the Constitution. Because an army was "dangerous in time of peace," he said, he himself "could never consent to a power to keep up an indefinite number." Seconded by Luther Martin, he made a motion that the peacetime army could never be larger than two or three thousand men.

As the presiding officer, Washington did not take part in discussions. He made only one speech during the convention, and that at the very end. However, delegates could often tell how he stood on an issue by watching his eyes. Astounded that such a motion as Gerry's could be seriously made, the Virginian did not trust to facial expression to convey his disdain—in a stage whisper heard throughout the room, he said that the proposal would be just fine if it were accompanied by one making it also unlawful for any enemy to invade the

United States with more than two or three thousand men. A chorus of members spoke in opposition to Gerry's plan. Are troops not "to be raised until an attack should be made upon us?" Limiting the appropriations of revenue would be "the best guard in this case." There was no reason "for Mister Gerry's distrust of the Representatives of the people." As must be obvious, "preparations for war are generally made in peace; and a standing force of some sort may, for ought we know, become unavoidable." The convention all but shouted down the proposal, which virtually all members thought was ludicrous. There apparently was not even a vote on it.

Gerry had better luck with two other ideas. He thought "To provide and maintain a Navy" was a clearer clause than "To build and equip fleets." On reflection, everyone agreed. Then he suggested including a clause from the existing Articles of Confederation: "To make Rules for the Government and Regulation of the land and naval Forces." That, too, went into the final version of the Constitution.

Then the convention turned to the last, and by far the most divisive, of the military clauses. "We are come now to a most important matter," said John Dickinson, "that of the sword." The militia. Who would control it, the states or the federal government? Unlike the nearly complete correlation of thought on the imperative for a regular federal force, no common denominator regarding the supervision of the militia ever surfaced in the convention. For one thing, sheer size was a factor. Everyone expected costs to keep the regular army relatively small except in emergencies, while the militia was more numerous by many fold. For another, the regulars would generally be stationed in remote posts, out of sight, while the militia touched every community in America. If the militia were to be relied upon for the defense of the nation, it would have to be made reliable. On that all could agree. But it seemed that none could agree on how to achieve that goal. Delegates staked out positions ranging the length of a long spectrum.

At one end stood those who supported Washington's contention, as expressed in his 1783 proposal, that all militia units should at least be regulated by the central government. At the other end glowered Elbridge Gerry, who thought state control over its own militia should be the last point of principle ever surrendered. If the convention should agree to place the militia under the federal government, he said, the Constitution "will have as black a mark as was set on Cain." Arrayed in between were several compromise positions. Some fraction of the militia might be placed under federal control. Appointment of officers might be shared. Perhaps only the regulations would be federal, to assure effectiveness when called to national duty. But no consensus emerged. Positions remained fixed. There was no evident way to break the impasse. Everyone in the room knew that the militia should be made more effective—Shays's insurrection had converted even the most reluctant. But each man there also knew that the states would forever remain emotionally possessive on the issue. As Dickinson had intimated, it was a question of whose hand would rest on the hilt of the local sword. Wisely, the delegates voted to turn the matter over to a committee before they adjourned for the weekend. It had been a long Saturday.

On Monday, 20 August, members introduced a number of additional provisions for inclusion in the deliberations of the Committee of Detail. Included among them were several with military import. A few were merely administrative—descriptions of the duties of the secretary of war, for instance—and they did not surface again. Some spoke to the lingering fear of a standing army: "No soldier shall be quartered in any House in time of peace without consent of the owner." "No troops shall be kept up in time of peace, but by consent of the Legislature." "The military shall always be subordinate to the Civil power." These were handled by incorporation into other clauses, by ignoring them as redundant, or by the later decision not to include a bill of rights. One, in a slightly different form, gained entry into the Constitution— "no grants of money shall be made by the Legislature for supporting military Land forces, for more than one year at a time."

As August dragged by, its days filled with debates on other issues, the military clauses filtered back from committee work. On the twenty-third, the one seeking to establish control over the militia returned. Members consumed a good portion of the day in an acrimonious march toward agreement. The committee's phrasing was: "To make laws for organizing, arming, and disciplining the Militia, and for governing such Part of them as may be employed in the Service of the United States, reserving to the States respectively, the appointment of the officers, and the authority of training the Militia according to the discipline prescribed by the United States." Gerry, as expected, was adamantly opposed. This is tantamount to "making the States drill-sergeants," he cried. "I would as lief let the Citizens of Massachusetts be disarmed" as to take away their command of the militia. Several members tried reasoning, defining the words of the clause to show that the states did in fact retain control of the militia. Gerry was not to be mollified. Other wordings were suggested, but none of them worked either. Finally, voting began on each portion of the clause. On the first part, only Connecticut and Maryland were opposed. Next, all agreed to let the states appoint officers. And, by a vote of seven to four, the final phrase on training passed. Despite Gerry's objections, the Massachusetts delegation voted for all three parts. His stubbornness was wearing thin with his own state colleagues. The clause went into the Constitution with only one minor change, the substitution of "Congress" for "the United States" in the final part. But the issue would be heard from again.

More details returned as August faded and September brought thoughts of the completion of the work. It was at this time that, in relooking the authority of the commander in chief, members qualified his command over the militia by adding, "when called into the actual service of the United States." State militia would remain under state command at all other times. On Wednesday, 5 September, the final three military clauses returned from committee. To the clause "To declare War" would be added the words, "and grant Letters of Marque and Reprisal," which would be followed by a phrase regarding rules for handling captures. To the clause "To raise and support Armies" would be added the words, "but no Appropriation of Money to that Use shall be for a longer term than two Years." And the clause addressing federal posts was changed to provide Congress, not the president, authority over all places purchased. The first of the three passed without comment, but Gerry objected to the other two. Letting Congress appropriate money for the army for two years rather than one, he argued, "implied that there was to be a standing army." He wanted appropriations made every year. Gerry was out of step in this instance with common sense. Given the travel conditions of the time, one-year establishments had already proven to be impractical, and Congress itself would operate on a two-year cycle. Nevertheless, he could not pass up the chance to warn once more that a standing army was dangerous to liberty, and in so large a country was not necessary anyway. He raised again—probably not looking at Washington—his proposition that if a regular force should be required it should be restricted in size. Gerry then denounced the provision authorizing Congress to acquire sites for military installations. Such a power could be abused, he said, "to enslave any particular State by buying up its territory." Moreover, the "strongholds proposed would be a means of awing the State into an undue obedience to the General Government." To remove any concern on that account, members agreed to insert words to the effect that Congress could purchase such places only with the consent of the legislature of the state concerned.

That brought to a close the creation of the primary war powers of the legislative branch. The Constitution proclaims that the Congress shall have the exclusive power:

- To declare War, grant Letters of Marque and Reprisal, and make Rules concerning Captures on Land and Water;
- To raise and support Armies, but no Appropriation of Money to that Use shall be for a longer Term than two Years;
- To provide and maintain a Navy;
- To make Rules for the Government and Regulation of the land and naval Forces;
- To provide for calling forth the Militia to execute the Laws of the Union, suppress Insurrections and repel Invasions;
- To provide for organizing, arming, and disciplining, the Militia, and for governing such Part of them as may be employed in the Service of the United States, reserving to the States respectively, the Appointment of the Officers, and the Authority of training the Militia according to the discipline prescribed by Congress;
- To exercise . . . Authority over all Places purchased by the Consent of the Legislature of the State in which the Same shall be, for the Erection of Forts, Magazines, Arsenals, dock-Yards, and other needful Buildings. . . .

It provides an interesting insight into the thinking of the Founding Fathers to contemplate how the army and the navy are treated quite differently in the Constitution. Congress may "raise and support Armies," while it may "provide and maintain a Navy." Furthermore, it may appropriate money for as many years as it wishes for the navy, but for no more than two years for the army. The reason for those distinctions? Navies do not have the ability to conduct a coup; only land forces can overthrow a government. The man on horseback does not come from the sea. The presence of the ghost of Cromwell can be detected in a comparison of those two clauses.

The convention's work was nearly done. Five men were appointed to prepare the final version to be signed and sent out for ratification. Three of them—Alexander Hamilton, James Madison, and Gouverneur Morris—had been struggling ever since those hectic days at the close of the Revolutionary War to establish a strong central government. They must have gone about their work with unusual relish, for they were now putting into words what they had tried to create five years earlier. If any delegate had taken the time to compare Washington's vision for a peacetime military arrangement with that laid out in the Constitution, he would have found an unusual congruence. Morris did most of the writing, the way Dickinson had with the Articles of Confederation. The Preamble came from his pen. ". . . establish Justice, insure domestic Tranquility, provide for the common defence, promote the general Welfare, and secure the Blessings of Liberty. . . ."

On Wednesday, 12 September, the committee brought copies of the final draft before the convention. For four days the members went over the familiar clauses yet again, repeating in many instances well-rehearsed arguments for or against. George Mason raised for one last time the bugaboo of a standing army. Recognizing that an "absolute prohibition of standing armies in time of peace might be unsafe," he nevertheless wanted to insert in the Constitution some enduring warning against them. He thought that Congress' power to organize, arm, and discipline the militia should be explained as being necessary in order "that the liberties of the people may be better secured against the danger of standing armies in time of peace." Randolph quickly seconded the motion. James Madison spoke in support, the third Virginian to weigh in on the matter, saying, "as armies in times of peace are allowed on all hands to be an evil," the Constitution should go on record as being against them. Others then rose to oppose Mason's motion. Gouverneur Morris said that the inclusion of such words would be demeaning to soldiers, would set a "dishonorable mark of distinction on the military class of Citizens." The motion failed by a vote of nine states to two, with Virginia and Georgia being the only delegations for it.

That Saturday, the fifteenth, was the final day of the Constitutional Convention, save 17 September, which was set aside for signing the document. The final speaker, taking the floor late in the afternoon, was Elbridge Gerry. He would not sign on Monday, he informed the other members. After enumerating his reasons, he said that the most significant of them was the threat a too-powerful Congress posed to the rights of citizens. Congress could, among other things, "raise armies and money without limit." Gerry was nothing if not consistent on this point. And he was consistently beaten down. The Constitution was ordered to be engrossed.

The military establishment etched into the Constitution reflected the checks and balances permeating the entire document. Power was shared between branches of the federal government as well as between state and federal authorities. The United States could maintain armed forces in peacetime, but only if funded by Congress. The president would command the military, but Congress would write the rules. State authorities would command the militia, but would meet standards of readiness set by Congress. The commander in chief would wage war, but only after Congress declared it. The president would end wars, but with the approval of the Senate. The commander in chief would deploy military forces, but Congress would determine their size and shape. The president would appoint and commission officers, but with the consent of the Senate. The president would command the militia when they might be federalized, but the states would appoint militia officers and oversee the training of the units. The federal government could field regular forces, but the states would retain authority to direct the militia. Congress could purchase sites for installations, but only with the approval of affected states. The federal government could keep the peace inside states, but only if asked to do so by the state concerned.

With all of that, the framers had taken a giant step toward minimizing if not eliminating the risk of despotism. They had rendered remote the likelihood of a coup by a man on horseback. Still, they had left the United States a formidable capacity to make war.

CHAPTER 14
THE RIGHT TO BEAR ARMS

Benjamin Franklin suffered from gout and stones and age. To ease his pain, the octogenarian president of Pennsylvania traveled around town in a sedan chair. Suspended on flexible poles, which acted as shock absorbers to avoid jarring the distinguished passenger, and carried by four sturdy inmates from the Walnut Street jail, the chair was one of the city's sights. On 17 September—the day set to sign the Constitution—the prisoners brought Dr. Franklin to the State House and deposited him in the east room, as they had done on so many mornings that summer. Franklin planned to make a speech on this final day of the convention.

As was his practice, he had written the address out ahead of time and given it to James Wilson to read for him. His own quavering voice did not carry well. "I confess that there are several parts of this constitution which I do not at present approve," Wilson said, reading Franklin's words, "but I am not sure I shall never approve them." Members listened intently. "For having lived long, I have experienced many instances of being obliged by better information or fuller consideration, to change opinions even on important subjects, which I once thought right, but found to be otherwise. It is therefore that the older I grow, the more apt I am to doubt my own judgment, and to pay more respect to the judgment of others." He continued with humor, logic, and an easy charm calculated to soften lingering resentments. It was a grandfatherly and masterful plea from the eldest member of the convention to those who might be inclined not to sign. Franklin went on

134

to urge those who might disagree with one part or another of the document not to make their objections public. "I cannot help expressing a wish that every member of the Convention who may still have objections to it, would with me, on this occasion doubt a little of his own infallibility—and to make manifest our unanimity, put his name to this instrument." Then, in an attempt to gain the maximum number of signatures, he proposed that the document should reflect unanimous approval by the states represented, not necessarily concurrence by each person signing. The speech and the ploy were effective.

Thirty-eight of the forty-one members present signed. John Dickinson, absent due to sickness, had authorized George Read of Delaware to sign for him, raising the number of names affixed to the Constitution to thirty-nine. Roger Sherman of Connecticut was one of those. He had signed the Declaration of Independence, the Articles of Confederation, and now the Constitution of the United States of America. Of the three who refused to place their names on the document, two were from Virginia: George Mason and Edmund Randolph. Elbridge Gerry was the third. George Washington signed the covering letter to the Confederation Congress, and gave instructions to the convention's secretary to carry the Constitution to the Congress in New York City. By then it was late afternoon. "The business being closed," Washington wrote in his diary, "the members adjourned to the City Tavern, dined together and took a cordial leave of each other; after which I returned to my lodgings . . . and retired to meditate on the momentous work which had been executed. . . ."

Writing the Constitution had indeed been momentous work. A miracle in many accounts. But the hardest labor was yet to come. Gaining ratification by the states would take more effort over more time.

Ten or so members of the convention who were also members of the Confederation Congress rushed back to New York to urge a quick approval by that body. They found opposition waiting. Richard Henry Lee of Virginia, for one, wondered why Congress should participate in its own dissolution. Why should the Confederation step aside to permit the formation of a dangerously powerful federation? He proposed that Congress should at the very least attach a Bill of Rights to the Constitution before forwarding it to the states. That proposal was defeated by what an ill-tempered Lee labeled caustically "a coalition of monarchy men, military men, aristocrats and drones whose noise, impudence and zeal exceeds all belief." On 28 September 1787, Congress submitted the Constitution to the states. The battle was joined.

For months the proposed Constitution was the hottest topic in the land. Newspapers carried all sides of the various debates over it. Town meetings examined it. Preachers addressed it from pulpits. Taverns were abuzz with talk of it. Factions pro and con bombarded citizens with arguments. Individuals took sides publicly. The mails bulged with letters urging one stance or another. Combinations formed. State conventions assembled to consider accepting or rejecting it.

During this time political labels solidified—Federalists were those in favor of the Constitution, while those opposed were called Anti-Federalists. Anti-Federalists did not like being tagged with that name. Considering themselves to be the proponents of a federal establishment, they thought of the others as nationalists or constitutionalists. But they were, in fact, just what the name implied: anti. Against. Negative. The truth was, they could offer no alternative. They were simply against the changes the Constitution would bring. Yet the country was ready for change. People were tired, bone-tired, of the humiliation of weakness. Their sour mood had led to the convention in the first place. There were only two apparent courses: to strengthen the nation, which the Constitution did, or watch the union splinter. And that splintering would be a failure of the most spectacular sort. When all arguments were boiled down to irreducible essence, Federalists were proposing a way to avoid that failure, whereas their opponents did not like the vehicle they were proposing. No matter how Anti-Federalists couched their complaints, their message sounded like "more of the same," which was the one answer a majority of Americans were unwilling to accept.

In every state lived men who found some aspect of the document not to their taste. Taxation, representation, state sovereignty, control over commerce—just to cite some of the more common complaints. Military issues ranked high on the list of most of the Constitution's opponents. Anti-Federalists were not slow to try to rekindle the ever-smoldering distrust of a standing army. They railed, too, against the extraordinary strength the commander in chief would have. But as much as anything else, they raged over the perceived threat of a federal takeover of the militia. Granting the central government the authority to bear arms was one thing, accepting limitations to the states' ancient right to wield military force was quite another. Elbridge Gerry had warned his colleagues of this at the convention. States would not go along with federal infringement of their control over their militia, he had said as emphatically as he could. That indeed proved to be the case. Significantly, many influential Federalists agreed with their foes on this point. A groundswell of support grew for an amendment to provide positive assurance that the militia would remain under state ownership and control.

Without an alternative form of government to offer, Anti-Federalists hammered at the public's fears in emotional attempts to block ratification. "It is much easier to alarm people than to inform them," pointedly noted a prominent Federalist. A candidate for the ratification convention in North Carolina told a gathering that the seat of government under the Constitution would be a walled city. "Here an army of 50,000 or perhaps 100,000 men will be fully embodied and will sally forth and enslave the people, who will gradually be disarmed." Robert Yates in New York proclaimed that Federalists were "avowedly in favor of standing armies." Patrick Henry in Virginia thundered that federal troops would "execute the execrable commands of tyranny." The president, Henry went on, if he were a man of both ambition and ability, would become an absolute dictator because he had "the army in his hands." General John Lamb, a Revolutionary War hero, warned of the same thing. General Washington may be safe enough, Lamb conceded, but what about "General Shlushington," who may succeed him? George Mason raised the specter of a Congress run amok. By promulgating onerous regulations, Congress could destroy the militia in order "the more easily to govern by a standing army." Luther Martin struck a similar theme, warning of the risk to the rights of individual states to bear arms. "As it now stands, the Congress will have the power . . . to march the whole militia of Maryland to the remotest part of the Union and Keep them in service as long as they think proper . . . reducing them to the situation of slaves." In Massachusetts, where Elbridge Gerry was a leading Anti-Federalist voice, demagogues invoked images of the Boston Massacre to underscore the danger of a standing army. Gerry enlarged the view, thundering, "Standing armies have been the nursery of vice and the bane of liberty from the Roman legions to the establishment of the artful Ximenes, and from the ruin of the Cortes of Spain, to the planting of the British cohorts in the capitals of America." He also resurrected the worry of military ascendancy through the Society of the Cincinnati. Under the Constitution, he said, "the Cincinnati would in fact elect the chief magistrate in every instance. . . ." In these and untold other ways, Anti-Federalists sought to strike the raw nerve of the fear of military tyranny. Across the land rang and rang again the names of Oliver Cromwell and Julius Caesar.

Against that flood of invective stood the Federalists. Logically, firmly, calmly—in notable contrast to the heated rhetoric of the Anti-Federalists—they refuted the wild accusations, concentrating more often than not on educating and informing rather than inflaming emotions. Aware of the instinctively negative reaction Americans had to the very suggestion of a standing army, they assiduously avoided ever strongly endorsing one, even to the point of speaking against it. "With respect to a standing army," announced Edmund Randolph, who had decided to support the Constitution after all, "I believe there was not a member of the federal Convention, who did not feel indignation at such an institution."

Writing under the pen name, *Publius,* Alexander Hamilton provided an articulate and insightful defense of the Constitution, going far to influence open-minded members of ratifying assemblies. He was joined in that effort by John Jay and James Madison; their combined output, known as *The Federalist Papers,* comprises a priceless legacy explaining the philosophy of the framers. Washington complimented Hamilton effusively, saying that the body of *Publius* articles would "merit the notice of posterity because in it are candidly and ably discussed the principles of freedom and the topics of government, which shall always be interesting to mankind so long as they shall be connected in civil society." Hamilton had been blunt in his defense of the federal government's power to use force. Wars, seditions, insurrections—these were "maladies as inseparable from the body politic as tumors and eruptions from the natural body," he wrote in paper Number 28. "Should such emergencies at any time happen under the national government, there could be no remedy but force." In Number 29 he showed how federal access to the militia would actually reduce the requirement for a regular force. "If the federal government can command the aid of the militia in those emergencies which call for the military arm in support of the civil magistrate, it can better dispense with the employment of a different kind of force." Bit by bit, Federalists made the case that the use of force was sometimes necessary, and that being prepared ahead of time was always essential.

That argument made sense to most Americans. It fit the world as they had come to know it. It was particularly compelling to those who had served in the military outside their own local region. In Pennsylvania, for instance, of the forty-four former officers of the Continental Army whose position on the issue was known, 100 percent of them supported the Constitution. Surviving militia officers who had never left Pennsylvania were for the most part against the Constitution, while those whose military duties had taken them beyond their state borders were virtually all supporters. Americans who knew by personal experience of the military weaknesses of the Continental and Confederation Congresses tended to be Federalists—and they tended to be leaders in their communities. Moreover, and quite significantly, as veterans of the Revolution they were very influential in state ratification conventions.

Amidst all that tumult, the ratification process unfolded. Pennsylvania became the first state to pass a resolution setting up a ratification convention. It did so in tragicomic circumstances. On 28 September, when the question came to a vote, the assembly did not have a quorum present. The nineteen Anti-Federalists had left, and later locked themselves inside a boardinghouse. Their plan, apparently, was to prevent a vote during that session, hoping that elections in November would bring an Anti-Federalist majority to power. Federalists, though, were not about to lose the momentum they had. Next morning, forty-five members were present, all Federalists—and two short of a quorum. A mob broke into the boardinghouse, bodily seized two of the hiding Anti-Federalists, and dragged them to the State House, where just twelve days earlier the Constitution had been signed. White with rage, clothing torn, bruised and scratched, the two men were slammed into their seats to the cheers of spectators in the gallery. With a quorum on hand, the vote proceeded. Predictably, the count was forty-five to two.

Despite Pennsylvania's unseemly if not undemocratic haste, Delaware was the first state to ratify the Constitution, doing so by unanimous vote on 7 December 1787. Five days later, Pennsylvania followed, with forty-six for and twenty-three against. Tempers were still hot, though. Just after Christmas, at a rally in Carlisle celebrating the Constitution, Anti-Federalists wielding clubs broke in and assaulted former convention delegate James Wilson. Smashed to the ground, Wilson would quite likely have been killed had not an old soldier thrown himself over his body and absorbed the blows until help arrived. All in all, it was an inauspicious beginning for a process aimed at bringing domestic tranquility to the land.

In quick order, three more states ratified—New Jersey and Georgia unanimously, Connecticut 128 to 40. The easy ones were finished. Massachusetts came in sixth, although not without a fight, and only after extracting from Federalists a prior agreement to seek several amendments. Still, the margin of victory was razor thin: 187 yeas to 168 nays. With some nudging from Washington, Maryland voted on 28 April 1788. The count was 63 to 11 to ratify. Nearly a month later, South Carolina became the eighth state to concur, by a tally of 149 to 73. Nine states were needed to put the Constitution into effect. Tension mounted at the Virginia convention. Not knowing that New Hampshire had approved the Constitution on 21 June (57 yes, 47 no), members thought their vote on the twenty-fifth would be the deciding one—and all of them knew it would be close. Virginia and New York had probably the strongest concentration of Anti-Federalists in the country. The untiring work of Madison, coupled with the knowledge that Washington would surely be the first president, won a slender majority. The count was 89 for and 79 against. The new nation was a fact, ten states having opted to join the Union.

Without New York, however, a large gap would exist, psychologically as well as geographically. In no other state was the effort to gain ratification such an uphill struggle as it was in New York. The indefatigable labor of Alexander Hamilton overcame awesome odds to deliver the state on 26 July 1788, with 30 for union and 27 against. Hamilton had able help from John Jay and others, but the final push putting the state over the line most likely came from the knowledge of all involved that up to that point ten of ten states had voted for ratification, leaving New York in a lonely group with renegade Rhode Island and faraway North Carolina. Sixteen months later, after the new Congress had proposed a Bill of Rights, North Carolina ratified, 194 to 77. Finally, on 29 May 1790, more than a year after Washington's inauguration, Federalists in Rhode Island managed to squeeze a positive vote out of that state. The count was 34 yea, 32 nay. The original thirteen states were in the fold.

Actually, the business was not yet done. Although the convention chose not to append to the Constitution a list of guaranteed rights, many of its members had wanted one. Subsequent experience in the ratification process had led a large majority throughout the states to conclude that something of the sort was in fact necessary. Without expressed intentions by several states to add such a list, ratification would have been much more difficult to achieve, and may well have faltered. When the new government assembled in New York City in 1789, keeping those commitments was included in its foremost order of business. Within a year and a half, the country had adopted the first ten amendments to the Constitution, known collectively as the Bill of Rights. Four of the ten addressed some aspect of the military establishment of the country, three of them directly in words and one in intent.

The second amendment proclaims, "A well regulated Militia, being necessary to the security of a free State, the right of the people to keep and bear Arms, shall not be infringed." This amendment sought to alleviate the widespread concern that Congress in its zeal to regulate the militia might emasculate it. The ability of a state to maintain a strong militia was secured by this vested right to bear arms. The third amendment evoked memories of the British occupation before and during the Revolution: "No soldier shall, in time of peace be quartered in any house, without the consent of the Owner, nor in time of war, but in a manner to be prescribed by law." In the fifth lies recognition that military discipline and the exigencies of uniformed duty required service members to forgo certain individual rights reserved to all other citizens. The final amendment in the Bill of Rights, among other things, helps insure that states retain control of their militia *and* continue to influence the quality of those forces.

In accepting the Constitution and the Bill of Rights, the people of the United States had chosen to submit themselves to a central government with power and authority, one charged to provide them a sense of security not enjoyed since they had been Englishmen. But they had also cautiously assembled a structure predicated on the protection of life, liberty, and the pursuit of happiness. The new ship of state set sail on a course painstakingly plotted to carry it safely down the winding and narrow channel between the shoals of chaos on one side and the reefs of tyranny on the other.

Someone at the conclusion of the convention asked Benjamin Franklin, "What have you wrought?" He responded, ". . . a Republic, if you can keep it."

PART 4

PRESERVE, PROTECT AND DEFEND

I do solemnly swear that I will faithfully execute the Office of President of the United States, and will to the best of my Ability, preserve, protect and defend the Constitution of the United States.

—The oath of office for the president, as specified in the Constitution.

CHAPTER 15
BETWEEN ANARCHY
AND MONARCHY

On 2 July 1788—twelve years to the day after the decision by the Continental Congress to declare the United States free and independent of Great Britain—the Confederation Congress declared the Constitution duly ratified. Members arranged for national elections to be held the following January, elections to produce the Constitutional Congress and the national executive.

By adopting the Constitution, Americans had moved away from anarchy. Of that they were reasonably certain. But had they embarked on a course leading to a New World form of monarchy? Of that suspicions abounded.

George Washington was amply aware of those widespread qualms. Waiting at Mount Vernon for the summons to serve, he contemplated the far-reaching implications of his early months in office. He understood well that his actions during that crucial period would shape indelibly the affection, confidence, and respect Americans would hold for the presidency. He would have to be strong; the times demanded order. Yet he could not be too strong; that would fan the sparks of suspicion, igniting disorder. He had to find a balance, a position fostering security and stability, while at the same time preserving liberty. A position between anarchy and monarchy.

As it happened, Washington had a good long time to ponder that imperative. Although his election was a foregone conclusion, it did not happen quickly or smoothly. The electoral college met on 4 February 1789. It voted unanimously for the Virginian, with John Adams of Massachusetts being selected less enthusiastically to serve as vice president. But the vote could not be officially recorded until the newly elected Congress met and the Senate chose one of its number to open the ballots in front of the members of both houses. Congress was slated to convene in New York City on 4 March, the day the Constitution replaced the Articles of Confederation. But the much-anticipated new government got off to a most inauspicious start: on its first day it did not have enough members present to conduct business. Worse yet, the entire month of March passed with no quorum. While delegates straggled into New York, Washington paced impatiently in Virginia. Finally, on 14 April, a road-weary messenger arrived to deliver a letter from the president pro tempore of the Senate notifying Washington of his election. Two days later the Virginian set out for the city where, six years before, he had bade farewell to the officers of the Continental Army.

The public reaction to his journey was nothing short of amazing. Citizens all along the route turned the trip into a frenzied celebration, a spontaneous march of democracy triumphant. Everyone wanted to see him, to cheer him, to fete him. He dutifully accepted the wildly enthusiastic greetings, and stoically submitted to some of the most unusual salutes imaginable. He was one week on the road, and then had to wait another week before his inauguration. He used the time to write a new inaugural address; the one he had prepared back in Virginia ran to seventy-three pages, which he wisely saw would not do. Congress, meanwhile, fretted over what title to use in addressing the new president. The Senate, prompted by John Adams, wanted something with a royal sound. Adams personally preferred "His Most Benign Highness." A committee settled on "His Highness the President of the United States of America and Protector of the Rights of the Same." Washington thought the whole issue was ridiculous—and perhaps he remembered that Oliver Cromwell's title had been "The Lord Protector." James Madison, a confidant of the president-to-be and a member of the House of Representatives, led the fight against so pompous a title. He won. The chief executive would be called simply "The President of the United States." In conversations beyond Washington's hearing, most continued to refer to him as "The General."

That the Congress could dally so long, and then worry itself over such a matter, was indicative of a refreshing degree of ease in the air. A blanket of relative calm had spread across the land, giving the country a slight respite from its time of troubles. Citizens had been able to breathe more optimistically in the year and a half between the writing of the Constitution and the formation of the new federal government.

A good bit of that calm had come from the very fact of the Constitution itself, and the universal expectation that George Washington would be taking over the reins of government. Americans could anticipate an end to the humiliation of weakness. Also, the aftershock of Shays's uprising in Massachusetts was still being felt. It had led to the mitigation, or at least the venting, of many factors causing internal tensions. Furthermore, accommodating to the changed circumstances of peace, the economy had recovered somewhat. Particularly noteworthy was the passage by Congress of the Northwest Ordinance in the summer of 1787, even as the Constitution was being written. That act had placed a coordinating structure over the wild lands west and north of the Ohio River, setting up a territorial government and providing for eventual statehood for regions there. The appointment of a governor and the promise of order brought a temporary lessening of conflict in the area. Events abroad helped, too. Turmoil in France as that country moved toward revolution focused European courts more on European issues, easing some of the pressure on the United States, especially with respect to British mischief in the Northwest and Spanish machinations in the Southwest.[1] All in all, it was a rather quiet moment in an era known more for turbulence than for stillness. That welcomed

---

1. When westward expansion in the nineteenth century pushed the frontier of the United States beyond the Mississippi River, "Northwest" and "Southwest" assumed their current geographical meaning. Histories then began describing the regions of earlier settlement and conflict as the "Old Northwest" and the "Old Southwest." In this book, set in the earlier time, the two terms are used in their original context. Northwest refers generally to the area of the modern states of Ohio, Indiana, Illinois, Michigan, and Wisconsin. Southwest refers roughly to the region of Alabama, Mississippi, Tennessee, and parts of Louisiana and Florida. Kentucky, originally the western reaches of Virginia, was geographically a wedge driven between the two regions, and a part of unfolding events in both.

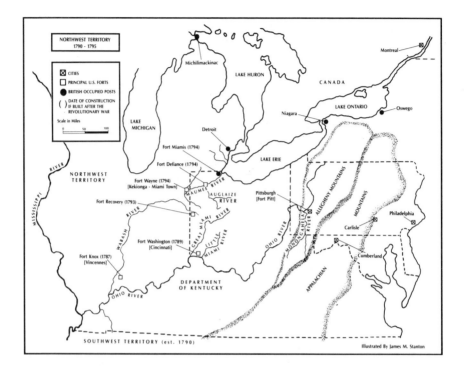

change was to give the new president a much-needed period of grace at the outset of his term.

Inauguration day, 30 April, dawned fair and noisy. Thirteen cannon blasts greeted the sun's first rays. No one seems to have remarked on the number. Tradition held that thirteen guns were to be fired in salutes, never mind that only eleven states were then in the Union.

Washington's day was quiet from then until noon, when he began preparing to be sworn in. He put on a suit of brown domestic cloth, as a way of advertising American products over imported goods, buckled on a sword, and rode alone in a coach to the intersection of Broad and Wall streets. The ways and windows along the route were stacked with shouting well-wishers, their mood bright, ebullient. In a second floor room of Federal Hall waited members of Congress, foreign dignitaries, and other officials. The Speaker of the House of Representatives and the vice president, in his role as presiding officer of the Senate, escorted Washington to a large portico, where he could be seen by the maximum number in the cheering throng below. There he placed his right hand on a Bible and faced the chancellor of the state of New York, Robert R. Livingston. The crowd grew silent.

"I do solemnly swear," Washington repeated after Livingston, "that I will faithfully execute the Office of President of the United States, and will to the best of my Ability, preserve, protect and defend the Constitution of the United States." The crowd roared approval.

When all of the activities ended late that night, the president could at last turn his thoughts from ceremony to action. To begin with, just how did one "preserve, protect and defend" the Constitution?

There was so very much to do. Flesh out the government prescribed in the Constitution. Get control of the country's foundering economic affairs. Establish the boundaries of the nation. Provide internal and external security. Gain international acceptance and respect. Earn the confidence of the people. The challenge was awesome—and wholly without precedent.

Washington was ever practical. Start with first things first. Hardly a thing could be done until an apparatus was put in place to do it with. The entire executive branch of the new government consisted of only two men, George Washington and John Adams. Congress must erect an administrative framework. Until that was accomplished, agencies set up under the Articles of Confederation would continue to function, although no one could say with certainty whether they should respond to Congress or the president. Establishing a fiscal program was also an immediate need. While the Confederation Congress could bequeath some agencies and policies, it had no money to pass along. So, building a structure of government and placing it on a solid financial foundation were the dual prerequisites for achieving everything else.

Well, that was not quite so. Above all, the foremost essential, in Washington's view, was to earn the confidence of Americans. He would have to secure their allegiance, to remove their suspicions of a too-powerful president, to allay fears of a standing army, to banish the specter of a man on horseback, to spike the talk of monarchy.

The president was committed to that end. Unity was his first aim, more important in the short run even than defense, for without a cohesive country security would always be a will-o'-the-wisp. Nation building, then, was his overriding priority.

Since Washington could not, in any event, act in the military sphere until Congress had completed its work of creating an infrastructure, he would make necessity a virtue. He would concentrate on "preserving" the Constitution by developing policies and programs and precedents aimed at promoting stability. "Protecting" and "defending" would have to wait until a mechanism for a defense establishment could be put into place. Although he had little choice in the matter, by putting off military initiatives he would quiet critics of the Constitution who had predicted that the commander in chief would constitute more of a threat to liberty than Indians and foreign foes combined. He was also quite fortunate in that the immediacy of dangers to the nation's security had for the moment receded. Obliged to wait anyway, the president could afford safely to do so. He could accept the calculated risk that there would be no early requirement for a resort to armed forces. The question was, how long would the respite last?

While he was prepared to postpone taking military actions, Washington worked from the very beginning to keep himself informed of circumstances in Europe and along America's forested frontiers. Henry Knox, the secretary at war, had kept him constantly abreast of affairs, especially those pertaining to the confrontations with western tribes. That relationship, of course, would continue. But the chief executive quickly expanded his circle of contacts. Just days into his presidency, he sat down with Arthur St. Clair, the governor of the Northwest Territory.

Could Washington have glimpsed the future, he would have been distressed to see in the fleshy face of his old colleague a source of some of his most bitter moments over the next three years—a man who would carry the administration and the country to war, and who would be responsible for the new nation's first military disaster.

At fifty-three, St. Clair was only four years younger than the president, and was a familiar face to him. Born in Scotland and becoming for a time an officer in the British army, he had later married an American and settled in Pennsylvania. After siding with the patriots and receiving a commission in the Continental Army, he had risen to the rank of major general, although his military leadership had been mediocre at best. After the war he had become prominent in Pennsylvania and national politics, ending up as the president of the Confederation Congress. He left that position to accept appointment as the first governor of the Northwest Territory in October 1787. For those who may have believed in omens, his arrival in the Ohio Valley might have given them pause. As the new governor rode into Fort Harmar, where a detail of soldiers stood at attention to present honors, a crashing thunderbolt brought a drenching downpour, chasing everyone to cover. He had subsequently spent considerable time beyond the mountains trying to forge a peace with the Indians. Returning to New York City for the inauguration, he had brought with him two recently signed treaties, but he did not consider his efforts to have been particularly promising overall.

St. Clair's report was pessimistic. Having been sent to treat with the tribes, he had found his hands tied by instructions that all but precluded a successful outcome. He had been directed to try to drive a wedge between the various groups of red men and had been forbidden to negotiate any adjustments to previous treaties. Land speculators wanted to be sure their investments were protected. Among them were many influential men inside the government itself, including members of Congress. Almost every army officer, from Harmar down, was a shareholder in one land company or another. Altogether, the speculators had enormous political clout. After spending a year or so gathering Indian leaders for a conference, and growing ever more aware of the implacably unbending attitudes of his own countrymen in the area, St. Clair had come to the conclusion that peace was probably unattainable. Settlers remained covetous of tribal territory, with land speculators stirring them to action. Whites were as brutal as the Indians, matching them in atrocity and devastation. Still worse, by retaliating against innocent tribes, white raiders were rapidly alienating those natives inclined to be friendly or neutral. The tribes, meanwhile, having banded into a loose coalition to confront the swelling surge of settlers, and being urged on by British officials, were growing more belligerent than ever. In addition to threatening settlements, warriors were also beginning to endanger commerce by attacking boats on the Ohio, Tennessee, and Cumberland rivers. Josiah Harmar's regiment of regulars remained unable to do much to control either side, but for its pains had begun to suffer losses steadily as the Indians grew increasingly hostile. Governor St. Clair had managed to convene a conference in December 1788, but some of the most warlike chiefs had refused to attend. Although treaties were obtained, and an uneasy truce seemed to be holding, St. Clair thought war was inevitable if not imminent.

As somber as that message was, Washington was actually more concerned over the explosive situation in the Southwest. Prodded by Spanish officials, supported by British suppliers, infuriated by American duplicity, the Creek confederation was veering toward open warfare. Able to summon several thousand warriors to battle, thereby greatly outnumbering the thinly spread white frontiersmen in the western parts of the southernmost states, the Creeks and their allies possessed greater potential for overpowering U.S. forces than did their fellow tribes in the Northwest. Moreover, they were ably led by an astute and well-educated half-breed named Alexander McGillivray, a product of both cultures who was not taken in by the double-dealing tactics of white negotiators and land speculators. Also, given Spanish intrigue and the connivance of several renegade Americans, the probability of a breakaway white nation establishing itself in the Southwest had to be taken seriously. The most recent intelligence of such a scheme, the so-called Spanish Conspiracy, had reached Washington at Mount Vernon as he was awaiting word of his election to the presidency. He set up a cipher to use with his informers because of the sensitivity of the subject and of its serious potential for enduring harm to the new nation.

In June, Henry Knox presented the president a wide-ranging analysis of the frontier problems, and laid out the limited options. Military action, he concluded, was not advisable in the Northwest. It would require larger forces by far than were available, and it would cost more than the United States could raise, especially considering the pressing need to fund "other indispensable objects." Moreover, he admitted, given the provocations and depredations of the settlers themselves, especially the often senseless ravages by raiding Kentuckians, aggression against the Indians was not a morally defensible option. In Knox's words, an offensive would "stain the character of the nation" at its very founding. The situation in the Southwest was similar, for most of the same reasons, except that military operations there were not only inadvisable, they were in all likelihood infeasible. Complicating matters, North Carolina was not yet one of the United States, which left South Carolina and Georgia physically separated from the rest of the union.

The secretary's recommendation for the Northwest, which Washington accepted, was to shift Harmar's undermanned regular units even farther west along the Ohio River, where they would be in a better position to block incursions from Kentucky. There they would try to keep the antagonists apart while negotiators continued efforts to forge a peace with all the tribes in the region between the Ohio and the Great Lakes. As for the Creeks in the Southwest, an all-out attempt would be made to preempt war by securing a formal treaty with them. The president ordered Knox to draft a suitable agreement, and he formed a commission to negotiate with Alexander McGillivray.

The months of the government's first year sped by, crowded with progress and blessed with rare tranquility. In the Congress, cooperation reigned. Members wasted little time before exercising their authority to raise revenue, and they began early to meet the unwritten commitment to send a Bill of Rights to the states for ratification. Around the country, optimism soared. Crops were bountiful; commerce was profitable; the people were hopeful. But the calm was deceptive. Events across the Atlantic in France and across the continent on the Pacific's shores, as well as in places closer to home, were raising as yet faint storm clouds.

Paris mobs overran the Bastille on 14 July, marking the beginning of the violent phase of the French Revolution. Lafayette, Washington's protégé, was in the thick of affairs that summer as the head of the National Guard. He interceded to protect the royal family, and for a while appeared to be in a position to help restore a semblance of order in the uproar that was France. News moved slowly; it was some time before word of the historic event reached New York. An exultant Lafayette sent Washington the key to the Bastille as a symbol of his country's release from despotism. The key, wrote the young French noble, was "a tribute which I owe as a son to my adoptive father, as an aide-de-camp to my general, as a missionary of liberty to its patriarch."

England had sighted opportunity in the difficulties engulfing the French court. Spain had long enjoyed a Papal-endowed sovereignty over the Pacific Ocean, which gave it a monopoly on the fur trade along the Pacific rim of North America, a monopoly British traders dearly wanted to break. English fortune seekers had surreptitiously established a fur trading station in Nootka Sound, on what is known today as Vancouver Island. Spanish forces, upon discovering the intrusion, responded firmly, seizing the station and three ships at anchor there. That gave England its opening. With Paris consumed by internal troubles and therefore not likely to rush to the aid of its close ally, London saw a chance to loosen Madrid's hold on the Pacific. Confident that the Royal Navy could easily handle the Spanish fleet so long as the French stayed on the sidelines, Great Britain took an overtly bellicose stance. Ministers demanded release of the ships, payment of reparations, and recognition of British trading rights in the area. The Nootka incident escalated rapidly to a state of near war. Hostilities between the two powers, one ensconced to the northwest of the United States and the other controlling territory to the southwest, would leave the new Republic in a most awkward position should fighting flare along the line of the Mississippi River. Again, though, distance and the slowness of communications delayed American realization of the rising threat to its peace.

In Kentucky that summer and fall, frontier leaders were not mollified by the shifting of Harmar's soldiers westward. The regulars established headquarters at Fort Washington (the site of Cincinnati)[2] and bolstered garrisons at Fort Knox (at Vincennes up the Wabash River) and Fort Finney (on the Ohio at Louisville). There, supposedly, they could "awe the savages from collecting in large bodies." Settlers were less than enthusiastic. They had long been incensed at the government's apparent inability or unwillingness to provide adequate security, or to demonstrate much concern in any other way. Even the presence of the commanding general and the use of the president's name on the fort, both aimed at symbolizing a newfound commitment by the government, failed to convince them. They saw the army's presence more as a brake on them than as protection from the Indians. And they were right. The move west had further dissipated the regiment's strength, leaving it less able to conduct operations against the tribes. Pleas for real protection continued to pour into New York City from citizens throughout the western lands.

Meanwhile, the new government began to take shape. Congress was doing its work well. It created the Department of War in August. The secretary *at* war became the secretary *of* war, and he answered directly to the president rather than to Congress. Henry Knox—by then weighing well over three hundred pounds—remained in the position. Congress

2. In January 1790, Josiah Harmar set up his base of operations in the new fortress built on the Ohio River between the Great Miami and Little Miami rivers, across from the Licking River in Kentucky. He named it after the president. That same month, St. Clair changed the name of the small settlement of Losantiville growing under the fort's protection. He called it Cincinnati after the controversial society of former Revolutionary War army officers.

also established departments of treasury and state, with the new secretary of state handling both foreign and domestic activities—except, of course, military and financial matters. Significantly, Indian affairs were placed under the secretary of war—the tribes were apparently considered neither domestic nor foreign. Lawmakers also set up the office of attorney general to give legal advice to the president. Alexander Hamilton became the secretary of treasury and Edmund Randolph received the nod as attorney general. For secretary of state, Washington wanted John Jay, but Jay demurred, asking instead to be chief justice of the Supreme Court in the newly activated judiciary branch of the government. The president next thought of Thomas Jefferson, who was en route back from France, where he had been serving as the U.S. ambassador. For the time being, Hamilton assumed the duties of state as well as his own. Washington had most of his team in place by the fall of 1789, and expressed pleasure at its quality.[3]

In September, Congress addressed several important issues pertaining to the nation's armed forces. After considering ways to "recognize and adapt" a military establishment, members legalized the existing regular army by confirming a 1787 law of the Confederation Congress, which had set the size of the regiment at 840 men. In response to a letter from Governor St. Clair, who lamented his inability either to provide safety to settlers in the Ohio Valley or to curtail the punitive raids of vengeful whites, the Senate included in the military bill au-

---

3. Since the Constitution left the vice president's role up to the president, Washington could have set a precedent giving that position considerable power in the government. He might well have used the vice president in some important way, such as a chief of staff, as a prime minister, or as a coordinator of the cabinet. But none of that was to be with John Adams in the office. Adams nursed an overweening jealousy of Washington and had been more trouble than help to him during the Revolution. The general had not forgotten. The two men had little if any personal attraction to one another; they were simply so different that they could probably not have worked well together. Benjamin Franklin, who knew Adams well, once described him as "always an honest man, often a wise one, but sometimes and in some things, absolutely out of his senses." Washington cut Adams out of his inner circle, relegating the vice presidency to the sidelines, where it has languished ever since.

155

thorization for the president to call into service such militia units as he might judge necessary to protect frontier communities. That proposal sparked immediate debate, with Elbridge Gerry leading the argument that such a provision would give the president the power to start a war in the West without coming to Congress for a declaration. Washington's support of the measure, as well as the strongly felt need of most members of Congress to respond to the urgent and pathetic appeals for security from Americans over the mountains, carried the discussion. The amendment passed—it would prove to be a key factor as events unfolded in the next year. Finally, members let Knox know that he should be prepared to provide them a proposal to regularize the militia when they returned in January. They adjourned on 30 September. It had been a full and productive five months since George Washington had taken the oath in Federal Hall.

When members of Congress went home, the chief executive embarked on a tour of New England. After telling Governor St. Clair to try yet again to talk recalcitrant tribes into smoking the calumet of peace, and authorizing him to muster up to fifteen hundred militia from Virginia and Pennsylvania if he and Harmar deemed it necessary, Washington set out in mid-October. He spent a month on the road, meeting people in all the New England states except Rhode Island, which he carefully avoided. That state—"Rogues Island," wags called it—remained the only holdout of the thirteen, for North Carolina joined the Union that November. Upon returning to New York City, the president plunged into preparations for the return of Congress.

A full slate of important work had to be accomplished as soon as possible in the new year. Washington and his cabinet used the weeks of early winter to lay the groundwork. Knox devoted much energy to completing the militia reorganization plan, which had been a salient element in Washington's "Sentiments on a Peace Establishment" submitted back in 1783. But the single most pressing issue was the national economy. From the time Hamilton had become the treasury secretary in September, he had been working on a three-part program aimed at placing the country on a solid and respected financial footing: the assumption by the federal government of all previous debts, state or central; the funding at face value of the entire debt, foreign as well as internal; and the chartering of a national bank. No aspect of the program would be free of controversy, so a struggle loomed in the attempt to enact it into law. Also certain to give rise to much emotional debate was the question of where to locate the permanent national capital—New York City, Philadelphia, Baltimore, and a site on the Potomac River were the leading contenders. The next session gave unusual promise of being an exciting one.

Meanwhile, national security issues continued to compete for the president's attention. He remained anxious over the bloody intransigence of white-red relations in the Northwest. Positions seemed to be hardening on all sides; few knowledgeable men could be found who believed the impasse would be broken without at least a punitive expedition against marauding Indians. Knox began to gather intelligence by sending patrols deep into the country north of the Ohio River. But the main requirement for that region appeared to be the suppression of a few out-of-control braves rather than the preparation for widespread war with the Indian nations. The principal threat, in the administration's view, continued to lie in the Southwest. There, negotiations to attain a treaty with the Creeks and other tribes were proceeding slowly. Washington had grown doubtful of Creek motives, suspecting McGillivray of holding out to see whether he could get the better deal from Americans or Spaniards. The chief executive's mind also turned during this winter to the problem of piracy on the Barbary Coast, and particularly to the galling fact that Algiers still held Americans hostage. With no navy, the country remained impotent in the face of such insults. Washington could only shore up the nation's relations with Morocco, hoping that the ruler of that state might be of some help with the Algerian potentate. Writing to his "Great and Magnanimous Friend" in Morocco, the president sent a request for assistance couched in copious flights of flattery. Obliged by weakness to resort to such virtual begging, the proud commander in chief must have cringed in frustration.

On 8 January 1790, Washington delivered the country's first State of the Union Address to lawmakers assembled in the Senate chamber. It was a brief presentation, but one rich in content. Financial affairs, education, improved roads, postal operations, a census, a uniform system of weights and measures, promoting inventions—all of these were important to the building of the nation. Security issues were not particularly emphasized, but neither were they overlooked. They included the militia organization, provisions for a strengthened regular army, and the manufacture of items needed for defense. It seemed clear from the president's words that building a sound country continued to be his top priority. Which it was. The sense of national unity was growing; the idea of a strong central government was taking hold. Washington did not want to retard that movement. Fortunately, conditions remained favorable. Although that worrisome thunder off in the distance may have sounded a bit more disturbing as the new year started, especially in the Southwest, the time of tranquility had not passed. Yet.

Most presidents have known a political "honeymoon," a time early in their tenure when criticism and controversy are muted. It rarely lasts long. Washington discovered his was fading in the early weeks of 1790 when he began trying to enlarge the regular army ever so modestly. Sad experience had shown that current numbers of soldiers in the northwestern sector were inadequate even for the basic task of manning their forts; the anemic units certainly were not up to conducting offensive operations. And there were no federal troops at all in the dangerous southwestern region. But if more aggressiveness seemed to be what was needed against northwestern tribes—and it was—and if war with the southwestern Indians seemed possible—which it did— prudence dictated acting ahead of time to strengthen the army. Washington deemed the moment to have arrived to pay more attention to that part of his oath requiring him to protect and defend. The frontier required more soldiers and more forts. In January, Knox asked Congress to authorize a total of 2,033 officers and men, an exceptionally conservative request that would merely have brought the army up to the size set during the crisis of Shays's insurrection.

Several lawmakers reacted with visceral hostility. Here rose again the phantom of a standing army. "Give Knox his army and he will soon have a war in hand," wrote one senator. "The first error seems to have been the appointing of a Secretary of War when we were at peace, and now we must find troops lest his office should run out of employment." Yet the majority of lawmakers conceded that a larger force was indeed necessary. Debate was hostile and lengthy, compounded by the legislators' unwillingness to attempt a reform of the militia, the greatest sacred cow of all. Finally, on 30 April, Congress boosted the size of the regiment to 1,216 enlisted soldiers by adding a battalion of some

400 men. That slight increase was hardly enough to help militarily, but was more than enough to hurt politically. The scant results elicited sarcasm from a New Jersey newspaper: "Five times the galleries shut; two or three committees chosen to consider the subject; and public expectation set on tip-toe; and all for *Five Companies* of men, and an additional *Major!!!*" The small expansion, especially coming so late in the year, did not give Harmar and St. Clair much to work with. Then, to help pay for the increase, the parsimonious legislators cut a private's pay from four dollars a month to three.

In May, Knox reviewed with Washington the deteriorating situation in the Northwest Territory. A year earlier he had urged military restraint, with reliance on negotiations. Now, however, having nothing much to show for that policy save a series of rebuffs and still more stories of savagery, and with frontier communities vociferously adamant in their claim that easterners were indifferent to their suffering, the secretary was inclined to use force. The trouble was being caused, he believed, by a small number of outlaw braves, maybe only two or three hundred. Shawnees and Miamis mostly. A mounted raid by four hundred hard men could scatter and subdue them. Washington agreed. On 7 June, Knox ordered St. Clair to begin planning for a swift strike by a hundred regulars and three hundred carefully selected militia.

In the meantime, other issues cried for attention, several looming larger than the matter of punishing renegade red men in the Ohio country. Domestic concerns stood high on the list.

When a faction led by James Madison appeared to be on the verge of stymying Hamilton's financial initiatives, and the various regions of the country remained at loggerheads over locating the national capital, Thomas Jefferson forged a compromise. The new secretary of state, who had not shown up in New York City to assume his duties until March, found seeds of solution in the weeks of dissension on the two issues. He sat down quietly with Madison and Hamilton to make a deal. Jefferson and Madison, Virginians both, would deliver the southern votes needed to pass the federal assumption of all debts, as well as the full funding of them, while Hamilton, the New Yorker, would arrange enough northern support to deflate New York's desire to retain the capital. The three agreed that, after a ten-year stay in Philadelphia, the capital would be located on the Potomac. George Washington was happy with both ends of the deal. He of course liked the idea of the capital being near Mount Vernon. And the funding bill would go a long way toward fulfilling his long-ago commitment to make every effort to assure that his Continental Army soldiers received the money owed them upon separation—although not many were likely to still be holding the certificates. That compromise removed the most contentious issues before Congress. Other domestic programs fared well, too, as the year unfolded. And Rhode Island voted for statehood in May, making acceptance of the Constitution unanimous.

Foreign affairs seemed also to be moving in the right direction. Great Britain had made informal contact with the new government in 1789, and Washington had responded by sending to London a private envoy, his old friend Gouverneur Morris. In March 1790, motivated by the crisis generated over the Nootka Sound incident, a British representative surfaced in New York. Because formal relations did not exist between the United States and Great Britain, the agent claimed to be speaking strictly unofficially. Nevertheless, he sought to assure the American government, through his contact, Alexander Hamilton, that "the Cabinet of Great Britain entertained a disposition not only towards a friendly intercourse but towards an alliance with the United States." The former colonies, he added, must certainly "find it to be in their interest to take part with Great Britain rather than with Spain." But, for so long as London kept garrisons in forts on United States territory and refused to meet openly with the new government, Washington was not about to commit himself to an arrangement with the English. He was delighted, however, by the opportunity so fortuitously opened to him.

Since Spain was obviously at a disadvantage in any conflict with England, the moment was propitious to push for concessions in Madrid's relations with the United States. The Americans could play Spain and Great Britain off against one another. Doing so would take some nerve, though, as it was not a risk-free opportunity. For one thing, a full British success would be a most unwelcome eventuality. Washington did not relish the thought of having "so formidable a people as the British" surrounding the United States, which would be the case if they held Canada, Florida, and the Mississippi Valley, "with their navy in front." For another, the frontier was always a powder keg, which could be ignited at any time by any stray spark. In that regard, the president wanted to exert as much control as possible over the frontiers. If hostilities should erupt, he wrote, "it is of the utmost consequence that they should be the result of a deliberate plan, not of an accidental collision."[4]

While keeping the unofficial channel of communications open with London, Washington began trying to reach policy-makers in Madrid. One route lay through Paris. He wrote to Lafayette, telling him that in a war between Great Britain and Spain the United States would remain neutral so long as "events will permit us to do so," and adding pointedly that America wanted "scarcely anything but the free navigation of the Mississippi." Asking his former aide to put pressure on Spain, he suggested that Madrid should not miss the chance to be both "wise and liberal" at the same time. The secretary of state, meanwhile, sent quiet word to Spanish officials that refusing to open the Mississippi by negotiations could lead to conflict, and perhaps to an American alliance with Great Britain. Spanish authorities understood the not-so-subtle threats. They were aware of the nearly continual plots, hatched by frontiersmen, to go down the Mississippi and take New Orleans by force, thus opening the river to their own use. In the face of a possible war with Great Britain, those threats assumed a new dimension.

The Spanish, wanting to keep Americans as far away from the Mississippi as possible, had long worked assiduously to establish buffer territories between the western part of the southernmost states and the Mississippi Valley. They had dealt simultaneously with Indian tribes already there and with white groups attempting to carve out separate countries. In 1790, two such efforts appeared promising; Washington tackled them both.

Georgia, with nebulous claims on much of the forested expanse embraced by Spain, had recently sold nearly sixteen million acres to land speculation companies. The region, lying mainly between the Mississippi and Yazoo rivers, comprised the principal territory of the Choctaw and Chickasaw tribes, and some Cherokee lands as well. Having divested itself of the area, Georgia also divested itself of any responsibility to control it. The speculators selected their own "governor," a soldier of

---

4. The president may well have been speaking from personal experience. The Seven Years' War had been ignited by "an accidental collision" in the back-woods of America between French forces and a contingent of colonials led by Washington himself.

fortune named James O'Fallon. That adventurer moved quickly to get on the right side of the three major forces in the area. To buy the support of McGillivray and the Creek nation, whose lands were not involved, he offered a major share of stock in the enterprise. To gain Spanish approval, he offered to create an independent buffer state. To win over the American government, he offered a military contingent with which to eject the Spanish. His timing was all wrong; the Nootka Sound crisis undercut all three efforts.

Spain, worried about England, did not want a confrontation with Americans just then. McGillivray, realizing that a Spanish alliance would work to his disadvantage in case of war between England and Spain, decided to accept the treaty proposed a year earlier by the Americans. Washington, wanting to stop white incursions into Indian lands, and knowing of Spain's reluctance to become involved in an interior squabble while anticipating a British attack, simply declared that the entire so-called Yazoo Scheme was contrary to existing treaties with Indians. On 26 August, he issued a proclamation forbidding citizens of the United States to be involved in the scheme, on pain of having to "answer the contrary at their peril."

How would the president enforce the decree? He had no troops in the area, and could probably not expect the militia to be responsive to a call for such a purpose. But he had an ace up his sleeve, a red one. Three weeks before, Washington and McGillivray, with great fanfare, had signed a treaty in New York City. That pact primarily settled land disputes between settlers and Indians. But unlike all treaties negotiated before, this one had special teeth. McGillivray, who controlled by far the most powerful fighting force in the Southwest, gained the authority to expel squatters, a provision his Creek warriors would gleefully implement. The well-educated half-breed understood the meaning of the term Machiavellian. One of the commissioners sent earlier to negotiate with the chief of the Creeks described him as having "the good sense of an American, the shrewdness of a Scotchman, and the cunning of an Indian." Washington himself may have put a finger on one of the reasons for McGillivray's success in bargaining with white men—he noted with apparent admiration the forest chieftain's ability to retain "his recollection and reason" even when rip-roaring drunk. The treaty also contained two secret provisions: McGillivray would receive a pension much larger than the retainer paid him by Spain, and, should a war between Spain and Great Britain interrupt the Creek's fur trade, they would be able to receive through U.S. sources the goods needed to sustain them. Interestingly, Spain was not displeased with the outcome, which was an unexpected bonus for the Americans. The Treaty of New York became the first such document to be ratified by the U.S. Senate.

Having thus secured his southern flank, Washington made another Machiavellian move to assure that the situation had a good chance to endure. When Congress established the Southwest Territory that year, in an act patterned after the Northwest Ordinance of 1787, the chief executive decided to preempt the speculators by coopting them into the territorial government. Getting advice from John Brown, a Kentucky congressman who had once been accused of plotting with Spain, he appointed a well-known land speculator as governor and placed other schemers in other positions. It worked. Although friction was always present where whites and Indians came into contact, and despite Spain's later return to its former policies when the Nootka Sound affair did not lead to war (Spain eventually gave in to British demands, thus averting conflict), the Southwest Territory ceased to be the foremost danger to peace in the United States.

As summer ended, the president, not imagining Spain would concede, remained quite nervous over the possibility of war between the two European powers. In a secret paper to his close advisors, he revealed that he expected one. "There is no doubt in my mind" that Spanish posts along the Mississippi would be attacked by an "operation from Detroit." But he was also well satisfied with the achievements so far of his administration. In his first year and a summer in office, he had successfully trod the path between anarchy and monarchy. His wisdom, good fortune, and firmness had brought an obvious sense of order to the country. Moreover, he had achieved that without waging a single campaign. Writing to Lafayette in August, he boasted that the recent diplomatic successes would give the United States "peace from one end of our borders to the other, except where it may be interrupted by a small banditti of Cherokees and Shawnees, who can be easily chastised or even extirpated if it shall become necessary."

The president was justified in being proud of his achievements, but, as events would show, not of his forecast. In fact, at that very moment he was about to take steps fated to start a bloody five-year war in the Northwest Territory.

CHAPTER 16
TOWARD WAR

It was moving time for the federal government. Congress adjourned on 12 August 1790, with intent to reconvene later that year in Philadelphia, the designated location of the capital for the next decade. President Washington devoted much of August to paying farewell calls on his New York hosts, tying up several loose ends of his personal and public affairs, and supervising the packing of his household for shipment south.

He was in an upbeat mood. By this sixteenth month of his presidency, he had seen his country make extraordinary progress. More, perhaps, than either he or anyone else would have guessed back during the ratification fight. Although focused on how much remained to be done in the two and a half years remaining in his term, he was quite pleased with the nation's direction up to that point, and of the distance it had traveled under the Constitution. He was in this state of mind when he had bragged to Lafayette of securing "peace from one end of our borders to the other." Eagerly anticipating a long vacation in the comforting embrace of Mount Vernon—wanting to be "as free from public care as circumstances will allow"—he launched into preparations for the trip, including ordering more than four hundred bottles of port to be sent ahead. However, he thoroughly relished the prospects of one special presidential duty. That fall he was slated to select somewhere along the Potomac a location for the nation's permanent capital. Washington may well have been happier in those fading days of the summer of 1790 than at any other time in his eight years as the nation's chief executive.

Into that rosy setting rode Arthur St. Clair. The governor of the Northwest Territory brought bad news. Back in June, when Knox and Washington had been concluding that a small, swift punitive expedition would be needed to bring Indian "banditti" into line, St. Clair, unaware of their thinking, had on his own begun preparing for an entirely different sort of operation. Messages passing back and forth in the following weeks, traveling the difficult route between New York and points along the Ohio, had revealed the crucial divergence in concept between the commander in chief and the governor. A pressing need to resolve that split had brought about this eleventh-hour meeting of the two men.

Washington's October 1789 directive to St. Clair had ordered the governor to contact the Miami Indians and various other groups living along the Wabash River to try once more to talk them into agreeing to a treaty. The United States did not want war, the president had emphasized. His policy was to draw the tribes into peaceful coexistence with the settlers through treaties and trade—military force was to be used to prevent conflict by serving as a shield for both sides. But, he had written, if those tribes still refused to come to terms and their braves remained a threat to the peace, St. Clair could take whatever steps, "offensive or defensive," that he and Harmar deemed necessary. That had specifically included the delegation of the presidential authority to mobilize up to fifteen hundred militia. Upon learning in June 1790 that the chiefs had rejected his latest overture, St. Clair had resolved to act. He headed at once for army headquarters at Cincinnati to begin planning with Harmar—by then a brigadier general—an offensive the two men had long contemplated. Their basis for doing so was Washington's October letter, not Knox's 7 June message stipulating a swift strike by four hundred mounted men.

High waters delayed St. Clair's arrival until well into July, but he and Harmar then moved decisively. They were thinking not of four hundred men and a raid, but of two thousand and a full-fledged offensive. They calculated the enemy not as a couple of hundred wayward natives, but as the whole of the Shawnee and Miami tribes as well as several bands living along the Wabash, a combined force capable of assembling about fifteen hundred warriors.[1] They saw the purpose not merely to punish the Indians, but to subjugate them once and for all by destroying their villages and by establishing a permanent presence on the Maumee River, which would keep the tribes under control and provide a counterweight to the British garrison at Detroit.

By August the offensive was taking shape. Regulars were assuming a posture for attack, and militia units were responding to a summons issued by Governor St. Clair as soon as he had obtained Harmar's agreement. He mobilized 1,500 men—1,000 from Kentucky and 500 from Pennsylvania. General Harmar had his campaign plans in hand, with logistical support calculated and supplies piling up.

But by then a cloud of doubt had begun forming over the entire scheme. The rules seemed to be shifting. Messages from the War Department were causing consternation. For one thing, when Knox's plan for a raid arrived, Harmar and St. Clair had found in it several glaring inconsistencies. Right away they saw that it was aimed at the wrong Indians, and the numbers on which it was based were way off. Furthermore, the regulars were infantry, neither trained nor equipped for mounted operations. If they could not be involved, the raid would rely solely

1. Tribal areas in much of the Northwest had become so compressed by 1790 that it was next to impossible to distinguish among them. That was especially true of the region of the Maumee and Wabash rivers, which were to provide the setting for most of the fighting in the early 1790s. Miamis occupied the area of today's northwest Ohio and northern Indiana, generally centered on the Maumee River. The Wabash River valley in Indiana was home to Piankashaws, Weas, and Kickapoos. Scattered along the watershed of those rivers were several other tribes or fragments of tribes, many of them refugees from earlier displacements by white settlers. They were mostly Shawnees, Wyandots, Mingos, Delawares, and Potawatomis. Ottawas and Chippewas from southern Michigan also ranged into the region. Altogether, that loose confederation had some twenty-five hundred braves at its disposal, but could realistically be expected to field only half that number at any one place. By way of comparison, in 1790 some four thousand whites lived in the Northwest Territory, mostly near the Ohio River. Kentucky had a total of around sixty thousand settlers. Their numbers increased daily, whereas the Indian population declined just as steadily.

on irregulars—and no one in the government wanted a campaign consisting only of Kentucky cavalry under the control of frontier leaders. Still more confusing, Knox had followed his 7 June letter with other instructions telling St. Clair to distinguish carefully between rogue groups and friendly Indians, to continue overall efforts to win the tribes' acquiescence through persuasion, and to offer a last-minute reprieve to inhabitants along the Wabash just prior to assaulting them. None of that made much sense in the context of a hard-riding, deep raid. Leaving Harmar to continue preparations, St. Clair set off for New York to consult with the president. His aim was to be sure the commander in chief fully understood the situation, and to gain his approval of the planned campaign.

The two men met, with Knox attending, in the midst of the hubbub of the government's move from New York to Philadelphia. The governor spoke forthrightly. His surprising report distressed Washington. The situation St. Clair portrayed was not at all what the president and Knox had had in mind earlier in the summer. But, despite a deep sense of chagrin, Washington found himself nodding in agreement with most of what he heard.

He could not refute the governor's estimate of the potential strength of the enemy, and he understood from personal experience the hazards of sending too small a force into hostile Indian territory. Timing, too, was a major consideration—the campaigning season was well along, and changes at this late hour could cause the year to be lost. Significantly, the militia troops had already been called out and were en route. Could they be paid and sent home without being employed? What would the westerners say if their expectations were dashed by a cancellation of the long-sought offensive? On a different level, the president still was quite concerned over a possible eruption of hostilities between Great Britain and Spain, and of the disruptive effect it might have on frontier communities. A large American force mobilized in the West could prove to be useful if the area did find itself somehow pulled into the fringes of an international conflict.

All things considered, St. Clair's forceful words were compelling. The lateness of the season, the militia already mobilized, a more robust opponent than previously assumed, uncertainties over foreign intentions in the area, the painfully obvious need to take some strong action to protect citizens on the frontier, repeated failures to convince the recalcitrant tribes to treat with the United States, the governor's strong feelings, Harmar's concurrence, the government in packing boxes—Washington and Knox could not see their way clear to modify or cancel the operation designed by the governor and the commanding general. The president reluctantly approved the offensive. Actually, as he read the situation, he had no alternative. The only part of the plan Washington turned down was the establishment of a fortified base on the Maumee. He thought it would be too costly and risky to maintain a garrison so far from the Ohio. St. Clair got everything else he had wanted. He started the long journey back to Cincinnati with the word to go.

While Washington would have wished for a more peaceful outcome to the confrontation in the Northwest, matching the one he had obtained with tribes in the Southwest, he was not unduly concerned. The endemic violence in the area had conditioned most citizens to the possibility—indeed, the probability—of a resort to arms. Many would have said the inevitability. Nearly every observer had come to the conclusion that the Indians would not treat unless the United States was prepared to compel them to do so. And, at last, reluctantly, the president was so prepared.

As he set out on the road to Mount Vernon, Washington's upbeat mood returned. His primary worry was over the eventuality of a European war spilling over and entangling the United States. A campaign to discipline some tribes in the Northwest was not novel in the long and brutal history of those brooding forests beyond the Alleghenies, nor was it seen as especially risky, particularly with the commitment of so large a force of regulars and militia. The commander in chief was confident. His foremost concerns were political, not military. It probably never crossed his mind that Harmar's force might be defeated.

CHAPTER 17
THE INDIAN WAY OF WAR

Take U.S. Highway 127 north from the Ohio River at Cincinnati to its intersection with Highway 24, then follow that second route to the shores of Lake Erie at Toledo, and you will have traveled a path of war. The two roads cut a swath through cornstalk forests for some two hundred miles, traversing a bright, bountiful rural region in America's heartland. It is an easy and enjoyable drive. But in 1790 there were no roads and the forests were primeval. The same journey then would have been an altogether different experience.

Climbing the steep banks from the river to a wide shelf where Fort Washington sat, the way northward led over a tousled crescent of low hills forming a backdrop for the fort. From those heights it continued past stations where groups of settlers, banding together for mutual protection from marauding Indians, had hacked communal clearings in the wilderness. Even those remote vestiges of white civilization were soon left behind. Having been bulldozed by glaciers in the Ice Age, the landscape becomes increasingly gentle, changing quickly from rolling hills to undulating contours to level land to flat. The soil is loam, deep and rich. There is little natural drainage. Absorbing and holding the abundant moisture accumulating from rainfall and melting snow, large reaches of the forest floor were constantly sodden. Occasional streams had etched shallow trenches into the mostly monotonous terrain, meandering lazily through marshes toward the great river to the south or the great lake to the north. Sunshine struggled without appreciable success to penetrate the canopy of interlocking tree branches, leaving

169

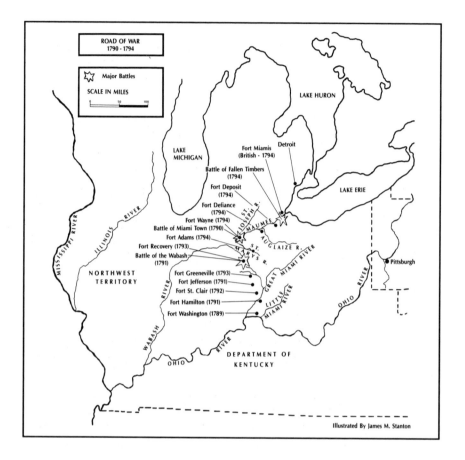

ROAD OF WAR
1790 - 1794

Major Battles

SCALE IN MILES

0   50   100

LAKE HURON

LAKE
MICHIGAN

Fort Miamis   Detroit
(British - 1794)

Battle of Fallen Timbers
(1794)

LAKE ERIE

Fort Deposit
(1794)

Fort Defiance
(1794)

Fort Wayne (1794)

Battle of Miami Town (1790)

Fort Adams (1794)

Fort Recovery (1793)

Battle of the Wabash
(1791)

NORTHWEST
TERRITORY

Fort Greeneville (1793)

Fort Jefferson (1791)

Fort St. Clair (1792)

Fort Hamilton (1791)

Fort Washington (1789)

Pittsburgh

DEPARTMENT OF
KENTUCKY

OHIO

Illustrated By James M. Stanton

the woods not only dank but dark. Dense morning fog often curtailed
the already reduced fields of vision. From time to time, the route crossed
a trading or hunting track, or encountered a trapper's bark hut, giving evidence of at least some human habitation. The black forest was
a vast hunting ground for the tribes of the region. Their villages sprinkled
the timbered expanse, with clustered wigwams and cultivated fields
providing rare breaks in the bleakness. The farther north the trek progressed, the larger and more numerous those communities became. But
still, the huge wilderness seemed to be virtually trackless. Seen from
some hard-won vantage point—perhaps a high limb of a tall oak growing
on one of the area's few elevations—the plateau of treetops would have
stretched sea-like to the horizon, disappearing in endless swells.

This was the daunting invasion route Arthur St. Clair and Josiah Harmar were contemplating. The mere thought of plunging very far into that foreboding forest was deterrence enough for all but the most adventuresome.

General Harmar's campaign plan called for marching a force of fifteen hundred militia and regulars some 150 miles to the center of the Indian lands, there to lay waste villages and fields and supplies, and to inflict casualties on warriors who would be forced to fight in defense of their homes. Natives not killed would be scattered and left destitute in the face of approaching winter. That central location was Kekionga, where the Saint Marys and Saint Joseph rivers combine to form the Maumee. It is the site today of Fort Wayne, Indiana. Whites called it Miami Village or Miami Town. Numerous other tribal villages stood in the vicinity, and much of the surrounding land had been cleared for farming. Fur traders had busy stations there—they took some two thousand packs of furs, worth twenty-four thousand pounds sterling, from the three rivers area in 1790 alone. Kekionga was also a strategic location controlling communications and commerce in the contested Northwest Territory, for it was a link between the Mississippi River and the Great Lakes. Coming from Lake Erie up the Maumee to Kekionga, one had only to make a short portage overland to reach the Wabash River, which flowed west toward the Illinois territory and then south past Vincennes to the Ohio. British forces had used that route in the American Revolution. Here it was that Governor St. Clair had wanted to establish an American fortress. However, the current intent of the campaign would be to clear the area of Indian forces, and to limit its further use to them by razing their villages. General Harmar would personally lead the attack, starting from Fort Washington.

A second column of about five hundred troops, under the command of Maj. John Hamtramck, would march from Fort Knox at Vincennes to attack villages up the Wabash River. Kicking off several days earlier and from much farther west, Hamtramck's move was a feint expected to draw the Indians' attention in his direction, giving Harmar a better chance of catching defenders unprepared in Miami Town.

Returning from his conference with President Washington, St. Clair reached Cincinnati on 22 September to find preparations for the expedition mostly completed—and a commanding general beside himself with frustration. The militia had begun arriving on schedule in

171

mid-September, but they were not the sturdy frontiersmen Harmar had expected. Few true fighters had come. Instead, they had hired substitutes, "a great many hardly able to bear arms, such as old, infirm men, and young boys." Many were foreigners, recently arrived in the region. They were described as "raw and unused to the gun or the woods." Nor did they arrive equipped to fight. Some brought broken muskets, having been told that artificers at Fort Washington would repair them. Others had no weapon at all. The militia from Pennsylvania did not arrive until 25 September. They were even less prepared for a military operation than were the Kentuckians, and only three hundred of the required five hundred showed up. The quality of the leaders seemed to be no better than that of the men. The best known Indian fighters had declined to participate, being unwilling to subordinate themselves to regular officers. Those who did report got into a fierce argument right away over who would lead the militia troops, with various factions declining to serve under one officer or another. Knox's proposal to reform the militia system, ignored by Congress, had been intended to prevent precisely this kind of debacle.

Harmar solved the command imbroglio by negotiating a deal with the senior militia leaders. Lieutenant Colonel James Trotter would direct the three battalions from Kentucky, Lt. Col. Christopher Truby would command the one from Pennsylvania, and Col. John Hardin would coordinate all four. Other difficulties could not be solved so quickly. There simply was no time to train the ill-prepared men and units, nor could Harmar wait for the missing troops to show up. With 1,133 militiamen, 320 regulars, three artillery pieces, and a large supply train, he set out on the new nation's first major military operation. But not without some trepidation. Casting a rueful eye on his militia units, he hoped they would "stick to the text, and not leave me in the lurch."

Why would a commander take such an unready force deep into hostile territory to face an enemy anticipated to be nearly as numerous, and who would be fighting on his own ground? The answer lies in the Indian way of war—and the assumptions about it made by white leaders.

Native warriors had advantages and disadvantages when fighting white forces. They were more at home in the forest, they normally had the initiative in deciding where and when to fight, they could assemble and disperse more rapidly, their reputation for savagery gave them a psychological edge in battle, and they were fighting for their homes and hunting grounds. On the other hand, they possessed less of the technological materiel of war. Artillery was not one of their weapons, and not all braves went into battle carrying firearms. Nor did the tribes have a command structure of the sort that had evolved in European warfare. "Chiefs" obtained their position because individuals chose to follow them, and no one could be compelled to fight if he opted out. Discipline was therefore unreliable, and the braves tended to function more as individuals than as members of a team. Importantly, too, they were not numerous. To put together a large force required intertribal alliances, with all of the difficulties inherent in coalition warfare.

For such reasons, the Indians preferred small war. Ambush, hit-and-run, sniping, terror, pilferage. Stealing pack animals might be considered in some instances a bigger victory than stopping a column of armed men. Despite the persistent views of decades of Hollywood directors, Indians were not inclined to attack palisaded forts in human waves. Nor were they prone to charge an unbroken line of trained soldiers. In fact, unless directly defending against a threat to their families and villages, they would virtually always fade away in the face of determined resistance, preferring to live to fight another day when the circumstances would be more favorable. When they did engage a major force, it was in all likelihood done in the form of an ambush, only in the rarest of circumstances in a pitched battle. That was the pattern well known to experienced Indian hands, and it conditioned their concepts for waging campaigns against the red men. Maintain technological superiority, keep the soldiers closed up so stragglers could not be cut off, prevent surprise, attack villages to force a fight—those were the ingredients of success. So long as the white unit held its discipline and cohesion, it had little fear of being beaten unless the Indians could muster a vastly superior force. And it was simply not imaginable that a contingent of troops the size the United States was sending under Josiah Harmar could be overwhelmed. Not in the Northwest, anyway.

Harmar, himself, reflected that thinking. Despite the miserable condition of the militia, he felt reasonably confident. The caliber of his regular troops was solid—the passage of years on the frontier had gradually transformed the rabble of 1784 into reliable soldiers with competent leaders. Had the militia units been as capable, he would likely have been overconfident if not downright cocky. He had led a small expedition into Indian country earlier in the year, farther east, and had watched smugly as the natives had scurried to avoid battle. The previous winter he had bragged, "If the word *march!* is given by proper authority, a speedy movement shall be made against the savages." He may have been speaking as much from frustration as from bravado, for, after years of chafing at the prohibitions against striking back at his tormentors, he was itching to go. He no longer referred to his foe as Indians, but as villains and savages.

On 26 September Harmar sent his militia, under Colonel Hardin, marching northeast from Fort Washington, away from the direct route toward Miami Town. Early reports, it could be hoped, might mislead the Indians in Kekionga. Hearing of Major Hamtramck's column threatening them from Vincennes, while the elements from Cincinnati seemed aimed elsewhere, they might become less vigilant in tracking the main body of troops. On the last day of September General Harmar left with the rest of his army, following the trail cleared by the militia. Meanwhile, Hamtramck was late. He was supposed to have started his movement up the Wabash by 25 September, but the militia from Kentucky had not arrived until 29 September. Although the Kentuckians showed up understrength and unready, the anxious major pushed off the very next day with only 50 regulars and 290 militia. The plan to divert the Indians' attention had already misfired.

Harmar was unaware of Hamtramck's troubles, but he knew that St. Clair had sent word to forewarn the British of the pending offensive, which might ruin any chance of achieving surprise if the march bogged down. (The governor had done so on orders from the secretary of war, who was concerned about an escalation of the fighting if the Crown's commanders interpreted American military movements as a threat to Detroit.) Harmar therefore pushed his units hard, but with full consideration for security requirements. He kept his flanks covered and took care to scout ahead. Nighttime bivouacs were set up in defensive squares, with the supply train squeezed into the center for safety. In that fashion, despite rainy weather, the column averaged about ten miles a day. Harmar followed the northeast heading until he reached the vicinity of modern-day Springfield, near the site of a battle fought during the Revolution between George Rogers Clark and Indians siding with the British. There he turned sharply to his left and pushed ahead on a line leading straight for Miami Town. On the morning of 13 October scouts ran across two Indians, managing to capture one. Under questioning, he revealed that the natives had been keeping Harmar's column under close observation, and had concluded that it was directed at Kekionga and nearby villages. He also said that the occupants there, with only a few hundred warriors on hand, were planning to evacuate rather than to await the soldiers' arrival. Harmar was distraught. He still had some thirty-five miles to go—at least three days' march even if he took some risks with security. The Indians would have made good their escape in that length of time. But a body of mounted men could cover the distance in a day's dash, so the general decided to detach a raiding party to try to catch the natives before they could get away. Because most of the mounted troops were in the Kentucky militia, Harmar entrusted the command of the strike force to Colonel Hardin. They were to start at dawn on the fourteenth.

Morning came cold and wet. Hardin did not get away until late, and then apparently became lost. By nightfall, he was only four miles ahead of the main body, having dashed Harmar's hopes of surprising his foe. It had not been a good day—in more ways than the commanding general realized. Far to the southwest, Major Hamtramck turned back that very day to return to Vincennes. After pushing up the Wabash for about ten days, the major had found ominous signs of impending resistance. Although no hostile Indians had been encountered, the soldiers were spooked. Many of the militia had already deserted, and the others were threatening to mutiny if the small column proceeded farther. They were afraid of an Indian ambush—and so was Hamtramck. Having no confidence in the fighting force he led, he terminated his mission and retraced his steps to the safety of Fort Knox. That day, too, the British commandant of Detroit responded officially to the message St. Clair had sent alerting him to the fact of the expedition. Runners had already been days on the road summoning help for the tribes who were the target of Harmar's column. Actually, British agents had alerted the Indians about two months earlier that the United States was readying an army estimated to be three thousand strong with the probable intent of establishing positions at Miami Town and on the rapids of the Maumee, near contemporary Toledo. While that early information had worried the native leaders, they had taken a wait-and-see attitude. This latest intelligence from Detroit had energized them to begin mobilizing, but it was too late. They had not yet assembled enough men to defend their homes against the threat posed by Harmar, even though scores of braves were pouring in from other sectors to join them. Accordingly, on that same busy 14 October, they decided to evacuate rather than fight.

Those living in or near Kekionga buried their corn, burned their cabins, and hurried on the fifteenth down the Maumee toward Lake Erie to evade the oncoming Americans. Hardin's lost day had handed them the time they needed. Harmar, unaware of his enemy's intentions or actions, hustled his main body onward, thankful that it was a clear day. John Hardin, recovering from his slack control of the day before, drove his men hard, covering some twenty miles to reach Kekionga in midafternoon. The Indians were gone. The area showed obvious signs of a frantic evacuation, revealing just what a near miss it had been. With no one to fight, the militia wandered off to rummage among the few huts not burning, quickly expanding their search for loot to nearby villages. The regulars looked on with a mixture of scorn and concern, worried that the Indians might return and catch them in disarray. One officer reckoned that fewer than two hundred warriors "might have beat us off the ground." Hardin wrote an exultant note to Harmar, telling him that Miami Town was theirs. Shortly after noon on 17 October, Harmar arrived to reunite his entire command. He had ideas of continuing on to the Wabash to strike at the Wea villages, but decided to go no farther after Indians lurking in the area stole more than fifty of his packhorses that night. Instead, hoping to find villagers hiding northwest of Kekionga, he sent out a body of soldiers under Lt. Col. James Trotter. Although Trotter had boldly insisted on leading the patrol, he became cautious when his outriders encountered and killed two braves. Satisfied with the two scalps, he returned. Hardin, with whom Trotter had argued vehemently for the overall command of the militia, was incensed by his rival's timidity. He demanded of Harmar a chance to take troops out the next day to restore the reputation of the militia. Harmar said he could.

On the nineteenth, Hardin left with about 180 men, including 30 regulars under Capt. John Armstrong. He took the same trail Trotter had used. Soon the patrol found Indians, who ran away at the sight of the soldiers. A contemptuous Hardin stretched his column out in pursuit. Entering an elongated meadow, with a swamp on one side and woods on the other, those up front saw a campfire at the far end, still burning, with an array of equipment lying scattered about. Surprised

Indians had apparently decamped in a hurry. The militiamen rushed gleefully forward to collect their booty. That was a mistake. Colonel Hardin had led his men toward the Eel River village of one of the best leaders in the annals of the Indian wars: Little Turtle, a battle chieftain of the Miami tribe. Little Turtle had set a trap, and Hardin had taken the bait.

Nature's spectacular spray of autumn colors had splashed the woods in brilliant hues. About 150 braves lay hidden, their war-paint patterns blending with the foliage. Patiently, they waited for their victims to fill the meadow. With the lead militia unit attracted to the abandoned gear, and Armstrong's regulars well into the clearing, warriors on the right poured a volley of musket fire into the astounded soldiers. They turned toward the gunfire, only to be blasted from behind by other Indians lying in ambush on the left. Reckless disdain turned in that instant to unreasoning fear. Leaving weapons and wounded, survivors bolted for the rear, where Captain Armstrong was hustling his men from column into line. All but nine of the militia kept right on running, passing through the regulars in headlong flight. In the chaos and smoke, Armstrong stood his ground, expecting other troops behind him to close up and join the fight. But those, too, panicked by their fleeing comrades, broke and sprinted back toward safety rather than come to the aid of their countrymen in the meadow. Little Turtle, seeing that Armstrong's small group had been abandoned, boldly ordered an all-out assault. Braves rushed from the woods, many brandishing tomahawks rather than muskets. Within seconds the fighting was hand to hand, and the dwindling group of whites was quickly overwhelmed. A mere handful avoided death by stumbling in the swirling smoke to cover in the swamp or the woods. Captain Armstrong splashed into a deep part of the swamp and escaped detection, but he had to remain in the cold water until nightfall, listening to the wounded being killed and the victory whoops of the red men.

When Armstrong and others straggled into camp the next day, and a head count could be taken, Harmar discovered that more than 120 men were missing, a large percentage of whom were assumed to have been slain in the meadow. Regulars were livid over the cowardice of the militia, which had led to the loss of so many of their comrades. General Harmar announced publicly that if there should be a repeat of the militia's "shameful cowardly conduct," he would turn his artillery on them. Hardin, humiliated, asked for permission to take a force back to the battlefield. Not trusting either the colonel or his troops, Harmar refused the request. He decided to leave the dead where they had fallen, burn the rest of the villages, and start back for Fort Washington before a larger number of Indians gathered. All that day and the next, the soldiers worked at razing anything useful to families living in the area. Then, at midmorning on the twenty-first, the chastened column began retracing its steps, covering eight miles before forming a bivouac.

On the way, Harmar had begun to consider sending a detachment back that night to waylay any Indians returning to Kekionga in the wake of the soldiers' departure. When a scout rode in with the news that a small number of the inhabitants had indeed begun returning, and that they were careless in their security, the general decided to try one more time to inflict casualties on the hostile natives. That was his mission, after all, but he was also smarting over the inglorious results of the expedition thus far. He resolved to send the detachment under the command of a regular officer. He chose Maj. John Wyllys, a Connecticut veteran of the Revolutionary War and a stout disciplinarian. The task force was composed of 60 regulars, 40 militia horsemen, and 300 of the best militia infantrymen. They expected to encounter at most a hundred braves. Colonel Hardin went along in charge of the militia, but under the overall command of Major Wyllys. The four hundred raiders began moving at 2:00 A.M. under a brilliant autumn moon.

To trap the Indians in the ruins, Wyllys planned to send half of the Kentucky infantry around to the left to block retreat along the Saint Joseph River, and the other 150 to the right to close the escape route down the Maumee. Once those two pincers were in motion, Wyllys would drive straight into the village with his regulars and the forty horsemen. The attack would take place at dawn.

Once again, however, the attackers' assumptions proved wrong. The Indians had detected the returning troops, and they were looking for a fight. Once again Little Turtle was in charge. With their numbers growing daily, and elated by the victory on the Eel River on the nineteenth, the tribes had determined to press the withdrawing U.S. forces. When scouts informed them that a column of soldiers was marching their way, they concluded that it must be coming back to retrieve and bury the dead. Little Turtle quickly devised a trap. The sudden American move had prevented the gathering of all the warriors in the area, but enough were on hand to deal the soldiers a serious blow. Some of the braves established an ambush at the ford on the Maumee near Kekionga.

In early light, Wyllys unsuspectingly approached the ford, his forty mounted troops leading, the regulars following on foot. When the horsemen were nearly across the river, a blaze of musketry cut into them from the opposite shore. Men and horses fell into the churning water in a surprised chorus of screams and oaths. The startled riders began returning fire, while the regulars scurried to form a line of support on the other bank of the Maumee. Crossing the stream not far to the right, the enveloping militia troops heard the sounds of battle. This time they reacted properly, turning quickly to go to the aid of the cavalry. Coming at the double-time from that direction they outflanked the Indians, who, seeing this new threat, broke off the fight and fled. Once reorganized, surviving horsemen joined the charging infantry in an attempt to chase down the small band of retreating warriors. Meanwhile, the regulars re-formed and started quickly after the others, not wanting to be left out of the hunt.

Major Wyllys hurried his troops across the shallow river and through the remnants of Kekionga. On the other side of the village they entered a charred cornfield, which had been torched a few days earlier by the Americans. Suddenly they were engulfed by a huge body of Indians springing from bushes bordering the field. This was Little Turtle's real ambush—warriors at the river had been decoys to draw soldiers into his trap. The fighting was fierce—and brief. Only ten of the regulars avoided death in the melee; Wyllys was not one of them. Hearing the unmistakable sounds of the struggle, both flanking elements marched toward the ambush site. But it was too late. After a short brush with the militia, the victorious braves escaped with relatively few losses— eyewitnesses reported about forty Indian bodies lying around the field.

Again failing to bury their dead, and even abandoning several of the wounded, the remnants of Wyllys's force, with Colonel Hardin commanding, scampered to rejoin Harmar and the main body. The entire column, considerably shaken by this second defeat and by the knowledge that surprisingly large numbers of Indians were in the area, headed southward. Harmar fully expected to have to run a gauntlet all the way back to Fort Washington. And he probably would have had to do just that but for the interjection of Providence. The Indians, by then about seven hundred strong, and with their blood up, had resolved to strike the whites as they withdrew. But in the evening after the battle there was an eclipse of the harvest moon, which some of the tribes took as an omen warning of great losses if they fought any more at that time. They chose therefore not to pursue the white troops, permitting Harmar's bedraggled column to limp back to the Ohio unopposed. Despite losing the chance to inflict still more casualties, the red men were ecstatic. They had thrown the soldiers "on their backs."

Hardin, Harmar, and St. Clair put the best face on the affair they could, but there was no concealing defeat. Successful armies do not leave their dead unburied; they do not desert their wounded; they do not return to garrison demoralized. As word of the repulse spread, finger-pointing started. Militia leaders talked disparagingly of Harmar's lack of courage and effectiveness, and reported that he was drunk most of the time. Regular officers railed at the militia's indiscipline in camp and cowardice in battle. Rumors of those charges and countercharges filtered back to Philadelphia, arriving ahead of the official word. The government was astounded. How could savages have inflicted such a defeat on the American army?

When Washington opened the new session of Congress in early December, he had scant information to refute or clarify the rumors. He explained the purpose behind the expedition, but could say little more. Clearly, though, further steps would have to be taken to achieve security in the Northwest. That imperative became even more pressing in light of Kentucky's imminent step into statehood. But Indians were not the only threat on the horizon. Affairs in France continued to inject a note of uncertainty into relations with that ally, and members of Congress needed no reminding that the English refusal to vacate its fortified positions on U.S. soil was a constant threat to peace, or that Americans still languished in Algerian prisons, or that the Barbary pirates were yet unchecked, or that English policies over fishing rights in the Great Banks reeked with arrogance. The president was also still concerned lest a conflict between Great Britain and Spain should involve the United States—word of the peaceful resolution of the Nootka crisis had not yet reached the capital—and he was particularly worried over the impact a naval war between the two would have on American commerce. And there was more. Militia reform was needed, arsenals had to be built, fortifications for "important and vulnerable" places were required. Notice was thus served on the members that defense issues were likely to consume much of their attention in the forthcoming session.

Dispatches describing the ill-fated campaign reached the capital a few days later. Lieutenant Ebenezer Denny brought them, along with his own observations of militia shortcomings. For nearly a month the capital was abuzz with talk, for it remained hard to credit the official accounts—many would prefer to believe that Harmar was a drunkard rather than to admit that the militia system had failed.[1] But when Capt. John Armstrong rode into town on 5 January 1791 to tell his harrowing personal account of the battles, including damning stories of militia failures, all had to agree that the nation needed to raise a differently structured army to deal with frontier security.

Moreover, word of widespread Indian raids flowed out of the West. Emboldened by their victory, angered by the devastation wrought by Harmar, sensing that the moment to roll back the tide of white migration was at hand, the tribes had decided to carry the war to the entire Ohio Valley, even back to the western reaches of Pennsylvania, where settlers had enjoyed a long period of relative quiet. That winter was the bloodiest the frontier had yet seen, providing any number of gruesome vignettes to energize the government to take action.

Early in 1791, a band of about two hundred warriors from the Maumee region ravaged the area near Cincinnati. They were led by Blue Jacket, a Shawnee chieftain who had played a role in fending off Harmar's invasion, and who was destined to be heard from again. On 10 January they encircled a stockaded strongpoint known as Dunlop's Station, about seventeen miles from Fort Washington. Displaying his numbers, Blue Jacket attempted to bluff the settlers and soldiers taking refuge inside the stockade into surrendering. The occupants—thirty-five men and an unknown number of women and children—decided not to trust themselves to the dubious mercies of the marauders. After a day of

---

1. While Harmar's competence as an independent commander of large forces could fairly have been questioned, the charge of drunkenness was not valid. He was later cleared by an investigation. Except for its impact on his reputation, however, the entire issue was moot, for his military career was ended by the battles in and around Miami Town.

desultory sniping, when it became apparent that the stronghold could withstand either attack or siege, the Indians turned to psychological warfare. At midnight they stripped naked a prisoner, a surveyor named Abner Hunt whom they had recently captured, and staked him spread-eagled to the ground within easy sight of those in the small fort. Kindling a fire, they inserted glowing coals from time to time into incisions made in the prisoner's arm and leg muscles. As the unfortunate surveyor screamed in agony, his torturers danced mockingly around his writhing body. Then, when the garrison still would not accept a summons to surrender, warriors built a fire on Hunt's abdomen and let it slowly burn its way into his entrails. Dawn came, the screams finally stopped, and the raiders disappeared into the forest.

The escalation of warfare in the West sped that story and a spate of others to Philadelphia. Rufus Putnam, a respected Revolutionary War veteran well known to New Englanders, and a leading land developer in the West, galvanized members of Congress with a widely read letter giving a vivid description of the red menace threatening to erase white settlements. There was no alternative, nearly everyone in government soon concluded—force would be needed. The army would once more be called on to campaign in the brooding woods north of the Ohio. It was without question, said Secretary Knox, "that another expedition must be made against the Wabash Indians."

At Dunlop's Station, when defenders had ventured out to recover Abner Hunt's mutilated body, they found on it two crossed war clubs—the Indians' declaration of war.

CHAPTER 18
LITTLE TURTLE TRIUMPHANT

The Miami Indians had in Little Turtle a devastatingly effective war chieftain. Me-she-kin-no-quah, as fellow warriors called this charismatic son of a Miami father and a Mohican mother, was perhaps in his fortieth year in 1791. Standing about six feet tall, dignified in manner, with a stern expression seemingly etched permanently into the contours of his face, Little Turtle inspired respect and admiration among reds and whites alike. A British officer said he was the "most decent, modest, sensible Indian" he had ever met. Observers noted how he always handled himself with the utmost decorum. Intelligent, realistic, bold, with an intuitive sense of the decisive moment in a fight, he was a most formidable foe. Opponents took him lightly at their own peril.

Yet that is just what Americans did in the aftermath of Little Turtle's humbling of Josiah Harmar. They blamed that galling setback on the U.S. Army's shortcomings, without giving due regard to its enemy's abilities.

Harmar's defeat, Washington and his advisors believed, had been caused by inadequate generalship and indisciplined militia. The commanding general had violated basic precepts by repeatedly splitting his force, handing the enemy opportunities to pounce on the separated detachments. Worse, he himself had failed to be at the scene of any of the clashes—generals were expected to lead, not push, their troops. For its part, the militia, untrained and unruly, had behaved abominably throughout the campaign, and particularly disgracefully in actual battle. The solution, it seemed obvious, was to find a new leader and to field a better army.

The commander would be Gov. Arthur St. Clair. Considered to be more a political than a military leader, he was acceptable to those who worried about a man on horseback. Moreover, he knew the region and its problems, and he had already forged links with leaders in the West. When Congress authorized the rank of major general, St. Clair got Washington's nod. He retained the office of governor of the Northwest Territory, giving him unusual power with both political and military clout.

Despairing of moving any meaningful militia reform through Congress, and aware that it would not help for the forthcoming campaign even if it could be done, the president and his secretary of war pinned their hopes on fielding a wholly federal force of some three thousand men. To avoid yet another fight over a standing army, they found a middle ground between regulars and militia, a hybrid called levies. Those troops would be short-term volunteers. Enlisted only for the duration of the campaign, levies would clearly not comprise a standing army, but they would be under federal command and discipline, and therefore would be more reliable than militia. They were also expected to be more economical than either regulars or mobilized militia. The new force would be built by adding one regiment of regulars (some of whom would garrison posts in the Southwest) and by raising the rest as levies. Henry Knox took that proposal to Congress in January 1791.

Alarmed by the desperate situation along the Ohio, and assuaged by the concept of levies, the legislators gave the administration everything it asked for. By the time it adjourned in early March, Congress had authorized a second regiment of regulars, had approved as many as two thousand levies for six months, had enabled the calling out of the militia for six months, had approved Washington's nominations of regular officers, had permitted him to make appointments of levy officers without Senate consent, and had appropriated the funds necessary for all of that. The members had also authorized two regular army generals—a brigadier in addition to the major general—and had provided for a quartermaster to handle the increased logistical burden of a larger military establishment. Then, perhaps hoping to gain heavenly sanction for American arms, they had constituted the position of chaplain for the army. All in all, that was quite an achievement for a democratic legislative body to accomplish in about six weeks.[1] True, it was March before they completed their work, only then enabling the executive branch to begin to execute, which seriously hampered the building of fighting units in time to go on campaign that year. But the basic problem was not slow legislative action. It was a combination of year-by-year authorizations and the begrudging, piecemeal construction of an army—for which Oliver Cromwell might be thanked.

The strategic plan for 1791 had three components: vigorous operations by irregular elements to gain time, a diplomatic offensive to prevent the Indian uprising from spreading to other areas of the frontier, and a full invasion of the hostile heartland.

Since the United States would need several months to recruit and assemble an invasion force, there was an evident need in the meantime to blunt the Indian offensive. Frontier settlements could not be left exposed to continued atrocities; terrorized citizens had to be protected. Fortunately, a means was at hand. Kentucky militia units were eager to be unleashed. Secretary Knox authorized them to conduct spoiling attacks north of the Ohio. That permission, it was noted, was "calculated expressly to gratify the people of Kentucky," who had long been critical of the central government's inept attempts to provide security. More importantly, though, the counteroffensive would also have the effect of throwing the savage marauders off balance, of seizing the initiative, of easing the pressure on settlers and frontier communities. It would be an economy-of-force operation staged and supported by state troops, freeing federal officials to focus on preparing the invasion.

Hardly had the realization of Harmar's defeat sunk in before the central government began to take steps to isolate those bands that had taken the warpath. Aware of ongoing efforts to kindle a coalition of all the tribes to resist white expansion everywhere, Washington and Knox

---

1. Congress also approved the addition of Kentucky and Vermont as new states in the Union. That action reduced the threat of a breakaway movement arising in the West, but it made the obligation to protect citizens in the western territories even more compelling. It also gave Kentucky a bigger voice in the federal government, helping to elevate frontier concerns at the seat of government.

feared that euphoria from the victory over Harmar might fan smoldering embers into flame. They were particularly concerned with keeping the Six Nations neutral to avoid a spread of the fighting into western New York and Pennsylvania. Special effort went into making overtures to Mohawk leader Joseph Brant, widely recognized as the most influential of the Iroquois chieftains. Angered by several recent depredations by renegade whites against his people, Brant was known to be wavering on the edge of war. While Washington hosted Indian delegations in the capital, special envoys traveled to contact other groups in their forest homes. Peace was the message they carried, along with reminders of the benefits of cooperation with the great white father in Philadelphia and warnings of the perfidious nature of British agents agitating for an uprising.

Once the red rampage was stalled and the movement toward a wider war was thwarted, the third and decisive element of the government's plan would start. That was to be St. Clair's invasion, slated initially to begin in the summer. The general was to march three thousand trained men—enough to overcome any feasible combination of tribes—straight to the source of hostility, Kekionga, where Josiah Harmar had been repulsed. This time, though, soldiers would stay there. They were to establish a permanent American fortress to provide an enduring presence, ending once and for all the ability of the Maumee and Wabash tribes to sustain resistance. That forward bastion would be securely linked to the Ohio River by a chain of posts to be erected along the route of advance from Fort Washington. Such a grand American position planted in the very heart of the Northwest Territory would also serve as a counterpoise to the British garrison at Detroit. Despite the cost, which had led to the rejection of the idea a year earlier, the fortress in the forest was now seen as essential. Establishing it was to be Arthur St. Clair's primary objective, a mission of such paramount importance that not even an agreement by the Indians to cease hostilities would prevent it from being carried out.

George Washington had lost his complacency. He sat St. Clair down in March and lectured him. The old soldier, whose personal experiences with Indians were painful to recall, told the new major general that his guidance could be wrapped up in three words: "beware of surprise." Elaborating pointedly, he admonished his field commander to "trust not the Indian; leave not your arms for the moment; and when you halt for the night be sure to fortify your camp—again and again, General, beware of surprise."

After the president finished, Secretary of War Knox continued briefing the commanding general. He was explicit, detailed, and forceful. St. Clair would not be able to complain, as Harmar could have, of vague instructions. For added clarity, the secretary put his directives in writing—the "principles of your conduct," he called the lengthy document. While Washington had focused on leadership as the key ingredient for success against the tribes, Knox hammered on the theme of discipline. If American soldiers simply stood and fought, he said, retaining unit cohesion and mutual support, they could not be overcome by savages, who fought as individuals. "It is to be presumed," he told the governor-turned-general, "that disciplined valor will triumph over the undisciplined Indians." Implicit in that widely held belief was a dangerous underestimation of the enemy. Beating a competent battle leader would require more than avoiding surprise and maintaining discipline—but arrogance would not permit whites to attribute military competence to red leaders.

St. Clair left Philadelphia on 23 March to return to his headquarters in the West. His troubles began almost at once. He was stricken en route by a severe case of gout. Incapacitated by pain, he languished near Pittsburgh for the better part of a month, not reaching Fort Washington until mid-May. There he found his regular regiment in disarray. The veterans he had counted on to form the core of the invasion force were leaving the service as rapidly as possible. Decimated by casualties in the 1790 campaign, units had been hard hit ever since by expiring enlistments. The men, their meager pay much in arrears, dissatisfied by conditions on the frontier, and aggravated by their government's shabby treatment of them, were not prone to reenlist. Of more than four hundred men whose hitch had ended that winter, barely sixty stayed on. Rosters showed only 264 soldiers present for duty in forts along the Ohio. Nor were recruiting statistics encouraging. Men willing to enlist were hard to find. Although most politicians had joined westerners and land speculators in support of the use of arms in the West, that cause was by no means a popular one with ordinary citizens in the East, especially in New England, where much of the 2d Regular Regiment was expected to be raised. And the army pay of three dollars a month was hardly inducement enough to overcome the unpopularity of uniformed service. By midsummer, the 2d Regiment could count only about 550 men. Nor was attracting privates the only problem. Qualified officers were hard to find, too. Four men in succession turned down an offer to lead the regiment, leaving it without a formal commander when it later went into battle. Worse still, established units had difficulties in keeping up their strength. When St. Clair consolidated the 1st Regiment at Fort Washington in July, it mustered fewer than three hundred soldiers ready for the campaign. Perhaps that many more were absent because of sickness or detached duty, with the remaining third or so of the spaces unfilled. Ominously, as had been the case in earlier years, a large number of those reaching the two regiments were riffraff scooped out of the gutters of eastern society, men unaware of and unprepared for the demands of army or frontier life. The commanding general would have to rely more than he had anticipated on the levies.

But that initiative was not approaching its promise. Enlisted principally in New Jersey, Pennsylvania, Virginia, and Maryland, the levy recruits were sent on to Pittsburgh for training. Although it was somewhat easier to attract men to short-term service as levies than it was to entice them to sign up for three years in the regular army, recruiters were unable to meet their quotas. Short on quantity, the levies were also short on quality. As a group, they were similar to the new regulars—singularly unsuited for the rigors of campaigning on the frontier. The freshly designated commander of the levies, former Indian Commissioner Richard Butler, was deeply disappointed as he watched them begin to drift into Pittsburgh for outfitting and training. A veteran of the Revolutionary War who had seen his share of misfit soldiers, Butler thought the levy recruits were the worst he had ever encountered. For their part, his officers and men returned the sentiment, behaving on the whole quite surly and insubordinate. They resented having a politician for a commander rather than a seasoned Indian fighter. Idling their time away in Pittsburgh that summer, the levies were ridden by dissension, disease, and desertion. The passage of time may actually have rendered them less rather than more ready to fight.

The combined numbers of available regulars and levies eventually rose only to about two-thirds of the programmed three-thousand-man force. As early as June, Henry Knox cautioned St. Clair that he should contemplate using militia if the recruiting environment did not improve quickly.

By the middle of the summer, when the magnitude of the personnel problem was fully evident, a second severely adverse factor had arisen to plague preparations. Logistical inadequacies. The Department of War, accustomed to supporting a small army living and operating on the cheap, was not ready on such short notice to either equip or sustain a body of the size contemplated.

Secretary Knox had begun putting the logistical apparatus in place just as soon as he had attained congressional authority. But time was then already tight—and his appointments to the key positions were extraordinarily ill-advised. For the newly created office of quartermaster, he selected Samuel Hodgdon, who had demonstrated glaring ineptitude as a logistician in the Continental Army. To another crony, William Duer, went the contract to supply the army in its forthcoming campaign. More corrupt than competent, both men showed greater initiative in furthering their own ambitions and filling their own pockets than in meeting their obligations to the army. Exacerbating his horrible choice of subordinates, Knox thereafter failed to supervise them. His lassitude had grown with his bulk; he no longer displayed the energy for which he had been noted in the Revolution. The result was chaos in the supply system.

Money for purchasing agents failed to arrive on time; supplies were too few and too late; equipment obtained was of inferior quality. From first to last, as one senior officer later remarked, the army was "badly clothed, badly paid, and badly fed." Neither Hodgdon nor Duer showed any eagerness to go personally to the scene of the buildup. In fact, Hodgdon, whose place as quartermaster was with the army's headquarters in the field, did not leave Philadelphia until June. He then tarried in Pittsburgh until late August, when Knox, goaded by President Washington, ordered him to move on to the West. He arrived at Fort Washington on 10 September, where he found with apparent surprise that "every thing was in the utmost confusion."

St. Clair was furious over the dismal performance of the contractor and the quartermaster. Inadequate supplies coupled with the shortage of soldiers forced him to postpone the start of his campaign from summer to fall. The powerful and proud fighting force he and the president had envisioned in March remained pitifully short of reality in August.

Meanwhile, the two preliminary phases of the strategic plan were meeting success. Diplomatic approaches to friendly and neutral tribes had for the most part built a firewall against the spread of native insurrection. Although the most recalcitrant leaders had rejected the peace feelers from Philadelphia, it was clear by summer's end that hostilities would in all probability be limited to the Northwest. At the same time, militia hit-and-run raids had effectively seized the initiative from the Indians along and beyond the Ohio. Those raids included two major penetrations of hostile territory.

The first had begun in May, when Brig. Gen. Charles Scott of the Kentucky militia assembled some 750 mounted troops at the juncture of the Kentucky and Ohio rivers. Scott, whose son had been killed in action under Harmar's command the previous year, was eager for retribution. Riding with him was a man whose name would be heard prominently in the years to come, Lt. Col. James Wilkinson. Also along, ready for yet another fight, was Col. John Hardin. Scott crossed the Ohio, feinted northward toward Miami Town, and then wheeled northwestward to strike at the Wea villages along the Wabash. Fortune rode with him. The Indians, anticipating that Kekionga would be the objective, had assembled nearly two thousand braves in the vicinity of that strategic center. When Scott's raiders reached their goal on the Wabash they found it all but defenseless; local warriors had hurried away just two days earlier heading for the expected battle at Miami Town. The Kentuckians quickly razed villages and crops up and down the river, killed several Indians, and rode away with a large number of women and children as hostages. Scott returned to the Ohio on 15 June, depositing the prisoners in a federal fort, where they would be held to gain leverage over braves from those villages.

When the main invasion had to be postponed, St. Clair dispatched a late-summer attack to keep the Indians off balance. James Wilkinson led that second strike, leaving Fort Washington on the first day of August with more than five hundred horsemen. Repeating Scott's ploy, he feinted in the direction of Miami Town before turning sharply toward the Wabash region. Again catching the Indians unawares, the militia laid waste the area around the village of L'Anguille and returned with more prisoners.

Altogether, American sorties into Indian country that summer sufficed to disrupt and distract the warring tribes and to gain time. On the other hand, the two deep thrusts also solidified the resolve of the threatened natives to resist the invasion force they knew was forming in the vicinity of Fort Washington.

The tribes were not of one mind over whether to continue their war with the United States or to seek conciliation while they were in a relatively powerful position. Although they had continued terrorizing white settlements through the spring, many of their chiefs had begun considering a less bellicose stance. In early July, the tribes met in a grand convocation to discuss opening negotiations with their enemy in an attempt to determine a mutually agreeable boundary for settlement. Many pushed for peace on such a basis, but the Shawnees and Miamis, their attitude freshly hardened by General Scott's raid, remained adamantly hostile. Joseph Brant later recalled that his militant brothers believed a people "so wicked" as the Americans would never keep any treaty they might sign. Although several of the tribes would sit out the upcoming campaign, the Shawnees and Miamis vowed to lead the others in resistance. If some among them were wavering, Wilkinson's penetration of their lands in August swayed them to fight.

During the early part of the summer, President Washington had been away on an extended trip through the southern states. Upon returning to Philadelphia in late July—about the time St. Clair was originally to have launched the invasion—he was first astounded and then incensed by the rampant lethargy that had delayed the campaign. He lashed out at Knox, igniting at last a sense of urgency in the War Department. Through August and into September, the secretary bombarded everyone involved, especially the hapless St. Clair, with directive after directive to hasten their work. The president was highly perturbed over the "unnecessary and improper" delays, Knox told them; preparations had to go forward with utmost haste. It was not until then that the quartermaster went to Fort Washington, or that General Butler moved the levies forward from Pittsburgh, or that St. Clair finally shifted his army away from the Ohio—or that he admitted that he would be required to mobilize some militia units after all. The word from George Washington was clear and not to be denied: the chance for a campaign that year must under no circumstances be lost, even if it meant going with troops not fully trained and marching on a marginal logistical base.

While the chief executive could hardly be accused of undue impatience—the campaign started more than two months late—the army lurched forth in abject unreadiness. That was the unfortunate fruit of the nation's gross inefficiency in preparing for war. Congress, the president, the War Department, commanders in the field—all shared in the blame.

191

Months of wasted time, followed by weeks of wasteful haste, doomed the army.

General St. Clair himself was not in good health. His gout returned from time to time, making the slightest movement excruciatingly painful. He may have been sick at heart, too, as he surveyed the sad condition of his understrength, undersupplied, untried army. Certainly he must have entertained a sense of déjà vu when he saw the number and caliber of militiamen answering his call to arms, which he had belatedly issued on 1 September. Far fewer than half of the 1,160 he had asked for showed up. But that was not the worst of it. Unhappily, those arriving were a mirror image of the rabble who had joined Josiah Harmar a year ago—substitutes for the most part, would-be soldiers even less fit for a military campaign than the woebegone levies. But the general put forth the best face he could. Although still in some hopes that more men would arrive, he reported to Knox on 23 September, "All seems now as if it would go well."

From the latter part of August through September, the area around Fort Washington was abustle with activity as the polyglot army girded for movement. Supplies of all kinds flowed in, and more fighters. Major General Richard Butler arrived in the second week of September, bringing levy units to bolster the rapidly burgeoning force. St. Clair began leaning forward by sending elements to Ludlow's Station, five miles away at a crossing site over Mill Creek. There the animals would have pasture and the soldiers would be removed from the "means of intoxication, which was very plentifully supplied at Fort Washington." He then sent Maj. John Hamtramck, who had come with his regulars from Vincennes, another fourteen miles farther to the banks of the Great Miami River, where he was to erect a stockaded fort. That bastion, named for Alexander Hamilton, would become the nucleus from which would grow the present city of Hamilton, Ohio. The post, astride the direct route to Miami Town, would be a staging area for the march, a depot of supplies, and a strongpoint to fall back upon if the need arose. The area's first frost came on 11 September, the day construction began.

A forlorn Josiah Harmar watched the hectic final preparations. When a court of inquiry, chaired by General Butler in late September, finally cleared him of charges arising from the repulse his army had suffered the previous year, he and his family left. Departing after seven years in the West, the former commanding general predicted failure for the upcoming campaign. The Indians could not be conquered, he warned, with men "collected from the streets and prisons of cities," and with officers "totally unacquainted with the business in which they were engaged." His was the sad voice of hard experience.

By the end of the month, Hamtramck's soldiers had completed the new fort on the Great Miami. It was time to start the campaign. The army numbered about twenty-three hundred fighting men—regulars, levies, militia—as well as about four hundred noncombatants. Included in that latter category were a large number of women and children, the unfortunate flotsam of war who had no place to go once their men left, camp followers compelled by necessity to trail along with the army. They would share its hardships—and its fate.

Wading the waist-high river and plunging into the forest on the other side, the expedition marched from Fort Hamilton on 4 October, exactly one month before its dark appointment with destiny.

Unlike the mounted raids, which were swift and brief penetrations requiring a minimum of supplies, this invasion was aimed at conquest and occupation. Staying power required armed might and logistical robustness. That meant infantry and artillery, of course, but also pack animals and cattle droves, flour barrels and powder kegs, wagon trains and tent camps, utensils and tools—in short, all of the necessities not only for fighting but also for living deep in an inhospitable and undeveloped country. For that reason, St. Clair remained for a time back in Fort Washington gathering and forwarding supplies and men as they continued to straggle in. Sustaining the operation would be unusually difficult, but absolutely imperative. The foibles of the summer had spawned an extremely fragile supply situation, forcing the commanding general himself to act as his own logistics staff officer at the eleventh hour.

The plan of march reflected President Washington's admonition to "beware of surprise." Each day the army stopped early and threw up breastworks to prevent a surprise in bivouac. Moreover, it moved cautiously, with everything tucked up close. General Butler, commanding in St. Clair's absence, began by building two parallel roads about two or three hundred yards apart, each twelve feet wide to accommodate the artillery and wagons. The first day he advanced one and a half miles. The next he shifted to hewing out a single road. He went three miles. By the time St. Clair rode into camp, the army had crawled only twenty-two miles in five days. The agitated commander chastised Butler for making such "very gentle" marches, causing strained relations between the two senior officers that lasted from that point on. But even with the anxious commander whipping the cumbersome column forward, it could lumber no faster than about seven miles a day. By the evening of the twelfth it was less than fifty new-road miles from Fort Hamilton. There, on a dominant knob near a stream, the general called a halt to construct another staging fort, this one to be named for Thomas Jefferson.

He had little choice other than to wait while construction proceeded. Barely a week into the wilderness, he found his supply situation was already critical. It would be imprudent, he reasoned, to push on before the depleted food stocks could be replenished. Although no contact had been made with hostile braves, morale was ebbing fast. Fatigued from the incessant labor of opening a road as they went, inadequately fed, often cold and damp, the soldiers were growing restless. Bad promptly became worse. The weather turned rotten. Drenching rains soaked and chilled the men day and night. A significant portion of the gunpowder was ruined by the wetness. Tents, improperly treated, leaked. Thousands of people and animals contained in the small area churned it into a morass. Cheaply made shoes began coming apart; poor quality clothing was already in tatters. Upper respiratory ailments afflicted virtually every person. Sleet fell on the seventeenth. A hard frost followed on the twenty-first, with ice a half an inch thick. Snow flurries struck. Horses began dying from lack of forage and care. Resupply convoys arrived late if at all, having been hobbled from the outset by heavy losses of packhorses to Indian thieves. St. Clair appropriated every able horse, including the personal mounts of officers, sending them back to supplement pack animals in a desperate attempt to move enough food forward. The army went on short rations. Morale hit rock bottom.

The militia became openly rebellious, and many of the levy soldiers began claiming that their six months of service had expired, or was soon to do so. They argued that the calendar had begun turning on the date of enlistment rather than upon their arrival at the rendezvous point. An entire unit from Virginia threatened to quit. Desertions were daily occurrences, and numerous. St. Clair, recognizing the validity of some claims of completed enlistments, let a number of the levies go home on the twentieth. He then clamped down in an effort to restore discipline in the rest of the army. Carpenters erected gallows. A court-martial held on the twenty-second sentenced three men to death—two for desertion and the third for shooting another soldier. With the army drawn up to watch, the three were executed the next day. Fearful that matters would only worsen if he kept the men in that grim camp any longer, and aware that a majority of his levies were calling 3 November their last day of duty, St. Clair resolved to march on toward Miami Town even though he had flour and cattle enough for no more than a couple of days. Leaving 120 mostly sick men and two of his ten artillery pieces to secure Fort Jefferson, he headed the sullen army northward on 24 October.

Arthur St. Clair himself was able to continue only by dint of extraordinary determination. Stricken with "rheumatic asthma" and a flare-up of gout in his left arm and hand, he struggled to keep pace.

Six miles from Fort Jefferson, when the worried commander halted the column for the night, he was greeted with news of a rash of desertions along the route of march. Unable to go farther without re-supply, the army waited in place until a string of packhorses reached camp on the twenty-eighth, bringing some clothing as well as food. Then, in warmer weather on the thirtieth, it started northward again. Hearing that a large supply train was finally en route with plentiful provisions, General St. Clair stopped the advance the next day in order to let the convoy catch up sooner. His jubilation turned quickly to dejection when a group of some sixty militiamen bolted from the camp, proclaiming their intention of returning to Kentucky and threatening to loot the precious rations on the way. The loss of those supplies could not be risked. It would leave the scarecrow army in a state of starvation, and would mean the end of the expedition. St. Clair ordered Major Hamtramck to take units of the 1st Regiment, about three hundred of the army's best troops, to pursue the deserters and to prevent the plundering of the supply train. With Hamtramck's departure, the effective size of the invasion force had shrunk to less than fifteen hundred soldiers. More than eight hundred had been lost to death, disease, desertion, or detached duty in less than a month.

Betting that the regulars would succeed in rescuing the supply train and in escorting it forward, and after the arrival of a small convoy carrying enough flour to feed everyone, St. Clair set his diminished force in motion on 2 November. To speed its march, he left much of the baggage in a temporary depot at the campsite. Sickness and pain had all but overcome the general. His gout had flared alarmingly. Riding was sheer agony. He resorted to traveling slung "like a corpse between two horses" in a jury-rigged litter. The tormented commander and the suffering column were a pair matched in misery.

In mixed rain and snow, the less encumbered army made eight miles that day. The next day it covered another eight in frigid weather before reaching a low crest of ground overlooking the Wabash River. There, near its headwaters, the river was only a shallow stream. Dusk fell as the last elements closed in. As usual, militia troops occupied positions outside the main body, providing an outpost line about two hundred yards on the other side of the Wabash. Soldiers built fires in the darkness to cook what rations were at hand and to ward off the penetrating cold. Exhausted, the army bedded down without bothering to throw up much in the way of breastworks. Discipline had crumbled in the face of unrelenting privation. Lax security was the result, but that was not a major worry—there seemed to be no Indians around, other than a few hunters. Beware of surprise, Washington had admonished. But that had been so very long ago, before men were cold and tired and gaunt.

The mound itself made a good defensive position. An expanse of about six or seven acres, it overlooked marshy bottoms along the Wabash in front and swampy land on the flanks. As measured by the army surveyor's line, it lay eighty-nine miles from Fort Washington. Erroneously thinking he was encamped on a tributary of the St. Marys River only fifteen miles from Miami Town, St. Clair decided to pause for a few days on that snow-sprinkled rise until the 1st Regiment could rejoin. Then, with his soldiers rested and fed, he would go on to seize his objective and establish a winter cantonment. He was wrong on all counts. His army had less than a day to live.

About two or three miles away, in the woods past the Wabash, waited more than a thousand warriors. Shawnees and Miamis mostly, with good numbers of Delawares, Wyandots, Ottawas, Chippewas, Mingos, and Potawatomis, as well as a scattering of others, including some Cherokees and a few Iroquois, and even some white men. They were spoiling for a fight. Their leaders—Little Turtle, seconded by the Shawnee, Blue Jacket—were ready to oblige them.

Unlike their opponents, the Indians were well provisioned and fully informed. British agents had seen to the former with several shipments of foodstuffs and equipment. And keeping abreast of the stop-and-go, plodding progress of the invading soldiers had been an easy task— made all the easier because there had not been the slightest attempt to disguise the direction of attack. Little Turtle knew where the Americans were, where they were going, what they intended to do, how many of them there were, and what their condition was. He had watched with growing delight as their morale and discipline deteriorated.

Having begun assembling in the vicinity of Kekionga upon receiving word of the advance of units from Fort Washington, the tribes were ready for battle as the autumn colors hit their fiery peak. Little Turtle had resolved to orient on the enemy force and to strike it en route rather than to stand passively in defense of Kekionga. Mightily encouraged by intelligence of supply problems in the struggling American column, he hustled his men south on 28 October. At that moment the two sides were about seventy-five miles apart. The native warriors hurried some fifty miles in four days. Stopping to find a suitable battle site, they were confident of success. A white supporter recorded that he had never seen them "in greater heart to meet their enemy." As braves were reconnoitering the terrain where their slowly advancing foe was expected to intersect the Wabash, U.S. troops reached the banks of that stream and made camp, apparently unaware of the presence of the Indian army. Little Turtle decided to assail them where they stopped. Quickly planning a coordinated assault to commence at daybreak, he had in mind not harassment or ambush, but encirclement and annihilation.

While moving into their attack positions during the night, warriors brushed into soldiers patrolling beyond the camp's outer perimeter. Shots were exchanged. But there was no reaction from the American command. One officer even went back to report to General Butler the sighting of braves in war paint. Still, no action was taken to rouse St. Clair or to alert the slumbering men. Thus, the Indians were poised in readiness when their unsuspecting enemies awakened to a reveille stand-to in the predawn darkness on 4 November 1791. They waited patiently as the soldiers answered roll and were dismissed. They watched the freshly stoked campfires blaze high. Then, as the first light of a sun not yet risen gave definition to trees and people on a cold, clear morning, they attacked.

Driving straight into the outposted Kentuckians came the main attack of Miamis, Shawnees, and Delawares. The remaining warriors, divided into two wings, rushed to get around the flanks of the encamped

197

army to seal off any escape. With the first war whoops and crash of musketry, the startled militiamen fled for the security of units behind the Wabash, splashing through the river and running pell-mell up the rise toward the defensive lines. Many never made it, as tomahawks and scalping knives accounted for the wounded and slow of foot.

Chaos erupted in the camp itself. Troops sleepily intent one moment on performing morning duties were rushing frantically for their stacked weapons the next. Officers shouted over the din, trying to assemble and form their men. Drummers beat the alarm. Artillerymen struggled to shift guns not emplaced properly the night before. Women and children, clustered in the center of the knoll, screamed in terror. St. Clair hobbled half-dressed from his tent, striving to make some sense out of the wild scene. The panicked militia survivors ran right through the camp, sowing still more disorder, stopping finally only when lured by the chance to snatch up food abandoned on cooking fires by frightened civilians. The rattle of muskets soon sounded all around the perimeter as the Indians completed their encirclement. Sniping from behind trees and logs, they poured a heavy volume of fire into the densely packed defenders. Very little return fire came from the bewildered soldiers, for they were still not sure just what was happening to them. Men began to fall everywhere; a musket ball killed St. Clair's horse as he was trying to mount. Cannon began booming, increasing the noise and adding to the thick, acrid smoke, but with no visible effect on the attackers. Gunners were aiming too high, harmlessly blasting tree limbs above the crouching braves. The morning air became dark with gunsmoke.

St. Clair, moving on foot and in pain about the encampment, rallying the men and steadying the leaders, courageously exposed himself to the densest fire. All around him aides and others fell victim to the bullets, and his own clothing was pierced time and again. For once in this ill-fated campaign, fortune seemed to smile on him. He was untouched. But personal bravery could not redeem months of professional failings. Slowly, as the sun climbed higher, he came to realize the seriousness of their predicament. Surrounded by what he supposed was a superior force of Indians, having no breastworks or other defenses, crowded into a tight area with little maneuver room, he had lost the initiative entirely to Little Turtle. The braves, moving stealthily from firing position to firing position, were taking a steady toll of the exposed soldiers, while suffering minimal casualties in return. As the grisly, one-sided attrition continued, the situation grew increasingly tenuous. St. Clair and others decided in desperation to launch a bayonet attack to push their assailants back.

Gathering about three hundred men, levies and regulars mixed, Lt. Col. William Darke, a levy officer, led a charge over the Wabash, pushing some three hundred yards before his attack lost momentum. The Indians, perhaps having anticipated such a counterattack by the "long knives," agilely sidestepped the onrushing soldiers. They shot at them from the flanks and then closed back in to enter the American position through the gap left in the defensive lines. The utter devastation they quickly wrought signaled to all the defenders just what was in store for the entire command. When Darke and his men fought their way back, they found a slaughterhouse where once the rear line of artillery and the noncombatants' tents had stood.

Dead and dying lay in macabre profusion, all scalped. Many of the wounded had been thrown alive onto the campfires. Nor had the women received mercy. Their lot had been not only the scalping knife but other mutilation as well. A shocked lieutenant of the 2d Regiment reported seeing some of the women sliced nearly in half, with "their bubbies cut off," and tossed to burn with "a number of our officers on our own fires." The Indians had occupied the position for only a bloody ten minutes or so.

Too late, it was becoming obvious to the beleaguered Americans that their opinion of the Indians' ability to wage war had been all wrong. Their foe this day fought not only with brutality and bravery, but with discipline and unity. The more professional force on the field was red, not white. Although outnumbered and outgunned, the Indians had the edge in training, discipline, morale, teamwork—and, above all else, in leadership.

The uneven contest grew quickly more hopeless. Painted and shrieking braves pressed ever closer, nimbly avoiding various efforts to beat them back. Many stunned soldiers simply stopped trying to fight, standing like cattle to be shot down from point-blank range. The army had ceased to be. What was happening was no longer battle, it was massacre. St. Clair realized that further resistance was futile—but surrender was tantamount to suicide. The Indians would take no prisoners. Shortly before nine o'clock he ordered those who could to attempt a breakout before they were all killed. Men unable to move would have to be abandoned. Major General Richard Butler, too badly wounded to join the retreat, was one of those left behind. He died at the battle site, sharing that fate with some eight hundred others, including almost all of the women, only three of whom are known to have escaped. So far as is known, those children not killed were taken into captivity.

The better part of those able to participate in the breakout in even a slightly organized fashion were the remnants of Colonel Darke's unit of levies and what was left—about 25 percent—of the 2d Regiment of regulars. A few hundred men burst through the thinner Indian lines in a rush, striking out in the direction of Fort Jefferson, twenty-nine miles to the south. As they passed through the area of contact between the two sides, they came across dozens of wounded Americans, their scalped heads steaming as cold air met warm blood. One captain, sitting numbly on the ground, his head "smoking like a chimney," looked up wanly to ask his fleeing comrades if the fight was over. For him and hundreds of others it was. The battle had lasted three hours.

The ragged retreat carried what was left of St. Clair's army to Fort Jefferson, with the first wide-eyed survivors staggering in that night. Many had thrown their muskets away; most were still in a state of shock; some had been scalped. The general, who had himself escaped on a packhorse, assembled as many of them as he could and moved farther south in the middle of the night. Stragglers, quite a few with severe wounds, continued to dribble in over the next several days.

Although some braves followed and harassed the beaten soldiers for a few miles, killing several along the way, Little Turtle made no concerted effort to pursue. Having seized the American position, his warriors had become intent on plundering the camp and murdering the captives. That ritual killing, accompanied by appropriate torture for selected individuals, and special savagery for the women, took time, permitting the American force to avoid complete annihilation. Had there been a determined pursuit of the routed whites, easy prey without weapons and helplessly strung out on the forest road, most would have been slain.

That night, as Major Hamtramck and the unused 1st Regiment helped recover the shaken men reaching Fort Jefferson, the Indians celebrated on the field of battle. It was an evening the ecstatic warriors would never forget. They marked out a piece of land about five hundred yards long, stripping all the bordering saplings and covering them with red-painted symbols signaling victory and life. They camped there, drinking captured whiskey, feasting on roasted cattle, admiring their eight newly acquired artillery pieces, and cavorting in the wealth of clothing and personal effects they had taken from bodies and found in deserted baggage. Exulting in the hundreds of corpses that would be left to rot where they fell, the victors boasted of providing a grand feast of white meat for the wolves.

The scope of their victory was astounding. About 650 U.S. soldiers had been killed, and up to 200 civilians had perished as well. Nearly 300 of those who managed to reach Fort Jefferson were wounded. Records of the shattered army are incomplete, but, by any accounting, close to 1,000 of the 1,400 soldiers who fought under St. Clair that day were dead, missing, or wounded. The toll of casualties for Little Turtle's force was 21 dead and perhaps 40 wounded. It was the most one-sided, overwhelming victory Indians had ever won from an American or European army, a record that has never been broken. Not Braddock's defeat, not Custer's massacre, not any other battle in three centuries of warfare—none of them can match Little Turtle's triumph on the Wabash.

CHAPTER 19
WASHINGTON FINDS A GENERAL

President and Mrs. Washington were entertaining at home on a chilly December evening in Philadelphia. During dinner an aide interrupted to say quietly that an important message had just arrived. Washington excused himself and went into a nearby room to read it—and thus learned of St. Clair's disastrous defeat.

He returned calmly to the dinner table, it was later reported, showing no sign of emotion and not mentioning the shocking news. After the guests had departed, at about ten o'clock, he went to his study where his secretary, Tobias Lear, was waiting. Then he exploded. Lear had never seen him angrier. Pacing back and forth, his large body shaking with rage, his voice drawn tight, he recounted his repeated instructions to St. Clair to beware of surprise, recalling even the very words he had used to caution his field commander. Two-thirds of the army dead or wounded! It was simply unthinkable that St. Clair could have blundered into so terrible a loss, incredible that he could have suffered a greater proportion of casualties in a backwoods fight with Indians than was ever inflicted on Americans by British or Hessian regulars in any battle of the Revolution. The ranting went on and on, all the more intimidating to Lear because it was so out of character for a man renowned for his self-control. The worst defeat ever for American arms! How could it be? It was almost as if the president's mind was rejecting the report, as if refusing to accept it would somehow render it invalid, would make it not so.

But it was so. Communities all across the West got the word well before it reached Philadelphia, and soon the entire country knew. St. Clair himself made no attempt to minimize the magnitude of the defeat, telling Knox up front that the retreat "was, in fact, a flight," and that he had returned to Fort Washington with just "the remains of the army." Others wrote as well; levy leader William Darke, for one, sent Washington a lengthy personal account of the entire affair. Lieutenant Ebenezer Denny, who had a year earlier also conveyed the bad news of Harmar's defeat, rode unhappily into town on 19 December to brief the president officially. Newspapers bannered the bitter news. "This is a fatal stroke to the United States," proclaimed one Maryland edition. A Boston broadside highlighted the human costs of the "Bloody Indian Battle" with two printed rows of little coffins.

A storm of controversy arose, seeming to blow in from every direction. Those who had been against waging war on the Indians felt vindicated. Antimilitary voices saw confirmation for their contention that a standing army was an evil genie best left in the bottle. Proponents of the militia used the event to excoriate the regulars. Westerners saw the debacle as further evidence of the central government's ineptitude in military matters. Federalists bemoaned the loss of life and treasure caused by the country's reluctance to field a competent, professional force. No one was neutral on the issue. By the middle of January, when St. Clair arrived in Philadelphia to face Washington, the uproar was at its peak.

For about a month, the president declined to respond to the public outcry. Once having vented his anger in private, he had begun to analyze the causes for failure and to search for solutions. The causes were readily apparent. First of all, the United States had not fully committed itself to the effort, settling instead on halfway measures in the raising of its army. Secondly, the force that was deployed had been inadequately trained and poorly supported. Thirdly, leadership had been sorely lacking. Obviously, the solution lay in correcting those failings. How to go about correcting them, though, was not so easy to see. How could Congress be persuaded to meet its Constitutional mandate to "raise and support" an army suited to the task? Washington decided it was time to take the issue on straightforwardly, to tell the members what was needed and then to let them vote it up or down. The basic question was really a simple one: Did the country want to win the West or not? Victory would require commitment, full commitment from both the executive and the legislative branches—which is precisely what the authors of the Constitution had envisioned when they had molded provisions for providing the common defense. The administration entered the fray in mid-January in the form of a memorial written by Henry Knox rebutting the bulk of the criticism, and with the submission to Congress of corrective legislation. The commander in chief remained convinced that his carrot-and-stick policy of negotiations and military pressure was the best approach. It would not work, though, without a strengthened stick.

The regular army needed to be composed of long-term soldiers—the dodge of using levies had been disastrous. Leaning on short-term soldiers of any stripe had once again proven to be a false economy. And two regiments were not nearly enough—five would be needed. Nor were numbers the only consideration—a raise in pay and an enlistment bonus would be necessary to attract a higher quality of recruit. A competent military could not be raised cheaply. In constructing an armed force, as in building a house, cutting corners carries the risk of collapse when the winds of war blow strong. That reality had to be faced. Neither could reform of the militia system any longer be avoided—bloody experience had made that evident to most observers. Additionally, the field commander should have authority to employ auxiliary forces, such as friendly Indians or volunteer cavalry. As for the army itself, reorganization was called for. It would be remodeled into a more effective structure for campaigning in the Northwest Territory. The legion system, suggested by Steuben back in 1784, would provide the flexibility needed in that forested fastness north of the Ohio River. It would be a combined arms team of infantry, artillery, and cavalry. There were to be four sublegions, each also incorporating all of the combat arms. Numbering about 1,250 men, each sublegion would be commanded by a brigadier general, giving the legion commander a robust chain of command. Logistics, too, must be upgraded; responsibility for purchasing would be taken from the War Department under lethargic Henry Knox and would be entrusted to the Treasury Department headed by energetic Alexander Hamilton. Finally, a new commanding general would be selected based primarily on his military talents rather than on his political connections.

Those reforms could not be implemented quickly. Fielding an effective army is the work of years, not weeks. A wiser Washington recognized that there could be no campaign in 1792. The new force must be carefully recruited, fully equipped, and painstakingly trained before being sent into battle against the likes of Little Turtle. There would be no hasty or halfway solutions this time. The president was deadly serious about preparing thoroughly and properly for combat. "We are involved in actual war!" he thundered. To pretend otherwise and to remain passive, he warned, would be "ruinous." Now he had to bring Congress and country around to that thinking as well.

Congress was balky. And not just because of the public furor. The annual price tag for the proposed five-thousand-man army would be a million dollars, a threefold increase over the existing military budget, and for that era an eye-popping figure. What was more, having so many troops under arms looked suspiciously like a standing army to a good number of the lawmakers. Because of the sensitivity of the subject, members conducted most of the debate in secret. Arguments were heated. Strange allies formed, as regional pressures often clashed with ideological differences and personal convictions. Elbridge Gerry, for instance, with New England not particularly behind the war in the West and he himself still essentially antimilitary, was nevertheless apparently supportive of the administration's plan. He felt that way, he told his wife, "because I seriously think we never shall have so good a president after Washington." Curiously, in light of later events, one of those speaking initially against the plan was a new representative from Georgia, Anthony Wayne.[1] When the bill addressing the size and composition of the army (militia reform was handled separately) came to a vote in early February, it passed easily in the House, but failed by one vote in the Senate. After learning that the president intended to replace St. Clair, and upon being assured that the administration would emphasize negotiations with the tribes, the Senate reconsidered, passing the measure by three votes. On 5 March 1792, Congress sent to the president "An Act for making farther and more

---

1. Although Wayne's Revolutionary War service had been as a Pennsylvanian, he had gone south after the war. Having failed in several pursuits, he had turned to politics, winning a disputed election to the U.S. House of Representatives. He had to vacate that seat in early 1792, and subsequently sought the position of major general in the new army.

effectual provision for the protection of the frontiers of the United States." It provided him the army he had asked for. Moreover, lawmakers agreed to raise the soldiers' pay and to offer an eight-dollar enlistment bonus. The country did indeed want to pay the price to win the conflict. After three years as commander in chief, Washington had finally been given the war-making authority he had thought prudent ever since the end of the Revolutionary War. Still, it was not granted by an overwhelming margin. The specter of a man on horseback endured—a section in the law cautiously required the disestablishment of the three new regiments "as soon as the United States shall be at peace with the Indian Tribes."

Washington turned at once to the matter of command. He told St. Clair that he would have to resign his commission to free up the vacancy for a new major general, but that he would be permitted to remain as governor of the Northwest Territory.[2] Then, at the end of March, the president obtained approval from Congress to appoint four brigadier generals, which would permit the reshaping of the army into the more flexible legion with its four maneuvering elements. Of all his decisions in this busy winter and spring, though, the former commander in chief of the Continental Army knew that the selection of the field commander would be his most important one. He sought advice from his cabinet; they surveyed the nation, seeking the best man.

The young country had no military academy (the creation of which Washington had recommended a decade earlier in his "Sentiments on a Peace Establishment") to provide a steady flow of aspiring battle leaders, nor had events since the Revolution widened the pool of potential candidates. Of the three men who had served as federal generals in the postwar period, two were in disgrace and one was dead. The president therefore turned to Revolutionary War veterans, drawing up a personal assessment of each of the surviving general officers.

There were six former major generals to be considered. None would do. Henry Knox was the secretary of war, a position that let Washing-

---

2. Congress conducted an investigation of St. Clair's defeat, establishing a precedent that the legislative branch had such authority to look into the operations of the executive branch. St. Clair was absolved of blame, perhaps because of his illness and his heroic actions during the battle itself.

ton tactfully omit the ponderously obese former artilleryman from consideration. Thomas Mifflin, the Pennsylvania governor, had been found incompetent as a senior officer in the Revolution. All the others were over sixty, and each had further disqualifying characteristics as well. Horatio Gates was despised by Washington; Benjamin Lincoln, described as "infirm," was physically unfit; William Moultrie had a spotty war record; Baron von Steuben, though able, was "ambitious and a foreigner." Five other officers had worn two stars as brevet major generals (brigadiers who had held the rank in special circumstances but who had never actually been promoted). Four of them, having "never discover'd much enterprise" as commanders, were considered to lack initiative: George Weedon, Charles Scott, Edward Hand, and Jedediah Huntington. Scott had done well enough leading the June 1791 raid into Indian country, but had not been impressive in his subsequent actions that year. The fifth brevet major general, Anthony Wayne, suffered in reputation for having too much initiative. In councils of war during the Revolution, he had invariably made a single recommendation: take the offensive. Washington considered him "more active . . . than judicious and cautious. No economist, it is feared. Open to flattery, vain, easily imposed upon, and liable to be drawn into scrapes. Too indulgent (the effect perhaps of some of the causes just mentioned) to his officers and men. Whether sober or a little addicted to the bottle I know not." No, Anthony Wayne—Mad Anthony as he was popularly known—was not the sort of man to entrust with an independent command.

The six brigadiers, as it turned out, had no standing in their former commander in chief's eye. Even Daniel Morgan, who "has been fortunate and has met with eclat," was a heavy drinker with questionable integrity. A brevet brigadier, Charles Cotesworth Pinckney, may have been the best candidate of all in Washington's opinion, but having had his wartime experiences cut short by becoming a prisoner of war when Charleston fell, he had never advanced further in rank. He would be too junior for any of the other ranking officers to serve willingly under him, and Washington wanted to fill some of the four brigadier positions with generals experienced in war. Rufus Putnam, a land speculator in the West, was another possibility hindered by the same liability. Actually, the man Washington probably most wanted, Henry "Light-Horse Harry" Lee, the governor of Virginia, was not even on the list of former generals. He had risen only to colonel in the Revolution. The same was true of James Wilkinson. So, having come up empty-handed in their first trip through the roster, the president and his advisors started glumly at the top again.

After more discussion, Washington whittled the names down to five: Lee, Pinckney, Wilkinson, Morgan, and Wayne. He preferred the first two, but only the last two had been actual general officers in the Revolution. To the president, that point was compelling. In an era when there were no professional schools to educate military leaders, and not much of a peacetime establishment in which they could gain developmental experiences, seasoning was all-important. He could not appoint one of the younger men, he confided to a disappointed Governor Lee, because "if any disaster should befall the army, it would instantly be ascribed to the inexperience of the principal officers . . . thereby drawing a weight upon my shoulders too heavy to be borne."

That left it between Daniel Morgan and Anthony Wayne. Thomas Jefferson's notes of the meeting spoke briefly of Morgan: "no head, health gone, speculator." Of Wayne he wrote: "brave and nothing else." Mad Anthony was a bull-like fighter who would bang his head into a brick wall "where success was both impossible and useless." Between the two, however, Wayne was the easy choice. He had more experience in command, he was probably more intelligent and certainly better educated, and he was more trusted by those who had served under him. Besides, Washington and Knox knew him well, and were reasonably sure they could work smoothly with him. The president spoke of Wayne's "many good points as an officer," and hoped that the weight of his responsibilities would either "correct his foibles or cast a shade over them."

Wayne's nomination, sent to the Senate in April, met with surprise and some resistance, particularly by Virginians who were backing Governor Lee. He was confirmed, James Madison wrote, but "rather against the bristles."

Not until George S. Patton rose to fame in World War II would America have another battle leader quite like Anthony Wayne. The two were cut from the same bolt of warrior fabric. Aggressive in war and fractious in peace; eager for battle but thoroughly conscientious in preparation; strict of discipline yet deeply caring of the soldiers' welfare; possessed of a blind spot for the bright plumage of uniforms but steely-eyed in a fight; students of military history as well as practical soldiers; egotistically self-important although unflinching when facing the mortal hazards of combat; flawed judgment but superb instincts. Each was reputedly the most profane general of his era, yet both had in super-abundance the charismatic power to inspire men. They sought and fought more than their share of battles. When Light-Horse Harry Lee sat down later to write his memoirs, he would recall: "General Wayne had a constitutional attachment to the sword, and this cast of character had acquired strength from indulgence."

Anthony Wayne may have been in the president's view the least worst of those available, but the tide of fortune often finds the unlikeliest of heroes to elevate. Mad Anthony was to prove to be a briliant choice, the man for his moment.

CHAPTER 20
THE EMBRACE
OF ADVERSITY

Time had not been waiting for George Washington to conclude his search for a new commanding general. Trying events continued piling up one upon another. Although St. Clair's cataclysmic loss to Little Turtle had been far and away the most galvanizing piece of bad news to cross the president's desk, it was only one of many. As the calendar opened on 1792, the country found itself increasingly caught in an embrace of adversity, a chilling squeeze fated to tighten over the next two years.

In retrospect, the start of the slide from the relative tranquility the nation had enjoyed in the first half of Washington's term could have been marked by the passage of a controversial taxation act in early 1791. Congress, needing revenue, had levied an excise tax on domestically produced whiskey. In the furor following Harmar's defeat, and in the subsequent debate over raising St. Clair's ill-fated army, the revenue act had passed handily, although not without rancorous arguments.

Excise taxes were nothing new—states had been using them for some time. But heretofore the central government had not. Quite expectedly, then, this proposed extension of the federal reach sparked immediate opposition from unreconstructed Anti-Federalists. Perhaps less anticipated was that geographical factors soon generated another powerful locus of opposition. Inhabitants of the more remote and rural parts of the United States resented and resisted the singling out of distilled products as the lone commodity to tax. In those less developed reaches, good distances and bad roads made the shipment of grain expensive. Converting harvested grain into liquid spirits made it easier to transport and market, which in turn made whiskey a rather more significant product in sparsely settled areas of the country than elsewhere. It followed that opposition to the tax loomed greatest where ideology and geography merged. That occurred principally in the western districts of states bordering the frontier, where independent-minded settlers distrusted the central government to begin with, and where distilleries had become extraordinarily important local enterprises. In no region was this more emphatically so than in the rough-hewn counties near Pittsburgh. Trying to enforce the tax there would lead to "war and bloodshed," warned Pennsylvania senator William Maclay. He was sure that "nothing short of a permanent military force could effect it." Although Thomas Jefferson had initially supported the tax, much later, when resistance stiffened, he concluded that the tax would require "war on our own citizens to collect it."

Proponents of the measure, noting that those living beyond the Alleghenies were already refusing with impunity to pay state levies, shot back that westerners seemed not so much opposed to a tax on whiskey per se as they were against paying any taxes at all. Many officials thought the excise on spirits was the best of all potential taxes. Virginia's tax collector went so far as to say optimistically, "It will become popular in a little time." Others thought like Congressman John Sevier of North Carolina, who, while not for the idea itself, did not adamantly resist because he thought his constituents were so far beyond the government's reach that they would never have to pay anyway. The issue was both complex and divisive. The whiskey tax generally pitted North against South, East against West, mercantile interests against agricultural concerns, city dwellers against rural inhabitants, and frontier districts against established areas. Old antagonisms all, better left alone because stirring them up was to the detriment of national unity. Washington was seized in the swirl of all those currents when, by mid-1792, the situation in western Pennsylvania had reached serious proportions, to include the violent harassment of collectors and the holding of public gatherings to proclaim a common resistance. Such purposeful incitement of domestic unrest could not be tolerated. The president was resolved to enforce the laws of the land, even if that meant using the army. Cabinet members recommended that he first put his vast prestige on the line in a proclamation aimed at impressing on the rebellious westerners the seriousness of their actions. He did so that September, then waited to see the effect.

The levy rubbed one other raw nerve. Political parties—"factions" in the parlance of the day—were taking shape about that time, adding a discordant new note to government. A faction beginning to coalesce around broad opposition to many of the Federalist programs found a ready-made cause in the tax on distilled spirits.

Washington himself remained above faction, indeed, fought against it, but he was unable to restrain his two most precocious lieutenants, Alexander Hamilton and Thomas Jefferson. Hamilton, the acknowledged leader of the Federalists, had been from the beginning a fervent spokesman for a strong national government. He had never deviated from that philosophical line. Jefferson, finding himself often bitterly at odds with Hamilton, and occasionally out of step with Washington, had drifted slowly into opposition. By the beginning of 1792 a coterie of like-minded men had clustered around the secretary of state. Buttressed by an array of supporters—regionalists from the South, a few remaining ideological Anti-Nationalists, critics of the administration on one policy or another, and several individuals worried over the growing personal influence of Alexander Hamilton—that cluster formed an expanding faction that would eventually evolve into the modern Democratic party. In one of those delightful ironies so often found in American history, the Democrats were known at first as Republicans. Only later, when the Federalist party had disappeared and "democratic" lost its connotation of anarchy, did the current name emerge. Republicans accused Federalists of harboring visions of creating a monarchy in America; Federalists asserted that Republicans were determined to undermine the United States by fostering mob rule. Early in 1792, Jefferson set up firebrand Philip Freneau to run a newspaper aimed at spearing Federalists; Hamilton responded in kind by founding a rabidly anti-Republican organ. Charges and countercharges bounced back and forth with a degree of malicious abandon modern readers would find both amusing and astounding. But it was not the least bit funny at the time. The increasingly vitriolic schism boded ill for the sense of national unity Washington had struggled so hard to foster.

Traumatic events across the Atlantic also widened the political split in America. France, America's first and staunchest ally, was sinking ever deeper into the morass of internal mayhem and external conflict known collectively as the French Revolution. Turmoil in that country could not fail to affect the United States, linked as the two nations were by treaty, commerce, memories of the wartime alliance, and, increasingly, a shared philosophy in a government aimed at elevating human freedom.

Symbolizing the closeness between the two countries, Washington kept on prominent display in his parlor both the key to the Bastille and an engraving of Louis XVI. He was particularly disappointed, then, when he learned in the summer of 1791 that France's National Assembly had voted to violate the commercial treaty with America by placing an import tax on tobacco and whale oil. Although the president accepted the setback calmly, trusting that the "disorders, oppressions, and incertitude" in Paris would eventually "terminate very much in favor of the rights of man," he was jarred by a message carried on a following vessel. The king and his queen, Marie Antoinette, had fled in a dramatic attempt to join loyal troops outside of France. Intercepted before reaching the safety of the border, they were returned under guard on Lafayette's orders. In the president's mind, that open rupture between the king and the reformers removed the legitimacy of the revolution. Jefferson, who had brought the information to Washington, recalled that he had never seen him "so dejected by any event."

Soon, neighboring nations turned on France, massing armies on its borders. Battles followed. Military defeats inflicted by Prussian and Austrian forces precipitated mass insurrection in Paris. Taking advantage of that unstable situation, radicals grabbed control of the Legislative Assembly (which had not long before replaced the National Assembly). They imprisoned the king, suspended the constitution, and set out to rule according to their own fierce beliefs. Lafayette escaped capture by his countrymen only to be placed in an Austrian prison. Word of the revolutionary takeover reached Philadelphia in December 1792, prompting jubilant celebrations among citizens who regarded the French Revolution as an echo of their own, but greatly concerning Washington, who knew better.

Fearful that affairs in France were reeling out of control, and anxious to have balanced reporting from a trusted minister, Washington had earlier sent his old friend Gouverneur Morris to Paris. Selection of that staunch Federalist had not been to Jefferson's liking, and the

Senate but narrowly confirmed him. Republicans were not so upset at the idea of a radical reign in Paris as was the president, and they worried that Morris was not sufficiently sympathetic to the spirit of revolution. But Washington wanted intelligence unfiltered by ideological bias. When the Terror started not long afterward, Morris reported accurately on the bloodbath. "We have had one week of unchecked murders in which some thousands have perished," he wrote. Jefferson reacted with equanimity, saying that "many guilty people fell without forms of trial and with them some innocent. Those I deplore as much as anybody. . . . But I deplore them as I should have done had they fallen in battle." Washington, who had commanded men in battle, felt otherwise. He was distressed by the Reign of Terror, and fearful for the life of Lafayette, his spiritual son. He could not comprehend why Jefferson's Republicans were ecstatic over the turn of events; he sided on this issue with Hamilton's Federalists, who were aghast at the bloodlust.

On the other hand, Republicans were not so happy with the English. When George III finally established relations with his former subjects, he did so while still insisting on continuing to control U.S. territory around the Great Lakes. His ambassador, George Hammond, submitted a lengthy justification for the British occupation of posts in the Northwest, which Jefferson promptly and forcefully demolished. Real explanations, both sides knew, were rooted in money and power. The profitable fur trade was a key reason the British had retained a presence in the region, their belief that the United States would dissolve was another. So, when the upstart new nation showed signs of surviving, London had sought to establish a cohesive Indian nation from the Ohio River to the Great Lakes to serve as a buffer between Canada and the westward-moving Americans. Despite those machinations, however, Great Britain wanted to avoid an open breach with the United States while war with revolutionary France appeared imminent. Accordingly, agents worked behind the scenes to incite the tribes while diplomats piously denied any such involvement. Aware of this double-dealing, but also anxious lest a situation America was not yet strong enough to handle should worsen, Washington and his cabinet played along by officially ignoring the British role in agitating the tribes.

Spain, too, was once again turning militant in the Southwest Territory. With Madrid and London drawn closer by their joint concern over the French Revolution, Spanish authorities in Louisiana and Florida felt free to act. Reports soon reached Philadelphia of reinforcements of soldiers and arms arriving in New Orleans. At the same time, Spanish agents began trying to turn the Creeks against the treaty McGillivray had signed in New York. Not a few of the braves took the bait and began taking scalps. Actually, the peace in the Southwest had been tenuous all along. Militant braves, operating more or less outside the reach of tribal authority, had kept the embers of war glowing. Then, a handful of southern chiefs, who had fought with Little Turtle against St. Clair, returned sated with blood. They raised the passions of bands in the Tennessee region. Young hotheads donned war paint. For their part, settlers in western Georgia, by choosing this time to violate provisions of the treaty, were not helping matters at all. Scattered clashes along the frontier set emotions simmering, Indian and American alike. Washington lodged strong protests with the Spanish envoy in Philadelphia, found a few regular troops to send southward, and energized William Blount, the governor of the Southwest Territory. But he could do little else for lack of military muscle. For a while, late in the summer and fall of 1792, he feared that "peace or war are now in balance" in the Southwest Territory.

Major powers were not alone in bringing grief. Algerians still held U.S. citizens in bondage, an outrage as much a persistent reminder of American weakness as it was a personal tragedy for the captives and their families. As minister to France in 1784, Thomas Jefferson had urged the use of force to free hostages rather than the paying of tribute. In 1792, however, as the official responsible for the matter, he could see all too well America's impotency. A country without sea power could not influence the Barbary pirates, and Congress was not interested in trying to find funds to forge a navy. The secretary of state had no recourse other than to ask the lawmakers to appropriate money to bribe the Barbary rulers. They complied, voting a hundred thousand dollars to grease palms in hopes of making a treaty. Jefferson, hearing that John Paul Jones had returned from employment in Russia, asked the naval hero to conduct the negotiations in Algiers. Unfortunately, Jones died before he could undertake the mission. The year ended with the woebegone prisoners no closer to freedom.

Meanwhile, back in the forests of the Northwest Territory, where war smoldered, negotiations with the Indian nations had started off rocky and had gotten worse. Although few in the government thought chances were very good for securing a peace until the warring tribes had been subdued, Washington was resolved to give diplomacy a sincere try. He had to. Only by pushing for a nonviolent solution to the war could he attain and hold political support for military operations. Personally, too, he preferred to win the West by parlay rather than by battle. Never since, in the long and troubled record of U.S. relations with Native Americans, has an administration tried harder to find an accommodation between the irrepressible white drive for "manifest destiny" and the unrelenting red resistance to that westward expansion. But the well of goodwill had been irretrievably poisoned by decades of atrocity piled upon atrocity—by both sides.

Nevertheless, Secretary Knox labored mightily. He brought friendly and neutral Indian delegations to Philadelphia, where he showered them with flattery and gifts in an effort to win their allegiance. Do not listen to the drums of war, he urged, and carry Washington's word of peace to those tribes continuing to fight. His representatives distributed silver medallions to chiefs throughout the disputed regions, molded ovals showing a picture of George Washington smoking a peace pipe with an Indian who has thrown his tomahawk to the ground. Emissaries also traveled woodland trails, taking conciliatory messages to hostile tribes. That extensive effort probably ameliorated the raging conflict somewhat. It might even have increased the number of Indians siding with the United States. But, in the end, it failed in its basic purpose of obtaining peace without bloodshed.

British officers turned away several "confidential agents" trying to reach the warlike chieftains. Indians murdered others. Knox then sent official spokesmen under flags of truce. Major Alexander Trueman, a Revolutionary War veteran and a survivor of St. Clair's disaster on the Wabash, left in full regalia from Fort Washington planning to go to the Maumee River. An Indian hunting party shot him en route. Departing Fort Washington at the same time, Col. John Hardin, whose inept leadership had contributed so much to Harmar's defeat at Miami Town, headed toward Wyandot villages on the Sandusky River. He, too, was slain before he could complete his mission. Rufus Putnam, appointed to one of the four brigadier general positions, went safely enough to Vincennes, but Indians in that area were already inclined to commit to a treaty in order to retrieve their women and children, who were still being held hostage after the raids of the summer of 1791. Putnam did sign a treaty with them late in the year, but it was rejected by the Senate the following spring. Thus, when most of the tribes met in October at a grand council to consider war or peace, Knox could only hope that cautious voices would carry the argument. They did not. After days of debate at the conference site, located where the Auglaize River flows into the Maumee, the strident Shawnees prevailed. The Indian position—reached with the help of British conniving—was uncompromising. Unless the Americans withdrew to the south banks of the Ohio River, warfare would continue. In the meantime, native raiding parties took a steady toll of settlers in the disputed lands, as well as of soldiers manning stockades north of Fort Washington. Little Turtle, leading a rather small band of marauders, embarrassed the Americans in November by delivering a costly blow to a Kentucky militia unit under the very walls of Fort Hamilton. This "desultory war," coupled with the uniformly unsuccessful attempts to persuade the most recalcitrant tribes to talk of peace, left Henry Knox a very frustrated man by the end of 1792.

Knox's frustration was aggravated by the perennial problem of fielding an army. Although Congress had mandated a major reform of the militia, which it was hoped might eventually result in a more standardized and reliable force, no one expected to see any practical effect in the near term.[1] So there was no alternative to raising the powerful regular army

---

1. On 8 May 1792, Congress passed into law "An Act more effectually to provide for the national defense, by establishing an uniform militia throughout the United States." Although it was less than Washington had hoped for—it left implementation to the individual states and contained no provisions for federal enforcement—the act nevertheless represented a major step forward. It required militia service of every able white male between eighteen and forty-five years of age, thereby placing the historic concept of a citizen army on a common legal basis throughout the Republic. It mandated minimum amounts and types of equipment, set standards for training, and prescribed the levels of organization, to include brigades and divisions. A separate bill, passed six days earlier, gave the president authority to mobilize whatever numbers of militia "as may be necessary" to enforce the laws of the nation. It was this act, not the one of 8 May, that would have a major impact on affairs two years later.

Congress had authorized that spring. Anthony Wayne reached Pittsburgh in June, where recruits were to assemble and where he was to mold such a force. If he had not recognized before then the magnitude of the task ahead of him, he soon did. Counting only forty recruits and a handful of dragoons, he wrote Knox: "I really feel awkwardly situated—a general without troops is something similar to a fish out of water." James Wilkinson, who had succeeded to command in the Northwest upon St. Clair's departure, and who had been made a brigadier general and Wayne's deputy, reported that he had only some seven hundred men to garrison all the posts along the Ohio, as well as those extending northward from Fort Washington. Wilkinson was told to try to hold fast against Indian depredations with that thin force, while Wayne himself concentrated on training a new army able to go on the offensive.

After setting up his headquarters in Fort Fayette, a recently constructed position in Pittsburgh not far from old Fort Pitt, the general began to build. Recruits trickled in slowly but steadily from the East. By August he had about eleven hundred men of very uneven quality. They looked depressingly like the castoffs of society seen every year since Harmar had first begun training soldiers on that same ground nearly a decade earlier. Supplies were slow in arriving, too, while the temptations of Pittsburgh—a frontier "Gomorrah," Wayne called it— inhibited the toughening process. It all sounded so familiar to old hands. But there was a difference this time around: the leadership of Maj. Gen. Anthony Wayne.

Drilling began immediately, and continued daily, with Baron von Steuben's 1779 drill manual being the Bible. Henry Knox had stated that "another conflict with the savages with raw recruits is to be avoided by all means." Wayne needed no convincing. Men learned to maneuver together in formation, to work as a team, to react instinctively. They learned to march and to dig. They learned to handle their muskets and to use their bayonets. And they learned to shoot straight by actually firing, a practice often previously neglected because of its cost in powder, but necessary nonetheless. From the outset Wayne imposed his will on the army. Discipline was unrelenting and swift. And harsh. Floggings occurred often, executions were not uncommon. Mad Anthony wanted the men to be more afraid of him than of the Indians. Knox and Washington both knew from personal experience that a responsive and reliable soldiery was an imperative, and so supported Wayne's brutal ways. Nevertheless, Knox expressed the hope that before long "there may be less call for the punishment of death."

Wayne worked hard to ready the Legion of the United States (as his army was called) for a spring campaign. He wanted to strike the tribes when they were weakened by winter. Knox denied the request to move that early—he anticipated having only half the Legion in place by the spring of 1793, and he knew of an effort in Congress to cut the army back even before it could be completed. Once again passionate diatribes against a standing army reverberated in congressional debates, along with unstinting praise for the militia as a better alternative. To block that antiregular pressure, the administration had to show that every possible attempt at negotiations was being made before resorting to arms. The president would appoint commissioners, and they must be given a chance to reach the tribes with an offer of peace. Wayne was sorely disappointed. He firmly believed strength was the only thing Indians would respond to. Send me to their next council, he said cynically, "attended with about 2,500 commissioners . . . among whom I do not wish to have a single Quaker."

The determined general decided at least to leave the morally debilitating town of Pittsburgh. In defense of their city's reputation, residents liked to describe how religious the community was. "A compound of worship on Sunday and whiskey on Monday," was an early saying. That left out five days. Wayne was pretty sure he knew what went on then, too. Selecting a site twenty-some miles downriver, which he named Legionville, he moved his men at the outset of winter. Free there from distractions, he was able to intensify the training program and tighten discipline even more. One of his company commanders, nineteen-year-old Lt. William Henry Harrison, a future president, clearly remembered the rigors and the results of Wayne's regimen half a century later. The general's school was indeed one of hard knocks, in which officers willing to endure and to learn prospered; Harrison was one of those who braced his "mind to encounter with cheerfulness" anything thrown at him and his men. The Legion grew taut and tough. Wayne conducted the most effective training program seen since Steuben had rebuilt the Continental Army in the snows of Valley Forge.

In the meantime, the administration succeeded in convincing Congress to sustain the strength of the Legion—with all frontier region votes supporting the regular army. Nevertheless, events beyond Wayne's control would preclude the Legion's commitment for more than a year after that first winter. Although Washington had hoped to give him a full year to forge an army, the field commander would actually have two.

That delay, of course, was not foreseen by the chief executive, who still expected to launch a campaign in 1793, the first year of his second term. But if the new year turned out to be as marked by adversity as 1792 had been, nothing was predictable.

The fact that Washington decided to accept another term at all was itself evidence of the difficult times. The aging and tiring hero had been looking forward to returning to a pastoral life at Mount Vernon when his tenure in office expired. Four years as president, he told close friends, was enough, especially in consideration of his years of arduous service before that. But it was not to be. Even though great gains had been made in shaping and solidifying the nation, much remained to be done. The country stood at a critical juncture, with pressures internal and external tugging forcefully in insidious ways. Given the divisiveness of the moment, no person other than George Washington had the stature to steer the Union forward—or perhaps just to hold it together. If he were to quit, intimates argued, he would be leaving with the frontier war unwon, with a defense establishment unbuilt, with a budding insurrection over taxes unsettled, with political factions ripping the government apart, and with foreign affairs in disarray. Attorney General Edmund Randolph wrote darkly of pending "civil war." He bluntly told the president that, in such circumstances, "you cannot stay at home." Heavy of heart, but knowing his duty, Washington agreed to serve again. He was elected unanimously. John Adams, George Clinton, Thomas Jefferson, and Aaron Burr split the votes for vice president, with Adams collecting the majority. Washington's second Inaugural Address set the standard for brevity: a terse two minutes. In repeating the oath of office on 4 March 1793, he might well have reflected on the depth of difficulties entailed in preserving, protecting, and defending the Constitution.

Less than two weeks into his second term, Washington learned that Louis XVI had gone to the guillotine. Soon afterward, word arrived of the expansion of the list of countries at war with France, notably Great Britain and other major naval powers. That meant the conflict would not be contained on the continent; it would inevitably become maritime, with the inherent risk of spilling over to involve the United States. Indeed, that was already happening, as French agents were making contacts to arrange for the outfitting of armed vessels to sail from American ports as privateers. Those agents were finding eager reception in most quarters as a supportive wave of emotion swept the country. The French Revolution, seen by many as the natural offspring of their own fight for freedom, met with widespread approval. For a time the passion led to extremes of expression, with the styles of revolutionary Paris becoming something of a fad. Disdaining "sir" and "madam" as titles too aristocratic, some of the more fervent sought to adopt what they deemed to be more politically correct forms: "citizen" and "citess." That change did not catch on, but it indicated the reach of the turmoil in faraway France. Sentiment in America ran demonstrably in favor of France, but practical considerations overruled emotion. The new nation could hardly take sides against Spain and England, the two European powers then occupying major portions of the North American continent. Neutrality was the only sensible course for the United States. But war is a vacuum. Washington realized at once that only quick and forceful action could keep the country from being sucked into the international struggle.

Congress was in recess and the president was at Mount Vernon. Summoning his cabinet, he rushed back to Philadelphia. Something had to be done immediately, which meant the executive branch would have to act alone. Calling Congress into special session would take too long. That raised questions not addressed in the Constitution—declaring war could only be done by Congress, but what about declaring peace? Were steps taken to prevent war within the purview of the president alone? Did the commander in chief's responsibilities include waging peace? Such issues of theory might have entertained Constitutional lawyers for decades—but Washington faced real and present exigencies that could not wait. He moved decisively to keep the country neutral, to restrain American citizens from entering the conflict in any way.

Debate in the cabinet was intense. The stakes were high, for both the security of the nation and the sanctity of the Constitution. A narrow but useful interpretation emerged during the discussions. Strictly speaking, taking a position on neutrality might have impinged on the Senate's prerogatives, but, since a state of peace already existed, the

221

president reasoned that he could continue it on his own. He determined to issue a proclamation to that effect. Chief Justice John Jay submitted a draft, which the others unanimously accepted. The document announced that the United States would "pursue a conduct friendly and impartial towards the belligerant powers." It warned Americans to avoid any action whatsoever that might appear otherwise, on pain of prosecution in the courts. Although the paper carefully avoided the word "neutrality," it was in fact such a statement, and was known then and ever after as the Neutrality Proclamation.

The proclamation was challenged at once in the midst of a crisis caused by one of the more curious figures ever to cross the pages of American history: the new French ambassador, Citizen Edmond Charles Genet.

Genet stepped ashore in Charleston on 8 April, to be met with a tumultuous reception. Americans thronged about him, avowing their interest in having French commissions to raid British shipping and, of course, proclaiming their eagerness to help France attack Spanish forces in Florida and Louisiana. Intoxicated by that outpouring of warmth, Genet spent ten days in the southern city, during which time he commissioned four privateers and excited a considerable number of hotheads over the possibilities suddenly opening to win territory at the expense of Spain. When he left for Philadelphia, he set out overland, stirring similar passions along the way. Washington, he concluded, was an out-of-touch conservative who could be bent or bypassed by the overwhelming revolutionary zeal welling up in the United States. Citizen Genet, transported by the spirit of the crowds he met everywhere, came to believe that he, not Washington, was the most popular man in America. By early May he had proceeded only as far as Richmond, where he heard for the first time of the Neutrality Proclamation. Suddenly energized to present his credentials in the capital, he hurried off for Philadelphia.

Times were tense in that city. A French vessel had seized a British ship in American waters and had tied the prize to a Philadelphia dock. Moreover, couriers brought word of other captures by corsairs commissioned by Genet. The British ambassador was beside himself; he protested heatedly to the American government. Washington, trying to find a fine line between the two sides, ruled that the British ship in Philadelphia should be returned, but, while no further privateering ventures could be undertaken, prizes won before the issuance of the

Neutrality Proclamation would stand. Into that electric atmosphere rode Citizen Genet.

The boisterous reception he received at the very seat of government prompted him to proclaim that he was as much a representative to the American people as he was to the administration. When the irrepressible ambassador finally called on the president in mid-May, he was so sure of his popular strength that he was grandly condescending. He thereafter set about simply ignoring the neutrality of the United States as he established French courts to handle the prizes hauled in by his privateers and launched a variety of schemes contrary to the stated position of his host country. In July he revealed to Jefferson a plan to foment an anti-Spanish uprising by French settlers along the Mississippi, a scheme that Jefferson neither stopped nor reported to Washington. By that time the city and much of the country were in an uproar, with people of all stripes taking one side or the other. Jefferson and his Republicans were staunchly pro-French; Hamilton and the Federalists were just as strongly pro-British. Both were working behind the president's back to push their own programs, and the resulting animosity made the city dangerous. Vice President Adams slipped weapons into his home for protection. He and others worried that not even Washington was safe from the threat posed by frenzied crowds roaming the city that frightening summer. Meanwhile, Genet continued his incredible adventures aimed at involving the United States in the war in every way he could, and in any way he pleased.

Finally, he went too far even for the ever-patient Washington. He began arming a captured British ship—the former *Little Sarah*—right under the nose of the government at dockside in Philadelphia. Worse, the warship boasted of having American cannon and an American crew. The captain defied orders to cease work, and sailed the vessel away before it could be seized. Furious, George Washington, after much debate in his cabinet, asked France to recall its impertinent ambassador, an unusually severe diplomatic step. Having thereafter no standing with the government, Genet soon also lost his position with the public by taking on Washington personally. When Rufus King and John Jay jointly published a letter describing how the Frenchman had insolently belittled the president, a groundswell of resentment brought the strange saga of Citizen Genet to an end. Infatuation with the mercurial ambassador had thinned anyway, and no matter what they might say or do, the people of America were not about to place anyone in higher esteem than the man they were already thinking of as the father of the country. The ensuing backlash supported Washington and scuttled Genet.[2] But the Frenchman's months of mischief had poured much gravel into the gears of government.

Nature, too, had contrived to help stem the ardor of zealots late that summer when it visited a devastating epidemic upon the capital city. Along the steamy waterfront, people began to turn yellow and die. The deadly fever spread rapidly to the other quarters of town, despite attempts to slow it by burning camphor, igniting gunpowder, and other desperate measures. Pestilence paced the cobblestone streets. Philadelphia was all but immobilized by death and fear. Washington wrote of "numbers dying daily." He was understating the case. Wagons hauled corpses to mass graves by the score. More than a hundred a day perished during the peak in October. Altogether, around four thousand died—no one really knows the exact number. Panic seized the city. Inhabitants who could get away did so. Washington himself stayed until the date he had previously announced for a trip to Mount Vernon, and then left. Alexander Hamilton fell ill, and appeared for a while to be on the point of death. The government was all but prostrate, with Henry Knox and the War Department picking up the bulk of the burden of administering. Crowds disappeared, having lost their enthusiasm for the French Revolution, or at least their enthusiasm for celebrating it in the face of a yellow fever epidemic. The scourge of the yellow death in Philadelphia—"the most appalling collective disaster that had ever overtaken an American city"—placed the mass murders in Paris in clearer perspective, making the French Revolution seem less glamorous.

With the advent of cooler weather that fall, the raging sickness eased. Warily, Washington called for his cabinet officers to assemble on 1 November in nearby Germantown. Not sure that Philadelphia was yet safe, he nevertheless felt compelled to resume affairs after a two-month hiatus. There was much to do.

---

2. France did recall Genet, but he wisely refused to return to his native country. Fearing the guillotine, he asked for and received political asylum from the very government he had worked so hard to undermine. He settled in New York, married well, and lived out his days there.

One area crying for attention was the Northwest Territory. The blue-ribbon panel Washington had sent in a final effort to try to arrange a peaceful solution to the conflict there had failed. The three distinguished commissioners—old soldier Benjamin Lincoln, former Virginia governor Beverley Randolph, and future Secretary of War and State Timothy Pickering—had reported in August that the Indians remained insistent on retaining all lands north of the Ohio River. After a year and a half of negotiations, the chiefs had budged not one inch. That meant war. As the chief executive and his advisors met on the memory-laden site of the Revolutionary War Battle of Germantown, where Anthony Wayne had excelled, that general was bivouacked with the Legion of the United States and a large formation of Kentucky militia deep inside hostile territory.

Wayne's shift from the training base at Legionville to the scene of war had consumed the summer and much of the autumn of 1793—and it had not been without problems.

Forced by direct orders from the secretary of war to avoid any buildup north of Fort Washington for fear of derailing the work of the peace commissioners, the perplexed general had found himself in a strategic straitjacket. A successful campaign would require careful work beforehand: notably, a logistical buildup, the prepositioning of troops, and the construction of forward facilities. St. Clair had marched into disaster by moving before he was ready. Wayne pushed his own preparations just as far as he dared before drawing a sharp rebuke from Henry Knox for moving too far forward and appearing too warlike. Gradually, as the year progressed, Mad Anthony quite sanely came to the realization that a decisive operation would probably not be feasible before 1794.

Bad news had dogged the campaign, beginning back in April when Wayne received word of his wife's death. That was followed by a professional blow when Knox informed him that the expedition would have to rely on militia reinforcements after all. Recruitment had lagged so much that the Legion could expect to have no more than three thousand men by the summer. A thousand or more mounted Kentuckians would be needed. Fuming, for he genuinely abhorred the very thought of going into battle with militiamen at his side, Wayne had loaded his men on barges and floated from Legionville to Cincinnati, arriving there in early May. Disappointments continued to tumble in. He learned that his supply contractors had not yet met their requirements to provide adequate rations to support a further deployment of the army. And his request to Kentucky governor Isaac Shelby to ready the mounted volunteers for service elicited the startling response that militia leaders would cooperate only if they did not have to subordinate themselves to the federal commander. They relented when Wayne exploded, but the episode did not improve the general's negative impression of the militia. The area around Fort Washington and Cincinnati proved to be too confining for the Legion, and too licentious for Wayne's concept of a Spartan environment for the men. Prevented by Knox's strictures from moving north right away, he carved out of woods some few miles distant a temporary encampment that he named Hobson's Choice. On top of all that, in circumstances reminiscent of St. Clair's experience of two years earlier, Wayne's health began to break. When word arrived on 25 August that peace had eluded negotiators and the command could at last shift to a war footing, the general's chagrin was at a peak.

The very circumstances Wayne had most feared had come to pass. Dragging out the search for a peace had indeed cost a campaign. The season was far advanced and the army was not ready. Logistical and operational preparations, held in abeyance to boost the chances of success in the negotiations, were barely begun—and Mad Anthony, despite his reputation for rashness, was not about to plunge unready into hostile lands as had St. Clair. For one thing, he could not forget the president's personal warning that a third straight defeat at the hands of the Indians "would be inexpressibly ruinous to the reputation of the government." But, even so, and as late as it was, he had no intention of remaining on the Ohio another winter. Wayne consumed September doing those things he had wanted to do months earlier to prepare to move. Then, after issuing a call to the militia commander, Brig. Gen. Charles Scott, to join him with his mounted volunteers, he marched north in early October at the head of about two thousand Legionnaires.

Following the old and by then much improved roadway St. Clair had cut, Wayne traveled easily but alertly, thinking—indeed, hoping—that the tribes might attack him en route.[3] In less than a week he had

---

3. The route included Fort St. Clair, a new position built in 1792 by James Wilkinson to cut in half the long stretch between Forts Hamilton and Jefferson.

closed in around Fort Jefferson, the end of his line of sturdy forts. The reinforcing Kentuckians began arriving, bringing his army to full strength for a fight—but the Indians seemed not the least inclined to start one, and he had no way that late in the season to force them. Needing a more suitable site to accommodate his sizable force, Wayne moved a few miles farther north and began constructing a major camp and defensive bastion, which he named Fort Greeneville in memory of his old comrade from Revolutionary War days, Nathanael Greene. Greenville, Ohio, traces its lineage to that fort. There the general reluctantly decided to sit out the winter—a decision made even easier for him by the ravages inflicted on his army by a siege of smallpox and influenza. Secure in his newly built stronghold, and with no prospects for a winter battle, he let the militia go home. His intent was to remain coiled in that forward location until his supplies could be built up in the spring, and then to strike at the Indian confederation.

While armed forces were not in such close proximity in the Southwest, affairs there, heating up even before being aggravated by Genet, had been turbulent throughout 1793. The frontier had suffered from a chronic state of alert as talk of Indian warfare escalated. All of the tribes, threatened on one side by militant Americans and agitated on the other by Spanish officials, had grown dangerously restive. Creeks, especially, had become ever more hostile. Jefferson complained in June that "Spain is unquestionably picking a quarrel with us."

When the Kentucky Democratic Society, a cover organization for pro-France and anti-Spain militants, circulated in December an inflammatory resolution to all inhabitants west of the mountains, Washington and his cabinet took it very seriously. Invoking memories of the country's revolutionary origins, the memorial urged westerners to prepare to attack Spanish forces along the Mississippi and to resist the pernicious policies of the federal government, especially the hated whiskey tax. Such incitement could not be shrugged off in light of the unstable situation in frontier areas. Violence lurked too close to the surface.

The road itself, a veritable highway by wilderness standards, reached all the way from Fort Washington to Fort Jefferson. Improving it had been one of the readiness steps Wayne had taken more or less against orders, and which had brought him a reprimand from the secretary of war.

The activities of Revolutionary War hero George Rogers Clark were indicative of the potential for an eruption. He had accepted a commission from Genet as a general in the French army, with the intent of leading an expedition against Spanish holdings. The veteran frontiersman quickly gained a considerable following in Kentucky, of course, but also in Georgia and South Carolina due to widespread inclinations there toward war. And Clark was only one of any number of freelancers who contemplated taking matters into their own hands. To say the area was a tinderbox was an understatement.

As President Washington pondered difficulties from over the mountains, other problems poured in from across the seas. When Portugal recalled a squadron of warships that had been cruising the Strait of Gibraltar, keeping the Barbary pirates out of the Atlantic, Algerian raiders had rushed out at once, spreading havoc among unprotected merchant vessels plying nearby sea lanes. American ships fell victim, and still more U.S. citizens were captured. By the end of November the number had ballooned to 119. But December brought an even worse situation nearer home. On top of its devious policies aimed at preventing Americans from making peace with the Northwest Indians, Great Britain suddenly began seizing U.S. vessels trading in the French West Indies. That winter, English authorities held hundreds of American ships in Caribbean harbors, their crews sweltering in fever-infested prison hulks.

A year earlier, President Washington had lamented that the United States was "encompassed on all sides with avowed enemies and insidious friends." With how much more emphasis he could have said the same thing as 1793 ended! The country was indeed assailed by enemies foreign and domestic. The new year was shaping up to be a fateful one.

PART 5
ENEMIES, FOREIGN AND DOMESTIC

I . . . do solemnly swear that I will support and defend the Constitution of the United States against all enemies, foreign and domestic. . . .

—Extract from the oath taken by all U.S. Army officers.

CHAPTER 21
FORT RECOVERY

Anthony Wayne could not wait out the winter. He simply could not. His head may have told him he had to hibernate at Fort Greeneville until spring, but his warrior's heart beat with the desire to do something active, to retain the initiative, to keep pressure on his foe. His heart won.

With a picked contingent of troops, he headed in frigid weather for the site of St. Clair's massacre on the Wabash, a cautious two-day march from Fort Greeneville in the direction of Miami Town. They arrived on Christmas Day, 1793.

The sight greeting them was gruesome. Hundreds of skulls lay scattered about. Bones were strewn everywhere, some still connected by sinew, skeletal remains framing in brittle silence both the scene of battle and the scope of disaster. Wayne and his Legionnaires slept uncomfortably on the ghostly field that night. The next day, they grimly gathered those macabre reminders of the price of unpreparedness and buried them in mass graves nearby. The dead, not honored much by their country when they fell—or in the two centuries since—had waited more than two years for the simple dignity of being laid to rest.

Even before that task was completed, Wayne began erecting a fortified position on the once-bloody knoll overlooking the Wabash. As work details started clearing an expanse for a sturdy blockhouse and palisaded enclosure, others began probing for St. Clair's captured cannon, buried by the victorious Indians shortly after the battle. Right away, tipped off by scouts who had been there with Little Turtle but who

231

had subsequently switched sides, they dug up three and incorporated them into the defenses of the rapidly growing fortification. Ultimately, the soldiers recovered most of the lost artillery. As soon as he assured himself that the outpost could withstand attack, General Wayne returned to Fort Greeneville, leaving behind an infantry company and a detachment of artillerymen.[1]

He was well satisfied with the week's work. The Legion's spring campaign would start that much nearer to its objective and, just as importantly, the winter operation would surely cause problems in the enemy's villages. The chiefs would be compelled to mobilize to meet what could very well be an all-out offensive, a reaction to a false alarm certain to bring added hardships in a winter already marked by unusual hunger and misery. Tribes in the area had previously been kept off balance and on edge by the Americans' late-autumn advance—a mental and physical dislocation that this latest incursion would only magnify. The initiative clearly rested with Wayne.

Psychologically, too, the general was making a powerful statement. By reclaiming and fortifying the very ground of the tribes' greatest victory, he was proclaiming, in symbolism his enemy would fully understand, the resurgence of American strength and the determination of the United States to persevere in the long war. To make sure the point was not missed, he named the new position Fort Recovery.

Wayne reached Fort Greeneville in time to celebrate the arrival of the new year. He and his staff welcomed 1794 with a sumptuous wilderness feast, including roast mutton, plum pudding, and even ice cream. A buoyant mood of anticipation permeated the remote headquarters. The army stood forward and ready; the men were carefully trained and well armed. And, while stocks of foodstuffs and other supplies were short of planned levels, the soldiers themselves generally went neither hungry nor cold. For men inured to hardship, it was an easy winter. Things

---

1. Some writers believe Wayne may not have gone personally with the troops. It is known that his health was not strong at the time, so he might have remained at Fort Greeneville because of illness. But he was often sick during this entire period and campaigned regardless. It would have been more in character for him to have led this symbolic expedition if he possibly could have. Either way, it was clearly done at his direction—and with his flair.

were different on the other side. Hostile tribes, suffering on the edge of starvation in makeshift camps, would have serious difficulty getting organized in the spring. For the Legion, the new year dawned full of promise.

As the establishment of Fort Recovery signaled a turnaround in the army's fortunes in the West, so too could it be considered a metaphor for the nation itself in the coming year. Although the United States began 1794 at a low point—the culmination of a decade of irresoluteness and bungling—the year would see the recovery of the country's sense of direction and purpose.

CHAPTER 22
PARANOIA IN PHILADELPHIA

Prospects may have looked good in the army's wintry encampment in the Northwest Territory, but the very opposite was true at the seat of government. New Year's Day 1794 in the City of Brotherly Love found an administration feeling besieged. George Washington and his closest counselors perceived the country to be under persistent assault by forces from within as well as from without, from both foreign foes and domestic opponents. Given that as the prevailing state of mind in Philadelphia, it is not reaching too far to say that paranoia touched the city that winter. With the responsibility for the security of the United States—of preserving, protecting, and defending the Constitution—resting squarely on his aging shoulders, the president particularly felt the pressure.

In the luxury of hindsight, we might venture today to suggest that the Republic may not have been quite as endangered as it appeared to be at the start of the year. But it certainly seemed so to those on the scene and in authority at the time. They were deeply and sincerely concerned for America's safety and future. Moreover, it must be remembered that a sense of paranoia does not preclude the actual presence of real enemies. And, in truth, the dangers were quite real enough; 1793 had brought a deluge of threats to the nation's peace and tranquility, a drenching downpour showing no signs of abating as the calendar rolled over to 1794.

Making matters worse, Washington found himself bearing an increasing share of the burden as his administration entered a period of major adjustment among its key players. Thomas Jefferson chose that dark moment to leave the government, submitting his resignation on the last day of 1793. Alexander Hamilton, weakened physically by his brush with death from yellow fever, was also hobbled politically by the incessant attacks from Republicans. Henry Knox was sinking ever deeper into lethargy, showing severe signs of burnout after nearly a decade as head of the War Department. Tobias Lear, the president's personal secretary, the rough equivalent of today's White House chief of staff, departed, leaving an administrative gap that proved elusive to close. And it had been some time since James Madison had shifted from trusted advisor to political opponent. Indicative of the degree of advancing isolation he felt, Washington that winter actually sought the advice of Vice President John Adams.

Never in the short life of the United States had external affairs contained greater potential for disaster. The wars of the French Revolution were escalating in reach and intensity, making ever more tenuous the balancing act of neutrality.[1] Walking that thin line between belligerents would have been difficult enough had all Americans hung together in the crisis, but they did not. Federalists thought inclining toward Great Britain was the safest course, whereas Republicans remained fixed in support of France. Avoiding entanglement in the European web of war required Washington to corral many of his own countrymen, as well as to convey a position of firm resolve to foreign capitals.

"Perfidious Albion"—General Washington's caustic phrase for Great Britain during the Revolution—appeared to have lost little of its perfidy with the passage of years. That had become infuriatingly evident when the president's failed peace efforts had uncovered for all to see how very deeply Crown officials had been involved in promoting and perpetuating the western fighting. And, on top of all of London's other cavalier provocations, English sea captains had resorted to impressing American sailors into duty on His Majesty's warships. To a great

---

1. Napoleon Bonaparte, a young artilleryman, was just beginning his swift ascent to power. His rise, launched amidst the turmoil of foreign strife and domestic chaos infecting France, would be precisely what so many Americans had long feared might happen in their own country—a charismatic man on horseback who would use the sword to become the head of state.

many Americans, the former mother country seemed inexplicably bent on goading its former colonies into conflict. A resurgent wave of anti-British sentiment, eagerly encouraged by Republicans, washed over the land. It was not weakened when word arrived that Canada's governor-general, Lord Dorchester, had begun to speak openly to the tribes of imminent hostilities between England and the United States. He had also promised them the aid of British soldiers. Visions of redcoats fighting alongside redskins elevated the clamor for war from fever to frenzy. Fortunately for the president, who was trying desperately to avert a clash of arms he knew the country was unable to win, French ships for a while that winter also abused U.S. vessels and crews. Although Paris quickly dropped that policy, realizing the politically counterproductive nature of such acts, the high-handedness nevertheless helped dampen the rising momentum in America for war with Great Britain. Still, foreign affairs were teetering drunkenly out of Philadelphia's ability to influence. Bluster could not suffice for force. Militarily naked, the United States had no diplomatic leverage other than withholding trade and trying to play the warring states off against one another, a course largely dependent for success upon the capriciousness of leaders in foreign capitals. When word reached Philadelphia that British troops had marched south from Detroit to begin raising a new fortification on American territory—Fort Miamis, a few miles up the Maumee River from Lake Erie—the president's concern deepened.

Spain, too, remained a worry. A special one. Washington and his cabinet dreaded the very thought of a combined British-Spanish campaign to eliminate U.S. claims in the West, a jolting possibility after the two countries set aside their differences in the common effort against France. Indeed, it was more than a possibility—Spanish and British couriers traveled up and down the Mississippi with messages probing the feasibility of a coordinated offensive against the Northwest and Southwest Territories. At that sensitive moment, Kentucky, following the lead of its aggressive governor, Isaac Shelby, was making warlike sounds not conducive to avoiding conflict in the West. That seized Washington's attention. On 24 March, he issued a proclamation threatening "condign punishment" for any citizen participating in a raid into the territory of any country at peace with the United States. Knox followed that with orders to Wayne to detach enough regulars to block the movement of freelance American armies down the Ohio. Wayne was freed to use "every military means" available to him to prevent the passage of groups "armed and equipped for war." In May, Knox also authorized the governor of Georgia to use militia or regulars to preclude attempts by persons in that state to campaign against Spanish posts. "What if the government of Kentucky should force us either to support them in their hostilities against Spain or disavow and renounce them?" the president asked his new secretary of state, Edmund Randolph. "War at this moment with Spain would not be war with Spain alone. The lopping off of Kentucky from the Union is dreadful to contemplate, even if it should not attach itself to some other power."

For their part, domestic affairs afforded Washington no respite, either. While external events veered toward some unforeseeable but frightening conclusion, internal pressures were reaching a dangerous point not experienced since the time of troubles leading to the writing of the Constitution.

Indicative of the strained atmosphere was the rising cacophony of negative—and anonymous—personal attacks on the president himself. Although Americans overwhelmingly revered the man who was the very personification of the country, having transformed him into a monument in his own lifetime, even he could not escape the poison of party strife. As Republican pundits perceived him to be tilting toward the Federalists, their criticism escalated accordingly. Washington never responded to those character assassins, hidden as they were behind pen names, but he felt anguish and anger nevertheless. Jefferson noted, before he left office, how Washington was "extremely affected by the attacks made and kept up on him in the public papers. I think he feels those things more than any person I ever yet met with. . . ." Though Jefferson felt sorry for the chief executive, he declined to curb his followers. For the outwardly stoic target of those scurrilous barbs, the cumulative effect was to heighten his sense of beleaguerment. Washington, who was most reluctantly serving a second term, must have been particularly chagrined in the spring of 1794 when one venomous writer tried to draw a parallel between the commander in chief's supposed aspirations and those that had once motivated Oliver Cromwell.

But personal attacks and party maliciousness were the lesser of his internal woes. The frontier, always a tinderbox, consumed untold amounts of his mental and emotional energy. Out of the West that winter came yet another reminder of the volatile environment there. Disgruntled

inhabitants of western Pennsylvania founded in February an extralegal organization they called the Mingo Creek Society. On its face it
was merely one more of the so-called democratic societies popping
up across the land, claiming as their antecedents the revolutionary
committees of some two decades earlier that had done so much to bring
about the break with England. But the Mingo Creek Society, arising
in a region already fraught with unrest and remote from central authority, loomed more ominous than most. For one thing, local militia
units eagerly embraced the society, and, for another, it quickly assumed
a militantly activist posture. Members lost no time in sending a blis-
tering remonstrance to the president and Congress. The bluntly worded
document demanded military action to break Spain's grip on the
Mississippi, blasted the federal government for failing to protect westerners
from Indian outrages, and announced the society's determination to
resist, with force if necessary, the detested tax on whiskey. The tone
was uncompromising. Reaching Philadelphia at a time of national crisis,
those arrogant words from the West reinforced the sense of paranoia
that had seized officials there. The Mingo Creek Society, by its own
description, smacked of treason. It also evoked disturbing memories.
Its threat of coordinated resistance to the excise tax cast in Philadelphia long shadows of Shays's Rebellion. Still worse, it appeared to
have the capacity of pulling together under one head the different groups
responsible for the spontaneous acts of violence against government
officials in the area. Galvanizing leadership, which had been missing
in Shays's movement, just might turn out to be present in the emerging Whiskey Rebellion.

Nor was the burgeoning civil unrest Washington's only worry emanating
from the West. While he at long last had a trained and disciplined force
ready to move against hostile tribes, thanks to Anthony Wayne's leadership,
troubling signs of insubordination were calling the army's reliability
into question. James Wilkinson, as thoroughgoing a scoundrel as has
ever reached a high position of trust and confidence in the nation's
armed forces, was agitating to have Wayne replaced as commanding
general of the Legion. Wilkinson, of course, had himself in mind as
the new commander. Being the deputy, or second in command, did
not suit the overly ambitious and utterly disloyal brigadier general.
By rumor, innuendo, and appeals to political friends, the Kentuckian
had been energetically undercutting his commander for months, de-

faming his character and belittling his professionalism. That effort was the talk of the army—officers took sides, supporting one or the other of the two generals. Wayne, whose autocratic ways made it easy for some of his subordinates to prefer Wilkinson, suspected the undercurrent of dissent was politically motivated, probably attributable to Republicans. He was apparently one of the few unaware of its true source. Washington and Knox, knowing of Wilkinson's earlier treasonous flirtation with Spanish officials in New Orleans, stood solidly behind Wayne, albeit with increasing nervousness. The ferment in the officer corps obviously added to the already large amount of uncertainty inherent in any military campaign.

In the Southwest, furthermore, an area that had once seemed more or less under control, but which had begun to experience serious friction, the framework for stability was on the very edge of coming unglued. Alexander McGillivray, the Creek leader who had personally been the primary stabilizing force in the region, died in late 1793. His passing left the tribes essentially rudderless just when the winds of war—whipped up by Genet's meddling, Spanish intrigue, militant Indian bands, and the intransigence of white frontiersmen—were reaching gale force. The forecast was foreboding.

From the president's vantage point, the entire national forecast was exceedingly bleak. Everywhere he looked loomed threats to the common defense or to domestic tranquility. In every quarter, it seemed, arose events fraying the bonds of union, disuniting the United States.

Washington was not alone in sensing the possibility of national dissolution in the torrent of threats. It was a widely held perception. One congressman wrote home, "You see the situation of our country, without money, and on one hand tormented by the savages of the West; in the East our commerce laid prostrate, and our citizens carried into cruel captivity by the Algerines; and moreover we are daily injured and insulted by that proud and vindictive nation, Great Britain, with whom war is almost inevitable." In June, the *Gazette of the United States* proclaimed that America had come to a climactic moment destined "to establish or ruin the national character forever." British consul Phineas Bond assessed the country's circumstances quite accurately in a report to London: "In every direction in which this country is viewed, its situation must be deemed exceedingly critical—critical in respect to the power of war—critical as to the continuance of peace—and immensely so as to its constitution and government." War, peace, union—a truly daunting triad of crises for any nation to face, however old or stable.

A resolute George Washington, leading a country new and far from stabilized, set to work to address all three issues before they could unravel the fabric of national unity. The Virginian's genius was that he always stood firmest just when adversity beat the hardest. In the crisis year of 1794, his sixth as president, he displayed that trait yet one more time. He may well have saved the Republic by his actions that historic year—without doubt he shaped its fundamental form in ways that would endure for more than two centuries.

CHAPTER 23
THE PEACE ESTABLISHMENT

With members prayerfully hoping the yellow fever epidemic was truly over, a nervous Congress reconvened in Philadelphia in December 1793. Washington was ready for them. It had been ten years since the Confederation Congress had rejected his "Sentiments on a Peace Establishment," a concept for a security structure for the long haul, not just for wartime exigencies. Ten trying years they had been for those responsible for the nation's safety. Facing the legislators to deliver his fifth annual address, the president sketched for them the outlines of a program required to promote the common defense at what he deemed to be a crucial juncture in the country's history. This was finally the moment, he reckoned, and not a bit too soon, to put into place a comprehensive military establishment. The various ingredients had been debated often, so nearly everyone involved was familiar with them. Several pieces, as a matter of fact, had already been enacted into law over the years. The ballooning war scare made passing the remainder seem almost self-evidently necessary.

Washington's vision of a suitable defense structure had been opposed ever since he had submitted it, first by Anti-Nationalists, then by Anti-Federalists, and, finally, by Republicans. Anti-Nationalists had for the most part faded from the scene as the confederation of former colonies had defied all odds and most predictions to remain intact in the aftermath of the Revolution. Anti-Federalists had similarly withered away once citizens embraced the Constitution. But, in a sense,

241

the two movements had lived on. A good bit of their antimilitary bias had found its way into Republican thinking.

Philosophically, Nationalists had become Federalists, a term at first big enough to cover virtually all of the Founding Fathers. Slowly, though, Jefferson's Republicans had splintered off, becoming an alternative political party rather than merely an opposition, and thus having more staying power than either Anti-Nationalists or Anti-Federalists had shown. Republicans and Federalists alike supported the form of government described in the Constitution—they agreed that power sprang from the people, that individual freedom was best promoted in a democracy, that authority should be shared between states and the Union. However, they found themselves in substantial disagreement on implementation, particularly regarding the shape and size of the Republic's military might. In seeking the proper equation of strength—to have enough but not too much—they fell on opposite sides. Federalists thought the country would be safer if it erred on the side of too much; Republicans believed it better to have not quite enough. Federalists feared being overcome by outside forces; Republicans thought the greater danger lay in being overthrown by the government's own forces. In short, Federalists found the idea of a large standing army comforting, while Republicans found it frightening.[1]

Congress had been out of town for several momentous months. There was much to talk about. The international scene had darkened dramatically during the adjournment, and internal affairs had also worsened considerably. War with one European power or another did not seem to be out of the question, and renewed conflict with the Indians appeared all but certain. Washington provided an update on the failed peace overtures to the western tribes. He announced that Anthony Wayne had orders to terminate the long conflict at the point of a sword, but he also restated his conviction that the United States could permanently end its prob-

1. It may be useful in avoiding confusion to pause again to recall how terms have evolved. The Republican party of the late eighteenth century is today's Democratic party. Federalists disappeared as a political grouping early in the nineteenth century. Today's Republican party was founded in the mid-1800s. Its first president was Abraham Lincoln, elected in 1860.

lems beyond the Alleghenies only "by creating ties of interest" with the Indians. Covering the difficult and quite unpredictable foreign situation, he explained his reasons for having issued the Neutrality Proclamation. Dangerous times had demanded decisive action, he reported. And the dangers had not abated. The sober-faced congressmen, listening intently, understood full well that the country stood at a crossroads of war and peace, of turmoil and tranquility. They were prepared—many were even eager—to hear the president's prescription.

He did not disappoint them. In his speech and in details subsequently provided, he described what steps he believed the emergency dictated. On top of a strengthened regular army backed by the militia organization provided for in the act of 1792, there were several other vital elements needed if the country were to have a viable overall defense establishment. Coastal fortifications to protect key harbors; a corps of engineers and artillerists; a navy; an institution to develop military leaders; places to manufacture arms; storage sites for the equipment of war.

Federalists, Washington felt sure, would be inclined to support such an ambitious program. Republicans, though, would find themselves torn. On the one hand, they would be fundamentally opposed to the creation of so powerful a military structure. On the other hand, their hostility toward Great Britain was so virulent that they would be pressured by their own policies to accept the president's program as a necessary evil. They could not very well contemplate war while voting against the very resources needed to wage it. That uncomfortable position, wrote Republican senator James Monroe, was indeed an "embarrassment" for members of his party. As for politicians who had committed to neither faction, the feel of war in the air, which intensified as the early weeks of 1794 passed, would also generally dispose them to side with the commander in chief. The climate in Congress had never been more favorable for decisive action.

An "Act to Provide a Naval Armament" passed early but not easily. Outraged by the renewed assaults of the Barbary pirates, and painfully aware of the country's inability to avoid insults even in home waters, a majority of congressmen were ready at last to consider creating a navy. But counterarguments remained strong. Cost worried some, for the upkeep of fighting ships was known to be quite expensive. Others feared that maintaining a naval force would detract from and weaken the primary focus on opening the West. Still others fretted over the ramifications of an increase in the total number of men in uniform. Senator William Maclay spoke for many when he warned that a standing army, an active navy, and a host of revenue officers would mean "farewell freedom in America." The debate ended with a compromise leading to a narrow victory for the administration. The government would get authority to build six frigates, but with the stipulation that construction would promptly cease should American prisoners be released by Algerians before the ships were floated. The day that bill was signed into law—27 March 1794—became, in effect, the birthdate of the U.S. Navy, despite the fact that the sea service, like the army, fell under the direction of the War Department.[2]

It was much less difficult to obtain a consensus on the urgency for erecting coastal defenses. While few congressmen expected an outright, ocean-borne invasion, all recognized the vulnerability of the nation's numerous ports to raiders from the sea. Moreover, it was a proposal both Federalists and Republicans could agree upon, for the defenses would provide security against all predators, regardless of the flag they flew. Congress appropriated funds to begin the extensive construction program at once, knowing that it would take years to complete. As it worked out, twenty-four of the squat bastions, bristling with a total of 750 guns, would be standing sentinel along the Atlantic coast by the start of the War of 1812.

To manage the construction and man the fortifications, the army would obviously need a large contingent of engineer and artillery troops.

---

2. The frigates, designed by Philadelphia shipbuilder Joshua Humphreys, would be about two hundred feet long and would carry up to forty-four guns and a crew of some three hundred. They were planned to be sturdy enough to slug it out with other frigates, but swift enough to escape larger warships. Construction began as soon as possible in different locations along the Atlantic seaboard. Some would see action before the decade was out. One, the *Constitution,* would still be commissioned—a floating museum—more than two hundred years later. Among the very best fighting vessels of their era, the frigates would provide then-President James Madison some of the few bright spots he would enjoy in the War of 1812. Ironically so, for, as a Republican member of Congress, he had energetically resisted the military expansion of 1794.

Accordingly, Congress passed in early May "An Act for raising and organizing a Corps of Artillerists and Engineers," a new organization to have a combined strength of more than a thousand men. It was to be formed by adding another eight hundred soldiers to the existing body of artillerymen. The corps would provide a small, standing cadre for each of the harbor defenses, with the expectation that local militia units would be available to flesh out the garrisons in response to a threat in any specific area.

Embedded in the act was a seedling fated to blossom rather quickly into the U.S. Military Academy. George Washington had begun trying in the midst of the Revolution itself to establish an institution to train and educate military leaders. In all the years since, he had never once wavered in either his conviction of the need or in his efforts to found one. When the concept surfaced in cabinet discussions in late 1793, Jefferson had argued against it, contending that a federal academy would be contrary to the Constitution.[3] Washington responded that he was "so impressed with the necessity" of creating one that he would recommend it anyway and let members of Congress "decide for themselves whether the Constitution authorized it or not." Congress sidestepped the Constitutional issue by giving the Corps of Artillerists and Engineers the mission of developing new leaders. The law established two spaces for cadets in each company of the corps, and authorized expenditures for "necessary books, instruments, and apparatus." The academy took root at West Point, the Revolutionary War fortress built to block the Hudson River in New York.

Congress also made provisions for arsenals and armories. The legislators set up a network of supply depots, and then authorized the

3. In another irony springing from the disputes between Republicans and Federalists over the shaping of the nation's military establishment, it would be President Thomas Jefferson who would formally found the Military Academy just eight years later. When actually shouldering the responsibilities of the commander in chief, Jefferson came quickly to realize that there was indeed a pressing and abiding need for a military academy. He determined then that there was no Constitutional prohibition after all.

opening of facilities at Springfield, Massachusetts, and Harper's Ferry, Virginia, for the production of arms and equipment by the federal government.

When they adjourned in June, congressmen could look back on a full and productive six months. On only one major defense proposal that spring had antimilitary voices won out: they turned back a Federalist proposal to raise a regular army of ten thousand or more men. A solid majority deemed that measure to be way beyond the dictates of the emergency, despite the apprehensions of the administration, which had alerted the states to prepare for a total mobilization of eighty thousand militiamen in the event of war with Great Britain. On virtually everything else a remarkable consensus carried the day. All told, lawmakers had completed building the basic military structure of the United States, finishing with firmness a sporadic, spasmodic effort that had been sputtering since the earliest days of the Republic.

None of those steps taken was really new or novel—the recommendations had been around in one form or another for a dozen years—but the sweeping nature of the enacted military programs was historic. For the first time, the United States had the framework for a complete defense establishment. Many of the separate parts were hardly more than embryonic, to be sure, and much debate and transformation would occur in the years to come, but the bedrock foundation was in place. And it was lasting. Its essence exists still, two centuries later. Modern Americans would recognize all of those elements central to today's defense establishment: an effective active army backed up by a nationwide network of reserve components; naval forces to secure freedom of the seas; defenses for the homeland; logistical complexes; an industrial base; and a system of professional education and training. Evolution would in time surface other considerations—air power and nuclear energy come quickly to mind—but the structure itself was set.

As if to underscore the determination with which it viewed the commitment to arms, Congress passed an act specifically outlawing the involvement of private citizens in military activities. Americans could no longer outfit privateers to serve the aims of other countries, or go on expeditions against neighbors not at war with the United States. Nor could they serve in foreign armies or accept foreign commissions. In effect, making war was a monopoly of the government, a pursuit denied to individuals or groups. The act also authorized the president to employ the land and naval forces "as shall be judged necessary" to enforce the law. When he signed it into effect on 5 June, Washington had a legal basis for his earlier order to Wayne to send Legionnaires to prevent Kentuckians from mounting an expedition down the Ohio against Spanish posts.

There was no mistaking the manifest will of the nation. Taking the long-avoided decision to acquire the strength required to protect its citizens, commerce, and territory sent a powerful signal of resolve to friends and foes abroad—and to those at home as well. The frigates were not even designed, nor were the other initiatives much more than ideas, before President Washington moved to take advantage of his newfound leverage.

He sent special envoys to Great Britain, France, and Spain—all with the mission of defusing the explosive international situation insofar as it related to the United States. John Jay, chief justice of the Supreme Court, went to London. Senator James Monroe received the nomination for the Paris assignment. Ambassador Thomas Pinckney moved to Madrid from his post in England. The militant mood in America sailed with each of the three—for the first time in its short life under the Constitution, the United States could approach negotiations affecting the common defense armed with more than hollow rhetoric. American representatives also pointedly let the Barbary rulers hear that keels were about to be laid for frigates capable of cruising the Mediterranean Sea, expecting the news to facilitate discussions for the release of captives. Power talks, the diplomats understood, and even potential power carries messages.

James Madison noted, insightfully if not admiringly, that the administration apparently planned "to supplicate for peace, and, under the uncertainty of success, to prepare for war by taxes and troops." To prepare for war, Washington had said many years before, was the surest way to keep the peace. By mid-1794, he finally had at hand the means to begin implementing that dictum: a peace establishment molded in concept after the one he had long ago envisioned.

By that point the pattern of America's abiding attitude toward its armed forces had become clearly discernible. Although a large proportion of the nation's citizens fully supported a powerful federal force, others remained suspicious. Some of them distrusted anything military, some only a standing body of regulars. Virtually all, however, recognized the imperative for fielding a competent force, and there was broad agreement that it must be reliable and affordable. That breakout in public opinion has not changed much in the two centuries since. Nor has the basic framework of discussion altered with the passage of time. From 1794 on, down through the decades, arguments would center not so much on whether to have a peace establishment, but rather on how large it should be and how ready.

Nations take positions and set courses using the sextant of policy and the compass of precedent. For the United States, 1794 was a turning point in both regards. In addition to witnessing the creation of an enduring defense policy, as embodied in the peace establishment, the year would also see two epochal precedents set in the use of military force: one in the name of the common defense, and one on behalf of domestic tranquility. Anthony Wayne would lead the Legion of the United States to decisive victory against British and Indian foes in the Northwest, and Washington himself would lead massed militia forces to suppress the Whiskey Rebellion. Combined with the adoption of comprehensive defense policies, those two precedent-setting events would indelibly demonstrate America's capacity and determination to confront its enemies, foreign and domestic.

CHAPTER 24
FALLEN TIMBERS

On one unrecorded day, quite some time before Anthony Wayne marched his Legion off into Indian country, a tornado roared over the Maumee River valley. Its swirling funnel touched ground along the north shoulder of the river, just south of the modern city of Toledo, Ohio. With incredible fury, the vicious winds cut a swath of devastation through the forest maybe a mile long and some four hundred yards wide. Hundreds of uprooted trees marked in gnarled profusion the location of the dark storm's brief visit to land. That chaos of twisted branches and broken trunks would also mark the site of the climactic battle in the campaign for control of the Northwest Territory, and would give the clash its name—the Battle of Fallen Timbers.

Anthony Wayne's intent was to keep the Indians off balance during the winter, build up his forward stockpiles of supplies, and then precipitate a pitched battle by driving to the heart of tribal territory as soon as spring thaws permitted. He set mid-April as the target for his advance. An aggressive program of probes, including the occupation of Fort Recovery in December, had accomplished the first aim. But the second proved to be more elusive.

Civilian contractors responsible for supplying Wayne's army were performing no more effectively than had those working for generals Harmar and St. Clair. Their pursuit of profit kept a lid on how much they sent forward in each convoy, while the Legion's long line of communications would have stretched their capacity in any event. Indians harassing the supply trains took a cumulatively heavy toll. What's more, unbeknownst to General Wayne, his disloyal deputy was actually hindering logistical operations. James Wilkinson, hoping to delay the Legion's advance so as to enhance his chances of superseding his commander, surreptitiously applied brakes to the supply system. A furious Wayne, although suspecting some sort of sabotage, turned his energy to correcting the problem rather than seeking its source. He muttered about the deviousness of Republicans, but placed the blame squarely on the shoulders of the contractors.

"Avaricious individuals will always consult their own private interests in preference to that of the public," he railed. "They will not part with so great a sum of money at any one time as will be necessary to purchase a large quantity of provisions in advance." The general, now "mad" in a different sense, peremptorily seized all the contractors' pack animals he could get his hands on and set about supplying himself. The situation improved markedly, but precious time had been lost. The offensive had to be postponed. "Thus will the public service always suffer," he concluded, "so long as supplies depend on a contract with private individuals in time of war."

Supply problems were not the only reason for moving the starting date back. Complying with Knox's order to block any illegal American attack of Spanish posts on the Mississippi cost the Legion a strong detachment of regulars, even as expected replacements for men with expiring enlistments failed to materialize. That complicated matters, although lower numbers than had been anticipated did not too greatly bother Wayne. He had more or less reconciled himself to using Brig. Gen. Charles Scott's Kentuckians anyway. In fact, he had grown to respect the militia general. Moreover, having a smaller force made his supply shortfall relatively less severe, for he would have fewer men to feed and clothe. Still, it was one more change to contend with.

Sudden hopes of achieving victory without a fight also slowed preparations. In January, a lone chieftain arrived under a flag of truce to propose opening peace discussions. Wayne, aware that the Indians were suffering cruelly that winter, and knowing that his very presence deep inside their lands had caused them to rethink their strategic situation, eagerly accepted the overture. He agreed to a month-long cease-fire in place, after which he expected all the tribes to come in and sign a treaty.

It was a false hope. Blue Jacket, Little Turtle, and others met in grand council and rejected the opportunity to treat. Part of their reason for deciding to continue in active opposition was the fiery address of the British governor-general, Lord Dorchester, in which he predicted war between the United States and Great Britain and held out the likelihood of assistance from the British army. Iroquois chieftain Joseph Brant, who vacillated between thoughts of war and peace, prophesied that the emotional speech would inspire his western brothers "to check General Wayne if he advances any further."

For his part, Lord Dorchester (who, as Gen. Guy Carleton, had turned over New York City at the end of the Revolutionary War to the victorious Continental Army) was quite concerned about the ultimate aim of the coiled and potent Legion. It could well be that "Mr. Wayne's intention is to close us up at Detroit," he surmised. To block such an attempt, he ordered in February the construction of a fortress on the Maumee River. It must be completed quickly, he said, and armed with cannon "of larger caliber than what Mr. Wayne can bring against it." By mid-April work was well along on the post, named Fort Miamis. That unexpected incursion gave Wayne yet another element to factor into his campaign planning: British military units inside his area of operations. Worriedly, he wrote that "the very quarter which I wish to strike at—i.e., the center of the hostile tribes—the British are now in possession of."

All told, the various events of the shifting scene that winter and spring combined to hold the Legion in Fort Greeneville nearly three months longer than the commanding general had originally planned. The invasion force was ready to move by the end of June, awaiting only the arrival of the militia reinforcements Wayne had called up. But the Indians struck first.

On the evening of 29 June, a large and well-guarded supply train reached the protection of Fort Recovery. The fort was to be a staging point for the invasion, and the supplies were meant to facilitate that movement. Tired soldiers tethered their animals and settled down for the night, securely—or so they thought—bivouacked on the edge of the two-hundred-yard cleared area around the walls of the fort. Which was just what the wily Little Turtle had expected they would do. The Indian battle leader had conceived a bold stroke to destroy the convoy and overpower the garrison in one swift assault early the next day. Soldiers camped outside the fort would have let their guard down, he calculated, while those inside, distracted by the early morning clamor of men and animals under the walls, would not detect the Indians' approach and would be caught by surprise. The capture of Fort Recovery would hand General Wayne a stinging reverse, all the more bitter because it would occur on the same bloody ground where the tribes had previously slaughtered St. Clair's army. Warriors still proudly recalled that victory as "the battle of a thousand slain." While the soldiers slept, Little Turtle and Blue Jacket moved a powerful striking force of perhaps two thousand braves quietly into place. It was the largest contingent of fighting men the Indian confederation could muster.

On a signal at seven o'clock, the mass of screaming warriors surged from the forest to overrun the encampment, quickly killing scores of the startled men. But, to their utmost consternation, the attackers found the gates of Fort Recovery shut and the defenses manned. A newly arrived commander, Capt. Alexander Gibson, required his garrison to stand to arms each morning, a practice he had not changed just because of the presence of a convoy. Maybe at that point Little Turtle grasped that Anthony Wayne's army would be an altogether different opponent than St. Clair's had been. As they crossed the open area, many of the charging Indians were slaughtered by a hail of musket and cannon fire. Others died under the walls when they could find no entrance. Howling in anger, survivors retired to safety in the trees.

The red host laid siege to the fort for another day, but to no avail. Captain Gibson and his two hundred men remained impervious to everything the lightly armed braves could throw against them. Seeing no way to win, and with their own casualties mounting alarmingly, the Indians killed all the animals outside the fort—some four hundred of them—and departed. As they were leaving, they had to swallow one last ignominy: Soldiers of Captain Gibson's heavily outnumbered garrison ran out of the fort to taunt them with vulgar gestures and jeering invitations to return and fight some more.

The initial impact of the battle was to delay somewhat the start of the Legion's advance. But the ultimate effect was one devastating to the Northwest tribes. The attempt to take Fort Recovery turned out to be their high-water mark. Never again would they be able to assemble on a battlefield as much strength as they had that day. Not in numbers, not in will, not in leadership. Combat casualties had been gruesome enough, but the galling defeat also convinced several of the smaller tribes, notably the more northern ones, to quit the coalition and return to their villages. Finally, the failure signaled the eclipse of Little Turtle. His role as the principal battle leader had been growing shaky anyway, for his people, the Miamis, were not nearly as numerous as the Shawnees. Blue Jacket soon emerged as the primary chief. But, for all his aggressiveness and charisma, he was not even close to being the equal of Little Turtle. Anthony Wayne was quite pleased with the outcome of the battle for Fort Recovery—he would have been ecstatic had he known how very severely his foe had been wounded.

When word reached Philadelphia of the British army's advance into American territory and the construction of Fort Miamis, the reaction was angry and vigorous. Holding on to posts the Crown had formerly owned was one thing, and bad enough, but this new affront was tantamount to an invasion by royal troops. It was an insult a sovereign country could not ignore, especially with John Jay in London trying to negotiate an end to frontier provocations. Washington was adamant. "You are hereby authorized in the name of the President of the United States," Knox informed Wayne, to engage British troops should it become necessary in the campaign against the Indians. Specifically, American arms could be employed to "dislodge the party" at Fort Miamis. Relieved to have that authority, and encouraged by the evidence of Washington's confidence in his judgment, Mad Anthony pointed his army northward.

General Scott's mounted volunteers had begun arriving from Kentucky in mid-July. The militiamen eventually numbered about sixteen hundred, almost matching the two thousand regulars Wayne had at hand. There was also a contingent of about a hundred Indians from Tennessee, mostly Chickasaws and Choctaws. They had come to help with reconnaissance, but were "resolved to have hair." Altogether, the invasion army was a hard-hitting and balanced force of fighting units—a combined arms team of cavalry, artillery, and infantry in flexible and mobile organizations. And it was responsive. Missing in the militia ranks were the excesses of independence and indiscipline that had been the hallmark of previous expeditions. Perhaps the impressive toughness and evident professionalism of Wayne's Legionnaires was a bracing influence for the Kentuckians. At any rate, Scott had his men firmly under control.

On 28 July, the eager and spirited soldiers left Fort Greeneville, taking the road to Fort Recovery. Next day at noon they passed that post, receiving joyous cannon salutes from the garrison, and plunged straight into "thickets almost impervious" toward the St. Marys River. Wayne's insistence on security and the marshy, almost swamplike terrain slowed the rate of march; the column consumed nearly three days in covering some twenty miles before intersecting the river.

There the general halted his men and began to raise another staging stockade, this one to be named Fort Adams in honor of the vice president. At this point, the Legion stood astride the old trail taken by Josiah Harmar to Miami Town four years earlier. That beaten path led off in a northwesterly direction, generally following the St. Marys River. Wayne had not confided in anyone what route he would take once Fort Adams was ready, or even where he was aiming. His own officers assumed he would order them on to Miami Town; British leaders, extrapolating from the line between Fort Recovery and Fort Adams, believed he might have Fort Miamis in mind. Both groups were wrong. The general's plan was in fact far more subtle—and astute.

When plotted on a map, the density of Indian habitation—people, villages, meeting areas, planted fields, trading posts, rudimentary roads, waterways—appeared as a huge barbell, two large weights connected by a sturdy pole. One concentration was centered on Miami Town, which had been the objective of previous offensives. The other was at the rapids of the Maumee, around Fort Miamis. The rod between the two stretched a hundred miles along the Maumee River valley.

Anthony Wayne intended to cut that rod at about its halfway point. That would put him between the two centers, in a position to threaten either, thus obliging the enemy to split his forces to defend both. After building a fortification to protect his rear, the American could strike first one way and then the other. As an operational concept it was simple—and brilliant. By maneuver alone he would virtually remove his foe's options and would change the odds even more in his own favor. He would thus assure that when battle came it would very likely be fought on his terms, not those of the defenders.

Fort Adams was far enough along to stand on its own by the third day of August. Leaving forty sick soldiers to guard it, Wayne moved on the next morning. He himself was probably in as poor a state of health as any of the men left behind. In addition to his chronic gout, he was bleeding internally. He had nearly been killed when a tree fell on him during the construction of Fort Adams. But he stuck his jutting jaw even farther out and pushed ahead regardless. Cutting a new road to the Auglaize River, the Legion briskly followed that stream to its confluence with the Maumee, arriving in strength on 8 August. That location was a traditional Indian meeting ground known as the Grand Glaize. The sudden and unexpected appearance of Americans stunned the Indians; those encamped in the area scattered just in time to avoid an encounter. Wayne was jubilant. He had seized the pivotal site merely by hard marching and shrewdness. To celebrate the bloodless capture of the "Grand Emporium of the hostile Indians," he issued each man a round of whiskey. But the soldiers did not have overly long to savor their reward. The general promptly started them scouring the area for food and forage, and sent scouts out to locate any assemblage of warriors. He also immediately began erecting an impressive stronghold on the high banks where the two rivers joined, and where each was about a hundred yards wide. Major Henry Burbeck, who had built Fort Recovery, supervised the construction. Not only would the fortress cover the army whichever way it moved, it would provide a safe haven to fall back on in an emergency. Mad Anthony was a bold fighter, but not a foolhardy one. Such careful attention to security would preclude a setback from becoming a disaster. Furthermore, the powerful bastion gave defiant notice that U.S. soldiers were on the Maumee to stay. "I defy the English, the Indians, and all the devils in Hell to take it," Wayne thundered. In his inimitable fashion, he assigned a descriptive name to the works: Fort Defiance.

With the initiative resting almost entirely in his own hands, the American commander tried once again to convince the tribes to capitulate without the necessity of more bloodshed. Five days after seizing the Grand Glaize, he sent the chiefs a final offer for peace. They promptly gathered in council to consider the proposal. Little Turtle spoke first. He urged his brothers to fight no more. In the long run, he said, the numbers ran against the red men. He reminded the others that the whites flowed in an unending stream from the east. "They are like the leaves of the tree. When the frost comes they fall and blow away. But when the sunshine comes again they come back more plentiful than before." He had also begun to doubt Great Britain's trustworthiness as an ally. (In that, he was insightful, but ahead of his time. Orders were actually on the way from London at that very moment telling Lord Dorchester to cede Fort Miamis and to avoid a fight with the Americans, but many weeks would pass before that message could reach the frontier.) Blue Jacket and other chiefs spoke in rebuttal, and British agents let it be known that they wanted the Americans to be stopped before they reached Fort Miamis. Little Turtle's star had set; the vote was to fight. The renowned battle leader would be relegated to a minor roll in the coming clash.

Reconnaissance verified earlier intelligence reports that large numbers of Indians, seeking food and security, had moved from Miami Town to the vicinity of Fort Miamis. Wayne therefore decided to head eastward first. In that direction lay better odds for precipitating the battle he sought. Dropping off a detachment to man Fort Defiance, the general crossed with some difficulty to the north bank of the Maumee on 15 August and began moving cautiously along the river's broad shoulders. By the eighteenth he was about ten miles from the British fort, still without major enemy contact, but with the feel of a fight strong in the air. Believing that an engagement was imminent, he paused briefly to erect a hasty fortification in which to have his troops stack all equipment and supplies not immediately necessary in battle. He called the position Fort Deposit. The enclosure would also serve as a rallying point should the looming fight not go well. Ordering Capt. Zebulon Pike to remain at Fort Deposit with two hundred men, Wayne put his lightened army in motion early on 20 August. Despite a painful attack of gout that made riding an agony, Mad Anthony mounted eagerly that morning. His adrenaline was pumping. This day, he was reasonably certain, he would encounter either Indians or Englishmen.

The Indians were waiting. More than a thousand of them, reinforced by about sixty Canadian militiamen who had painted their faces in an attempt to blend in with the natives. The tribes planned to ambush the Americans where the tornado had prepared natural breastworks for the braves to hide behind and fight from. They had improved the position by cutting off the second growth of brush and saplings about chest high. Their plan was a good one. Musket fire from these barricades would halt the advancing soldiers, causing the column to telescope as leading units went to ground and those in the rear shoved forward. Then warriors hidden on the high bluffs a few hundred yards north of the river would fall on the Americans' left flank, pinning them against the river. Although the Indians would be outnumbered, the chiefs believed that the terrain and the audacity of the scheme of maneuver, not to mention the fighting prowess of their warriors, would make up for the disparity in numbers. And, always before, American troops coming under sudden fire in the open had either frozen in place or bolted to the rear. There was no reason to expect different behavior this time.

Judging the rate of Wayne's advance, Blue Jacket concluded that his foe would enter the trap on 19 August. He had not anticipated the day-long halt to build Fort Deposit. That led to problems. The Indian custom was to fast for a day before going into battle; the chances of surviving a wound in the abdomen were greater if the intestines were empty. Accordingly, the braves did not eat on the eighteenth. When the whites failed to appear, the red men fasted again on the nineteenth, and slept on their arms a second straight night. With the sun high on the twentieth and no enemy yet in sight, many of them, tired and hungry, began to drift disgustedly back toward Fort Miamis. That lack of discipline cost them dearly, for the leading elements of the approaching Americans arrived at that moment of disarray, gaining surprise rather more than being surprised.

Taking advantage of the level flood plain of the Maumee, dry and firm at that time of the year, Wayne had marched his army in a formation ready for combat wherever and whenever he found the enemy. He had divided the Legion's infantry units into two wings, with Brigadier General Wilkinson commanding on the right and Col. John Hamtramck on the left. A mounted brigade of Kentuckians protected the army's open left flank, while the Legion's horsemen secured the right along the river. The rest of General Scott's mounted troops brought up the rear, a reserve to be committed after the battle opened. Well to the front as an advance guard was a select battalion under Maj. William Price. That security element had the mission of triggering initial contact to give the main body time to deploy as circumstances dictated. Thus arrayed, the Americans moved warily eastward for nearly five miles before Major Price's skirmishers came across the tornado-torn opening in the timber. The men, already sweltering under a hot sun, began picking their way through the debris.

Braves who had remained at their posts opened fire. With gaps in the line caused by those who had left, the opening volleys were not as effective as Blue Jacket had hoped they would be. Price's men returned the shots and fell back, stumbling into Wilkinson's leading troops and causing some confusion. Wilkinson promptly stabilized the situation as commanders in both wings began forming their units into line along the edge of the tornado's path of destruction.

Wayne rode forward, his piercing hazel eyes sparking with excitement. Listening to the sound of Indian musketry and making a quick visual survey of the terrain, he determined the location of the hostile positions, guessed Blue Jacket's plan, and calculated with surprising accuracy that he was facing about a thousand warriors. His instinctive feel for a battlefield had evidently not waned since the Revolutionary War. Using his aide and adjutant general to carry orders to subordinates, the general rapidly organized an attack.[1] The Indians, expecting to launch a charge against disoriented troops, would instead be on the receiving end of one made by very determined soldiers. Seeing that the maze of fallen trees would be too difficult for cavalry, Wayne directed his mounted units to the flanks. General Scott was to take his entire force around the Indians' right and fall on their rear. The Legion's dragoons would try to turn the Indians' left by cutting through at the river's edge. Infantry units were to drive straight into the enemy lines. They were to chase the defenders from cover, Wayne directed, "at the point of the bayonet." Then, once the concealed braves were exposed, the infantrymen were to deliver "a close & well directed fire." Wayne later wrote that all of those orders "were obeyed with spirit & promptitude."

1. The aide was Capt. William Henry Harrison. Riding at one point between the two sides, he narrowly escaped death. Harrison went on to attain high command himself in another war and victory in a battle that would always be linked to his name. He later became the ninth president. In his case, the hazards of combat turned out to be less deadly than service in the White House.

Hamtramck and Wilkinson waved their men forward. This was the moment the months of training had all been aimed at. With bullets clipping branches above their heads, would the soldiers stand up and go toward the source of death? Would they follow their officers or their instinct for survival? The training paid off. Unhesitatingly, the disciplined soldiers rose and moved toward the enemy, muskets carried vertically, bayonets sparkling in the bright sunshine. Working their way through the obstacles of blown-over trees, the men established a solid line near the Indian positions. From there, they delivered one carefully aimed volley with stunning effect, and then charged headlong and howling with bayonets leveled. The Indians panicked. "We were driven by the sharp ends of the guns of the Long Knives," said one chief later. Actually, they threw down their muskets and ran, he admitted. Soon the entire surviving body of defenders was in flight.

So rapidly did the fleeing warriors cover the two miles to Fort Miamis that General Scott's Kentuckians never got around them. The Indians simply moved faster on foot than the horsemen could beat through the tangled underbrush on the high ground above the river. Legion troopers, however, did break through on the right in time to strike the retreating stream of hapless Indians, most of whom were by then armed only with knives or tomahawks. Swords flashed and fell, killing until arms grew weary from the work. That intermingled mob of blood-splattered riders and frantic natives swirled nearly to the walls of Fort Miamis before the Americans broke off their pursuit. British soldiers watched from behind closed gates.

Exultantly, Wayne assembled his force in the vicinity of Fort Miamis. He knew that he had gained a grand victory. The Indians, suffering hundreds of casualties, had been totally routed, and the Legion was in uncontested control of their villages and fields. The British, moreover, penned inside their fort and apparently neither willing nor able to help their native allies, had been neutralized. American losses were surprisingly light—33 killed in action and 100 wounded, of whom 11 later died of their wounds. Wayne could not resist bragging that, whereas his men had been taught "to *believe* in the bayonet," the enemy had been taught to dread it. He was more right than he knew, for the will of the tribes to fight anymore had been shattered in that brief but momentous battle on the Maumee.

What to do with the British garrison in Fort Miamis was the next issue. Wayne paraded his soldiers near the walls, postured, provoked, even mocked the defenders. But the British commander, Maj. William Campbell, refused either to surrender or to be goaded into firing on the Americans. Neither he nor Wayne wanted the onus of being the one to start a war over a fort. Besides, the American commander, with only a few "pop gun howitzers," knew he could not take the well-constructed position by storm or siege without incurring heavy casualties and consuming excessive time. Wisely, Mad Anthony decided to ignore the British and get on with his primary mission—forcing the tribes to talk peace.

For days American units scoured the region around Fort Miamis, destroying anything of use to the Indians and pillaging British storehouses. When the formerly bustling community was reduced to charred rubble and blackened fields, and when his fallen soldiers had been buried on the battlefield, the general marched his army back up the Maumee toward Fort Defiance, moving slowly enough to destroy Indian habitations along the way, ranging miles on either side of the river. Left behind amidst the ruin and ashes was Major Campbell's thoroughly discredited garrison at Fort Miamis.

After strengthening Fort Defiance and leaving it in the hands of a powerful complement of Legionnaires, Wayne continued his scorched earth advance along the Maumee to the second Indian stronghold at Miami Town. He arrived on 17 September, and occupied it without opposition. His troops repeated their process of devastating the countryside. There, however, he gave further notice of the United States's intention to retain its hard-won dominance in the Northwest Territory. Soldiers, as accustomed by that time to building as to marching, raised another imposing fortification on the site of Harmar's 1790 defeat. It was named Fort Wayne, "by the will of the Legion," the honoree modestly reported. (It grew to become the present-day city of Fort Wayne, Indiana.) This post, the president and his field commander both believed, was the most important one between Canada and New Orleans. It stood at the strategic center of the Northwest Territory. Controlling that center had been the objective of both Harmar and St. Clair. Its seizure by Wayne, whose indirect approach to the site had assured a nearly bloodless conquest, was the death knell for organized resistance in the area.

In October, a courier from Lord Dorchester informed the American commander that a message from London had called for a halt to hostile actions pending the outcome of negotiations with John Jay. On the thirteenth, Wayne released General Scott and his Kentuckians to go home, stating outright that they were the best militia soldiers he had ever seen. The elated commander was unstinting, too, in his praise for the officers and men of the Legion, almost lavish in several instances. He had good words to say about Wilkinson's performance, but that did not dissuade the inveterate schemer from continuing his efforts to have Wayne removed from command. It mattered little; the glowing results of the campaign could hardly be dimmed by such pettiness. While the war was not formally ended, it was over for all intents and purposes. The British had been mightily embarrassed, and the Indian threat had been reduced to sniping from frustrated diehards.

Soldiers completed Fort Wayne late in the month. The general gave command of the bastion to Colonel Hamtramck, who had been serving in uniform in the West longer than any other officer. He then left for Fort Greeneville, reaching his headquarters there on 2 November amidst much fanfare. Boastfully but accurately, he recapitulated his hugely successful campaign in a report to Secretary Knox, calling it "an arduous & very fatiguing, but a Glorious tour of Ninety Seven days," which had covered altogether more than three hundred miles in primitive conditions.

Mad Anthony had earned the right to indulge in a bit of self-satisfaction. After all, wars are celebrated by the victors in the immediate afterglow of success. They are evaluated in the more lasting light of history, however, by examining a country's performance in four distinct categories: national direction, military strategy, operational art, and tactics. The first lies in the domain of the president, the commander in chief. The second is shared between the commander in chief and his top military leaders. The third is the responsibility of the commanding general in the theater of war. The fourth falls to those actually engaged with the enemy. Success in war is generally determined by the degree of competence with which each level is implemented and by the synchronization and integration of all four. The scorecard of the Fallen Timbers campaign reflects a superb performance by the United States in each of the four. Decisive victory was the result. At every level, that campaign remains a classic for study by would-be war-makers.

At the national level, Washington painstakingly forged a consensus for a resort to arms. Political and diplomatic activities were harnessed to help the military effort. The president and the secretary of war issued the field commander a clear mission. They provided the necessary resources, and then they let Wayne use his judgment in the theater of war. Strategically, taking the offensive to seize and retain the heart of Indian power was the one course capable of achieving the national aim quickly and at relatively small cost. More passive and less risky courses, carrying the virus of indecision, would likely have prolonged the conflict with the ultimate losses of people and treasure being much higher. Operationally, Wayne's insertion of the Legion into Indian lands by establishing Fort Recovery gave him the initiative. His subsequent isolation of the two centers of Indian power by building Fort Defiance between them led to the rapid attainment of his strategic objectives with minimum risk and cost. Finally, his outstanding tactical handling of the army achieved a resounding battlefield victory. That tactical success was the direct result of Wayne's preparation of his force, of the training and discipline he subjected it to over two long years.

The entire Fallen Timbers campaign demonstrated a point important in the maturing of the new nation—the government had discovered the ingredients for waging war successfully. Competent leadership was high among them.

With that in mind, the much respected historian of the U.S. Army, Russell F. Weigley, has written of Anthony Wayne: "With good reason he could be called the Father of the Regular Army."

CHAPTER 25
THE ARMY OF THE CONSTITUTION

As Anthony Wayne was making preparations in July 1794 to launch the Legion, an armed uprising far to his rear engulfed the area around Pittsburgh in anarchy. Resentment over the excise on spirituous liquors erupted in widespread violence. Rebels suppressed civil authority in western Pennsylvania, particularly in the counties of Allegheny, Washington, Fayette, and Westmoreland. That insurrection initiated the final phase of the antitax resistance known as the Whiskey Rebellion—and it presented the president his first major challenge to meet the Constitutional requirement that he enforce the nation's laws.

The chief executive had been warily watching the long-simmering trans-Allegheny region ever since the levy on liquors had become the law of the land. Strategically important, both militarily and politically, and verging on the edge of lawlessness even in the best of times, Pittsburgh and its vicinity had always been a source of serious concern to the president. Moreover, the issue of taxing whiskey boosted the area's significance, for a surprisingly large part—some estimates ranged up to a quarter—of all the stills in the United States operated in those counties. Pennsylvania's frontier citizens had from the very outset resisted efforts to collect the tax, but this latest episode of violence, coming at a time when the central government was feeling beleaguered anyway, lent the rebellion an even more ominous tone than it might otherwise have had. Finally, Washington saw in the angry and overt disobedience of the law a clear parallel with Shays's Rebellion. Both were popular movements in remote areas to protest the actions of a distant government. Both carried seeds of civil war and disunion. Both posed a direct affront to the government's responsibility to insure domestic tranquility. Shays's uprising, though, had been against state authority, while the Whiskey Rebellion directly challenged federal law. The framers of the Constitution, having been moved to their work by the thoroughly frightening experience of Shays's Rebellion, could hardly have taken the whiskey rebels lightly. Washington did not.

He had thought to act against them after their initial outburst some three years earlier, but when they had appeared to be responding to reason he had waited. Congress, meanwhile, took steps to remove several of the more onerous provisions of the levy act. Hoping that would end the problem, Washington had nevertheless made clear to members of his cabinet his resolve to enforce the laws if the violence persisted. Giving guidance to Alexander Hamilton, whose Treasury Department was responsible for collecting the taxes, the president had laid down two imperatives for planning. "The Constitution and the Laws must strictly govern," he directed. That principle would be inviolable. Furthermore, he warned, "the employing of regular troops [must be] avoided if it be at all possible to effect order without their aid; otherwise there would be a cry at once, 'The Cat is let out; we now see for what purpose an Army was raised.' " The commander in chief was ever sensitive to the country's fear of a man on horseback.

By late 1793 resistance had flared again. Rioters beyond the mountains had torched a collector's house, and were physically coercing anyone attempting to cooperate with the government. Washington offered a reward for the arrest of the vandals, and he issued in February yet another proclamation aimed at ending such lawlessness. Hamilton sent a treasury official to investigate the situation, but angry inhabitants blocked the agent's efforts and threatened him with bodily harm. He scurried back to Philadelphia, escorted out of the region for his own safety by some regular army cavalrymen. By June, not a single still had been recorded. Hamilton insisted on enforcement. David Lenox, the U.S. marshal for the district of Pennsylvania, rode west in mid-July to serve writs on several known violators. Those writs would require the westerners to appear in court in Philadelphia the following month, even though Congress had recently amended the law to permit hearings in local courts. Lenox and his bag of writs proved to be the spark igniting the explosion.

It was harvest time. Farmers, assembled in the fields to help one another with the hot work, were in the habit of fortifying themselves with ample amounts of the very whiskey they so jealously guarded from the tax collectors' grasp. Thus it was rather easy to reach large numbers of local inhabitants, who would at the same time be inclined to be more excitable than might have been the case in a more sober season.

Lenox delivered writs without incident on 14 July, and went on to Pittsburgh. The next day he started out again, accompanied by John Neville, the senior tax official in that part of Pennsylvania. The two rode into an area influenced heavily by the Mingo Creek Society. Word spread rapidly of Lenox's mission. A mob formed, composed of perhaps forty men who had been imbibing in the fields. The motley gang chased the two officials from the area; Lenox returned to Pittsburgh and Neville went to his estate near that city.

Militiamen meeting nearby—pursuant to the government's countrywide call for the readying of eighty thousand men for a possible war with Great Britain—got wind of the ruckus. The citizen-soldiers became enraged at the news. Declaring themselves a council of war, they dispatched about forty armed men to capture Lenox. Thinking he was at Neville's house, the group surrounded that structure and its outlying buildings on 16 July, and demanded the marshal's surrender. Neville and several of his slaves, ready for just such an event, opened fire from the windows, killing one of the attackers and wounding several. The ad hoc posse retreated in considerable disorder.

That bloodshed triggered an uproar. Around five hundred men, gathering on 17 July, formed a militia organization under command of Maj. James McFarlane. Like Shays, McFarlane was a Revolutionary War veteran. He and his men set out noisily for Neville's home, intending to force him to resign his position as chief revenue collector. Neville, meanwhile, had reinforced his defenses with more men, including a detachment of eleven regular soldiers from Fort Fayette in Pittsburgh. He himself was in Pittsburgh when the horde of agitated locals descended on his fortified compound. A brisk firefight followed when the defenders refused to turn over the complex of buildings. Major McFarlane was killed, several of the soldiers were wounded, and Neville's house was burned to the ground.

Rebellion escalated rapidly after that sharp encounter. The insurgents occupied Pittsburgh, hijacked the mails, burned buildings belonging to known or suspected opponents, and openly contemplated seizing Fort Fayette to get at the federal weapons and ammunition stored there. A massive muster at Braddock's Field on 30 July showed the extent of the revolt: upwards of fifteen thousand men assembled there in rowdy protest against the government. Rebels held sway in virtually every part of the four counties. Law-abiding citizens were terrorized into going along with the insurgents or leaving. One moderate observer later wrote: "The flame . . . spread with an infatuation almost incredible; for some time the voice of reason could not be heard nor durst scarce be uttered."

Dark news of mayhem began arriving in Philadelphia late in July. By month's end enough details were available to convince President Washington that patience and proclamations would no longer suffice. Anarchy reigned. The time for action was at hand.

His legal basis for acting sprang directly from Article II of the Constitution, which required the chief executive to "take Care that the Laws be faithfully executed." The same article made the president the commander in chief of the "Militia of the several States, when called into the actual Service of the United States." He did not have to agonize over whether or not to use regular troops—Anthony Wayne had the Legion fully committed in the Northwest Territory. The only option was to mobilize a force composed of militiamen.[1]

The details by which the president would fulfill his responsibilities had been enacted into law in the calling-forth act of 1792. Congress had passed that law pursuant to its Constitutional mandate "To provide for calling forth the Militia to execute the laws of the Union, suppress Insurrections and repel Invasions." The act stipulated:

That whenever the laws of the United States shall be opposed, or the execution thereof obstructed, in any state, by combinations

---

1. Establishing the precedent of using regular soldiers would await his successors. The next two presidents, John Adams and Thomas Jefferson, would each have occasion to quell domestic disturbances—and both would employ regular units.

too powerful to be suppressed by ordinary course of judicial proceedings, or by the powers vested in the marshals by this act,
the same being notified to the President of the United States by
an associate justice, or the district judge, it shall be lawful for
the President of the United States to call forth the militia of such
states to suppress such combinations, and to cause the laws to
be duly executed. And if the militia of the state, where such
combinations may happen, shall refuse or be insufficient to suppress the same, it shall be lawful for the President, if the legislature of the United States be not in session, to call forth and employ
such numbers of the militia of any other state or states most
convenient thereto, as may be necessary. . . .

The act went on to specify that the president, before actually committing the mobilized militia units, would issue a proclamation to
"command such insurgents to disperse and retire peaceably to their
respective homes, within a limited time."

Washington had previously resolved that every aspect of the law
must be scrupulously followed. Sending American soldiers to suppress
American citizens was serious business. He knew full well that the
first time it was done would be precedent setting; it had to be done
right. Furthermore, it would be a test of the viability of the Constitution itself—in the attempt to insure domestic tranquility, armed forces
could not subvert the very integrity of that document by working outside
the permissible boundaries set by the framers. Pertinent to that very
point, George Washington would call the nationalized force he was
about to assemble the "Army of the Constitution."

The very first step to be accomplished was to obtain a statement
by an appropriate judge certifying that opposition to the laws in the
counties near Pittsburgh was "by combinations too powerful to be
suppressed" by normal means. Washington sent the evidence of that
assertion to Associate Justice of the Supreme Court James Wilson. As
a member of the Constitutional Convention, Wilson had argued hard
for a strong central government. He had also twice in his lifetime been
the victim of mob violence. He was not likely to look with much empathy
upon the unrest in the West.

While awaiting Wilson's response, the president turned his attention to another prerequisite—a determination that Pennsylvania authorities

themselves either could not or would not call forth their own militia to solve the problem.

Washington convened a joint meeting on 2 August with his cabinet and state officers. He suggested that Gov. Thomas Mifflin should mobilize the Pennsylvania militia, but the governor declined. He claimed to be unsure of his authority in the first place, and doubted the capacity of his Pennsylvania troops to restore order in any event. To act alone would have required more political courage than Mifflin could muster. The excise on whiskey was a federal levy, he countered, so federal soldiers should enforce it. The meeting became a bit testy, but Mifflin would not budge. In a written follow-up, he stated his opposition to the use of military force—a politically safe position since any troops would be employed against Pennsylvania citizens—and passed the buck to the president. The federal executive, he wrote, must determine what measures were needed to enforce federal laws. He did vow, however, to cooperate fully in whatever course was chosen.

By 5 August, the president was ready to move. Associate Justice Wilson had issued a certificate stating that opposition to the laws in Allegheny and Washington counties was too powerful to be overcome by ordinary means. And the governor of Pennsylvania had claimed that the situation was beyond his power to handle unaided, opening the door for summoning militia from other states (Congress was in recess, not due to reconvene until November, which met another provision of the law). At a cabinet meeting the next day, Washington announced his decision to mobilize a militia army. He agreed, however, to take one additional prudent step recommended by Secretary of State Edmund Randolph. Before marching against the rebels, he would send commissioners to ascertain beyond a shadow of doubt that only military power would serve to restore civil authority. On 7 August, the president issued the proclamation required by the 1792 law. Charging that those in revolt were guilty of treason by committing "overt acts of levying war against the United States," he directed "all persons being insurgents" to disperse and return to their homes by 1 September.

On the eighth he named three commissioners: Attorney General William Bradford; Sen. James Ross, a native of Washington County; and Associate Justice Jasper Yeates, a member of Pennsylvania's Supreme Court. Combined in those three appointments were links to federal, state, and local levels of government, as well as to the executive, legislative, and judicial branches. Washington empowered the commissioners to offer amnesty in return for assurances that the whiskey levy would be untrammeled in the future. They were told to hurry to the scene of rebellion, for an army was even then being readied.

Secretary of War Henry Knox conveyed the president's call for troops to the governors of Pennsylvania and three neighboring states. He asked them to raise a total of almost 13,000 men—5,200 from Pennsylvania, 3,300 from Virginia, 2,350 from Maryland, and 2,100 from New Jersey. Units were to be ready to march on call, and to expect very little advance notice. The president soon increased the number requested to 15,450. He did not intend to err by sending a force too small for the task. Deploying overwhelming strength, the old soldier knew, would give him the best chance for a quick, decisive win with the least number of casualties. While the three commissioners went west to assess the extent of the insurgency, the four governors plunged into the daunting task of mobilizing a militia army larger than the Continental Army had been during most of the Revolutionary War.

In not one of the states did the mobilization go smoothly. While the militia act of 1792 had established standards of training and readiness, it had left to the various states the responsibility for checking and enforcing. That responsibility had not been met. To the chagrin and embarrassment of officials in the four involved states, the failure to have done so now became publicly and painfully evident.

Things went best in New Jersey. That state had completed its earlier requirement to prepare the militia for a potential war with Great Britain, so detailing units to be ready "to march at a moment's warning" was relatively easy. Governor Richard Howell simply turned to Maj. Gen. Elias Dayton, the commanding general of that force already embodied, and ordered him to detach fifteen hundred infantrymen for the whiskey campaign. Cavalry and artillery components would come from other militia elements, as well as from Dayton's command. The governor planned to march west, too. The men responded in good fashion; New Jersey actually exceeded its quota. But getting compliance from those called was one thing, getting them outfitted was another. Supply problems plagued the entire operation, causing many of the state's troops to be late reaching the rendezvous point—indeed, some were so late that they missed the expedition altogether.

Maryland's governor, Thomas Lee, encountered complications caused by the need to put down a small uprising in the western parts of his own state, where sympathizers of the whiskey rebels threatened the arsenal at Frederick. His method of raising his quota also hindered progress. Instead of calling for men from specific areas, he directed each militia unit in the state to provide a certain number of soldiers, a method bringing in individuals who were often strangers rather than groups of soldiers used to working with one another, which in turn assured that the organizations to be formed would lack cohesion, at least initially. Worse still, not enough volunteers stepped forward, so officers had to resort to a draft. Maryland also experienced supply problems, and many formations arrived late in the assembly areas, with some in such a state of disrepair that they were turned back. Governor Lee was deeply disappointed in the overall results. "I have had to encounter Difficulties arising from the striking Inefficiency of our Militia Law," he complained. "If I have not been able to accomplish the Force required by the President the fault is not mine."

Virginia's Henry Lee faced added distractions because of his state's strategic location. He accordingly distributed quotas to areas in consideration of their proximity "to the point of service, by regard to the protection of the frontiers from the Indian enemy, and by attention to the seaboard in case of sudden war." To help bring into the fold Virginians from the western counties—who themselves were generally opponents of the whiskey levy—Lee appointed old warhorse Daniel Morgan as commander of brigades to be raised there. That turned out to be a very shrewd move, for Lee's fellow Virginians did not rush to the colors. The Old Dominion's portion of the overall army was eventually raised without resort to Draconian measures only because so many additional men answered Morgan's personal appeals. Still, there was much delay in filling the ranks. Citizens' reactions ranged from a palpable lack of eagerness to outright mutiny in a few instances. On top of the necessity to motivate reluctant militiamen, Virginia suffered its full share of the seemingly universal state of chaos in the supply system. Throughout the mobilization process, Governor Lee had been very worried, and with good cause. He decided to personally lead his state's contingent.

Not surprisingly, Pennsylvania had the worst time in fielding its force. As with the other states, logistical shortcomings hobbled the call-up, but problems with people were far more serious to begin with. State Adjutant General Josiah Harmar received virtually no response to his initial call to arms. The former commander in the West was probably not very surprised at the absence of enthusiasm. State soldiers had no heart for marching against their western comrades. Nearly a month after the orders had been sent out, a mortified Governor Mifflin had to face the bitter fact that Pennsylvanians were sitting on their hands in silent protest. Decrying "so essential a defect of power of the officers" that they were unable to enforce the mobilization, he told Harmar to "resort to the spirit of patriotism" to attract volunteers. The governor also announced pointedly that officers should either support the effort or resign their commissions. He himself set out on a barnstorming, three-week speaking tour to drum up volunteers. While some might not agree with the Congress, he argued forcefully in village after village, no citizen in a democracy could condone armed insurrection. Nor could the militia permit the "reputation" of the state to be tarnished by refusing to march alongside the armed forces of neighboring states, who were coming, after all, to help restore order inside Pennsylvania itself. Appeals to patriotism and pride worked—although the full quota went unmet, the governor finally fielded a respectable body of men. Like governors Lee of Virginia and Howell of New Jersey, he marched at their head.

All of those difficulties should have been entirely predictable. They were the fruit of a decentralized and neglected militia system. For all its defects, though, that was apparently what a majority of the American people preferred. The system provided neither the state nor the federal government a readily effective organization, nor a reliable one. But local communities felt that it gave them local protection. Furthermore, in time and with much energy, it could produce a substantial if not a professional force for state or federal use. Two months after he called forth the Army of the Constitution, President Washington could count about two-thirds of the planned manpower in ranks. That may sound meager by today's standards, but, as historian Robert W. Coakley concluded, it was "a considerable accomplishment under the circumstances" prevailing in the young Republic.

While the four governors struggled to raise their contributions to the army, Washington turned to putting together the structure of command and to building a logistical apparatus.

Henry Knox took a lengthy leave of absence in early August, returning to Massachusetts to attend to some pressing personal matters. That Washington let him go at such a critical moment says much about his true opinions of both Knox and Hamilton, who promptly assumed Knox's responsibilities. The president knew that moving fifteen thousand men over the mountains to fight would require a Herculean logistical effort. That was sure to be the crucial element in the entire campaign, and Knox was simply not up to it. Hamilton was.

The president was less concerned than the governors themselves over how long it was taking them to recruit their men—he had warned for years of that very likelihood unless the militia system could be improved, so he was not surprised. Besides, he fully anticipated that the time consumed in patching together a logistical structure would at least match and maybe exceed any delays due to recruitment difficulties. Even when assembled, the army could not march until it had the capacity to sustain itself.

Leadership was the next ingredient addressed. In that regard, Washington's own role had to be determined. Would he, as the commander in chief, personally lead the army to Pittsburgh? The Constitution was silent on the subject, but debates in the Constitutional Convention on that very point certainly returned to Washington's memory as he pondered the decision. Delegates had been divided in that hot summer seven years before; some thought the president should never assume the mantle of a general in the field, others asked what kind of leader the nation would have in a commander in chief who could not command. In the end it had been left for events and George Washington to determine—and now the moment for setting the precedent had at last arrived.

Washington was of two minds. He had no personal ambition to go campaigning at the age of sixty-two, and he was very conscious of the image it might present of a "man on horseback." Yet a tug of duty told him that if Americans were to kill other Americans on his orders, he could not be elsewhere. The responsibility was too grave to delegate. But perhaps the commissioners would succeed and the army would not have to be used after all. He temporized. He would lead personally until the army was assembled and was prepared to cross the mountains, and would decide only then what to do next.

First reports from the commissioners were pessimistic. They thought the situation had probably deteriorated to the point that only "the physical strength of the nation" could right it. Attorney General Bradford, believing that the rebels might prove to be too tough for militia units, recommended that the president consider supplementing the army with regulars. Based on that intelligence, Washington had increased the numbers of men needed from the states. He also directed Gov. Henry Lee to find as many riflemen as he could to serve under Brig. Gen. Daniel Morgan, who the western insurgents especially feared. The passage of time would not alter the commissioners' initial impressions. From start to finish they forecast futility in any attempt to terminate the rebellion by extending an olive branch. A small, vociferous faction of westerners actually advocated civil war; others, vowing to resist the whiskey levy at whatever cost, were "numerous and violent." The two groups joined in terrorizing their other neighbors into acquiescence. The army would be needed, the commissioners finally reported in late September.

Washington did not wait for that final word. He had heard enough already. As the proclamation date of 1 September approached—the date set for the insurgents to disperse—he asked Henry Lee to take command of the entire expedition "if I do not go out myself." To demonstrate civilian control, the top three positions beneath the president would be held by governors. Mifflin, a Revolutionary War veteran, would have the second spot behind Lee, and Governor Howell would be third in line. Lee, who had always aspired to high military command, accepted at once. "My grief for the necessity of pointing the bayonet against the breasts of our countrymen is equaled only by my conviction of the wisdom of your decision to compel immediate submission to the authority of the laws," he wrote Washington. Some movement of troops took place in late August, but when September arrived with the whiskey rebels still in defiance, Washington issued orders for the full assembly of the army. Pennsylvania and New Jersey troops were to rendezvous at Carlisle, Pennsylvania, while those from Virginia and Maryland were to gather at Cumberland in Maryland. The commander in chief ordered the governors to start their contingents at once, with the expectation that the entire force would be assembled and under federal control by the end of September. On the twenty-fifth of that month, Washington issued another proclamation. Because rebellion persisted, he asserted emphatically, a powerful army was "already in motion to the scene of disaffection."

Five days later, accompanied by Alexander Hamilton, Washington left Philadelphia on the road to Carlisle. Always before, his drink in the field had been rum. But the politician had overtaken the general— on this command tour he switched to whiskey. Otherwise, he must have experienced familiar sensations as he set out yet again to join an army

273

preparing for battle. Having Hamilton at his side would have helped to trigger some of those sensations. During the Revolutionary War, he had commanded through a close group—his "family," he called them—of bright, young officers. Hamilton had been the best of the lot. The younger man's comforting presence apparently overrode any qualms the chief executive may have had over taking his controversial treasury secretary along. Republicans thoroughly distrusted Hamilton, and were sure to be suspicious of his proximity to military power.

When the two stopped for the night in the village of Trappe, a messenger caught up with them. He carried marvelous news from the West. Anthony Wayne had defeated the Indians in a major battle on the Maumee, had embarrassed the British, had devastated tribal lands up and down the Maumee, and had established fortified positions in the very heart of the hostile area. It was the first really good news to come out of the tortured land north of the Ohio since Washington had become president. Wayne had succeeded handsomely in his mission of defeating foreign enemies; now it was up to Washington and the Army of the Constitution to match that success by restoring domestic tranquility.

The sight that greeted the commander in chief when he and Hamilton rode into Carlisle on 4 October was in several ways depressingly similar to the one he had witnessed when he had first joined the Continental Army on the outskirts of Boston nearly two decades earlier. This army, too, was one in name only. It had to be whipped into campaigning shape quickly. The bulk of the men, having arrived "in a very disjointed and loose manner," had to be organized into a cohesive structure. The nature of the recruiting had brought together a strange mixture of men. Many looked very much like those caught up in previous canvasses—misfits, foreigners, those down on their luck, youngsters—but others were from society's elite, coerced by calls to their patriotism to volunteer. Welding them into closely knit teams would take some doing. Supply matters were also in disarray. Those had to be sorted out to provide the units "with necessaries for their March, as well, and as far, as our means would admit." And, very importantly, a sense of discipline and purpose had to be imposed. Expecting that "the whole country would be given up to execution and plunder," the troops were only too eager for the chance to "skewer the Whiskey men." New Jersey soldiers, particularly, were in a vengeful mood. A satirical piece written in the West had derisively referred to them as a misfit rabble, a laughable "watermelon army." Again and again, the commander in chief hammered on the theme of control, of proper conduct, of the primacy of civil authority. Hamilton, preparing headquarters directives and orders for President Washington as he once had for General Washington, wrote: "It is a very precious and important idea that those who are called out in support and defense of the laws, should not give occasion, or even protest to impute to them infractions of the law." Soldiers in the Army of the Constitution had to be above reproach in their deportment. They could not desecrate the Constitution in the act of defending it.

Within a week, the work of forging reliable units had proceeded far enough to start some of them on the road to Bedford, where they were to make final preparations before jumping off on the attack westward. As readied elements left Carlisle, with others still flowing in from staging areas in New Jersey and Pennsylvania, Washington departed to check the progress of the other wing at Cumberland. Arriving on 16 October, he was pleased to find the basic work of organization well along. Major General Henry Lee had been energetically doing the same things to prepare the Virginia and Maryland contingents that Washington had done with those at Carlisle. After only three days there, the president left with Lee for Bedford, a day's ride away.

At that final assembly area, Washington announced his decision to turn the field command over to Lee. He himself would not lead the army over the mountains. He had reached that decision only a short while before, probably upon seeing the condition of the men in Cumberland. Two primary factors brought him to that conclusion. Foremost was compelling evidence that the rebellion had all but collapsed. When the rebels had finally come to realize that the federal government was actually intent on marching against them with a huge army of somewhat dubiously disciplined soldiers, led by a determined President Washington in person, they had lost their starch. Those in the ranks melted away to return to their homes, while many of the leaders and those most guilty simply fled westward—some two thousand of them altogether. Resistance was likely to be sporadic at most, and the mountain passes would almost surely not be defended. Secondly, and significantly, Washington had the utmost confidence in Light-Horse Harry Lee. The army would be competently led.

At Bedford, the president stressed the importance of the expedition. Its purpose was "nothing less than to consolidate and preserve the blessings" of the Revolution. Soldiers had a special role in a democracy, he said: "The essential principles of a free government confirm the provinces of a military to these two objects: first, to combat and subdue all who may be found in arms in opposition to the national will and authority. Secondly, to aid and support the civil magistrate in bringing offenders to justice." Once more he reminded the men that they could do nothing more important for the government than to campaign with "a conduct scrupulously regardful of the rights of their fellow citizens," and to comport themselves with "exemplary decorum, regularity and moderation."

Leaving Hamilton with Lee, where he would serve as the senior civil official of the federal government on the expedition, Washington returned to Philadelphia. He reached the seat of government near the end of October, after almost a month's absence.

On the way back, encountering inadequately outfitted militia units straggling westward, he ordered those not yet near the rendezvous points to be turned back. "The Army which is already advanced is more than competent to any opposition that can be given by the insurgents," he explained. All told, General Lee had perhaps eleven thousand men under his command. Still, as recently returned Henry Knox said, that number was now "superabundant." The army's very presence and size had in essence assured its success before it had ever had to fire a shot— a most effective way to win a victory. Historian Coakley aptly summed up the achievement: "Given all the obstacles to recruitment, organization, and supply, accomplishing the assembly of the militia from four states at Bedford and Cumberland only three weeks past the deadline of 1 October was a tribute to the steadfastness and prestige of the President, the driving energy of Alexander Hamilton, and the diligence with which the four state governors had worked to fulfill their purposes."

All thereafter was anticlimactic. Lee led his army over the mountains in two columns, starting on 22 October and arriving at the end of the month after a harrowing march through truly awful conditions of weather and terrain. That miserable crossing was by far the most demanding part of the entire campaign to subdue the Whiskey Rebellion. It was described by one of the participants, with perhaps a touch of hyperbole, as "more difficult than any expedition during the Revolution or even Hannibal's passage over the Alps." Once he brought his frazzled army through that ordeal, Lee rapidly took control of the scene of rebellion, rounded up those who could be accused of crimes, sent about twenty rebels to Philadelphia for trial, set up Daniel Morgan as the commander of an occupying force of some twelve hundred troops, and returned the rest of the men to their homes east of the Alleghenies. By the end of November the Army of the Constitution was disbanded. Morgan's occupation ended the following spring. Washington granted a general pardon for all insurgents, and later extended it to the only two to be sentenced to death for the insurrection. The whiskey levy was collected thereafter.

The success of the Army of the Constitution "did not assure the allegiance of rural America," wrote historian Thomas P. Slaughter, "but it did demonstrate the federal government's commitment to a perpetual Union and its ability to enforce that commitment hundreds of miles distant from the centers of its power." He was quite correct. That was a message sent loudly to all enemies, foreign and domestic.

The president was almost boastfully proud of the results. He exulted in having brought the Whiskey Rebellion to a close "without spilling a drop of blood." He was also gratified that a large body of armed men had operated amidst a hostile if awed population without serious incident. One of his recent biographers put it succinctly: "Not a single person was hurt, virgins who were so inclined slept undisturbed, the army paid for everything it used." That may have been too rosy a summation, for there surely were scattered incidents of "misappropriation." Fence rails, for instance, have always seemed to be irresistible to passing soldiers—they make such ideal wood for campfires. And some of the captured insurgents were definitely treated with less than total kindness. Nevertheless, discipline prevailed. Washington was justified in being satisfied. The occupation was indeed a mild one.

But, withal, he was most pleased with the resounding signal sent to a watching world. He had never lost sight of his international audience. As historian Slaughter noted, he had all along wished to show foreign capitals that "the power and majesty of this young nation were not to be trifled with." The long-held assertion of many "that without the protection of Great Britain we should be unable to govern ourselves, and would soon be involved in anarchy and confusion," Washington wrote triumphantly, had been dealt "the most conclusive refutation." The United States was here to stay.

CHAPTER 26
1795 AND BEYOND

Because of an unusual confluence of significant events, some years cast larger shadows on the future than others. In the history of the United States, 1794 was such a year.

The outlook early in 1794 had been, to put the best face on it, grim. Just twelve months later it was surprisingly good. Adversity had not disappeared, but the embrace was no longer of the death grip variety. In that calm January of 1795, Vice President John Adams wrote his wife, "In the Senate we have no feelings this session; no passion; no animations in debate. I have never sat in any public assembly so serenely." It was a weather change—and welcome.

The country rejoiced in the splendid resolution of the Whiskey Rebellion. The government's authority had been reestablished, and it had been done without bloodshed. While the dollar costs of mounting the campaign had been high, Washington squelched complaints on that score. "No money could have been more advantageously expended, both as it respects the internal peace and welfare of this *country* and the impression it will make on *others*." What is more, the president's judicious and scrupulously correct use of the militia under the provisions of the 1792 law satisfied lawmakers that military power could in fact safely be entrusted to the nation's commander in chief. That precedent led promptly to an easing of legal restrictions on calling out the militia, and later to a permanent grant of authority to the president to employ regulars in addition to militia in event of domestic disorders. Less and less was there talk of the chief executive becoming a Cromwell.

Citizens were likewise ecstatic over the defeat of Indian power in the Northwest. The decisiveness of Anthony Wayne's campaign became fully evident in the terms of the treaty he imposed on the tribes. Gathering at Fort Greeneville in the summer of 1795, the chiefs ceded to the United States the entire territory south of a line running east-west through Fort Recovery. That opened vast tracts of land north and west of the Ohio to unopposed white settlement, leading before long to statehood for Ohio and other territories there. Further clashes over hunting grounds would occur before the Indians were to be completely subdued, and more battles were to be fought in the Northwest during the War of 1812, but peace as Americans then defined it was a reality. The Ohio Valley—from Pittsburgh all the way to the Mississippi—was, for the first time in the history of the nation, reasonably safe for travel and settlement.

In the Southwest, too, conditions had improved remarkably. Washington's strong stand against freelance military operations, backed in law by Congress, had dampened local desires to assail Spanish posts. Anthony Wayne's Legionnaires, guarding the Ohio with announced intent to turn back any expedition, further cooled them. Moreover, Spanish officials, realizing that they may have stirred up more resistance than they could handle, backed away from their bellicose agitation of the tribes. All of that, as well as reverses in a series of small clashes with Americans along the frontier, had had a cumulatively calming effect on Indian thoughts about an escalation to war. As in the Northwest, the final chapter of red-white conflict remained in the future—several bloody battles, to include a Creek civil war, would be fought early in the next century. But for the time being the war drums were muffled. Settlers could move into lands west of Georgia, and Tennessee could launch its race to statehood.

Abroad, affairs improved in just about every quarter. Two of George Washington's three special envoys enjoyed a large degree of success in Europe, and the Barbary potentates at last agreed to come to terms. Worried by the construction of American warships, the pirates signed treaties and released hostages, ending that dark chapter in U.S. history.

John Jay had concluded the negotiation of a treaty with Great Britain late in 1794, but the hazards of war and winter weather delayed its arrival in the United States until the following March. Its reception was decidedly mixed—no one seems to have been satisfied with the entire document, and partisan politics made it even more controversial than it would have been on its own account. Jay was roundly excoriated by many critics at the time—and by many historians since. Yet, as Washington and his advisors eventually decided, and as the Senate expressed in approving all but one of the provisions, the good gained outweighed the negatives. Notably, Great Britain agreed to remove redcoats from forts occupied on American territory, the United States would regain much of its former commerce with England and its possessions, and commissioners would meet to sort out other differences. All told, the treaty would enhance America's probability of avoiding entanglement in the European war. That point was especially compelling. Peace would be precarious, as events were to prove, for neutrality was not an easy or a simple course in those perilous times. But avoiding war with the country possessing the world's mightiest navy was virtually an imperative, particularly considering how imminent hostilities with Great Britain had appeared early in 1794.

In Madrid, Thomas Pinckney used the Jay Treaty as a wedge to extract unheralded concessions from the Spanish court. Spain had concluded for reasons of its own to withdraw from the war with France, an act certain to put Madrid at odds with London. In that event, the Jay Treaty held out the possibility of an alliance between the United States and England that would threaten Spanish possessions in the New World. Furthermore, American power itself was growing ever stronger in the West. Spain thought a negotiated arrangement would preserve its possessions, whereas otherwise they might all be lost in some future confrontation. The Treaty of San Lorenzo, completed in 1795, opened the Mississippi and gave American merchants preferred treatment in the port of New Orleans. It also settled the boundary between the United States and Florida at the 31st Parallel, and gained Spain's promise to cease inciting the Southwest Indians. Gleeful senators lost no time in ratifying it.

Treaties with Algiers, Tunis, and Tripoli were not nearly as satisfying morally, but they did at long last gain the release of Americans held in Barbary Coast prisons. It cost the United States nearly a million dollars in ransom money, with more to be paid annually in bribes. Assuring safe passage for American ships also entailed giving the rapacious pirates a warship and other arms. The Senate reluctantly approved the arrangement as the best deal the country could get until a navy could be built. Congress authorized construction of the frigates to continue.

The one nation with which affairs did not improve at that time was France. French authorities were horrified by the news of the Jay Treaty, and were worried that the special relationship between the United States and their country might be ending. Ambassador James Monroe, who assumed the curious position that he was a representative of the American people rather than of the president, must answer to history for the devious role he played. Unable to rise above party affiliation, he undercut his own government repeatedly. At the same time, however, he strengthened the belief widely held in Paris that most Americans persisted in supporting the aims of the French Revolution and remained committed to the treaties binding the two countries. That may have helped dampen inclinations among French leaders to take a more belligerent stance. President Washington replaced Monroe in an attempt to project a more coherent policy. Still, he knew that the revolutionary government in Paris would be dissatisfied with anything the United States did short of rejecting neutrality to side with France—which he fervently intended to avoid doing. A continuation of the love-hate relationship was, therefore, about the best that could be hoped for. In the supercharged European atmosphere, a tenuous state of peace with France was not the worst of results.

Internally, any improvement in political harmony was difficult to see. A reading of partisan newspapers would have provided scant evidence of a diminished level of bickering between political parties. Maybe that is simply an inescapably endemic condition in a democracy. At any rate, it has not changed much in the two centuries since. What did change was the nature of the debate over the nation's military structure.

The framework for a defense establishment completed in 1794 would last from then on, more or less unchallenged, with future political battles fought for the most part around peripheral military issues or over responses to evolving threats. Jeffersonian Democrats (Republicans), upon becoming the dominant political power, used and improved—and even eventually expanded—the military instrument created by George Washington and espoused by Federalists. Despite their antimilitary rhetoric, Jefferson and his Democrats were not pacifists. The country's vision of its future transcended individuals and political parties. That is why the 1794 consensus over the shape of America's defense establishment has endured, while parties have come and gone.

An undercurrent of distrust would persist—the ghost of Oliver Cromwell has never ceased haunting the American psyche. That subliminal inheritance from the Founding Fathers has prompted repeated references to the sacrosanct nature of civilian control over the military, and has even engendered from time to time a renewed outburst of antimilitary expression. Americans can never forget—it is in their philosophical genes—that an army "should be watched with a jealous eye." They expect the nation's soldiers to know their business, of course, but even more emphatically do they demand loyalty to the Republic. The words of the officers' oath—to support (loyalty) and defend (competence) the Constitution—were not crafted without purpose or intent.

All in all, the far-reaching results of the climactic year of 1794 became obvious in 1795 and beyond. That is not to imply that those successes somehow meant the end of troubles. They did not. History had many more crises in store for the young nation. And some of them were imminent. For that matter, the year may have reflected as much a beginning as an ending. At the very least, though, it was a seminal moment in the ongoing story of the making of the United States. The promises so grandly proclaimed in the Preamble to the Constitution—to provide for the common defense and to insure domestic tranquility—had been transformed from rhetoric to reality, from paper to precedent.

George Washington had written back in 1783 that the "immediate Safety and future tranquility of this extensive Continent depend in a great measure upon the peace Establishment now in contemplation." By 1795 the foundation of that establishment had been put in place and had been tested under pressure. That there were more tests to come did not lessen the importance of those results already achieved. The one immutable purpose of government is to assure the security of the state. That can only be done with a military both loyal and competent. After 1794, an abiding congruence of purpose existed between America and its army.

AFTERWORD

The creation of America's defense establishment in the dozen years ending with 1794 was the result of the fascinating interplay between the times and the men living them. The times were a part of that period which has been aptly termed the "Age of Revolution." It was an era unlike any other. The men, though, were in most respects not too unlike those living before or after. They possessed in normal measure the whole array of human attributes, good and bad, weak and strong, wise and foolish.

In one critical way, however, they were distinctly not normal. They had vision. Not all of them, and none of them all of the time. But enough sufficiently overcame self-interest and parochialism to enable them to forge a future to match their dreams. Because they did, the United States became a continental and ultimately a global power. It could have been otherwise.

The names of many appear in the narrative. But their lives and their work did not end with 1794. Some, in fact, made their greatest contributions afterward. To follow them through the years is to follow the continued development of the special relationship between America and its army. Summarized below is what happened to a few after 1794.

George Washington finally escaped to Mount Vernon in the spring of 1797. He had less than three years left to live. When the long-simmering problems with revolutionary France threatened to boil over into war in 1798, President John Adams called him out of retirement and appointed him commander in chief of the provisional army being raised, with the rank of lieutenant general. The old soldier reluctantly responded one more time to his country's call. But the danger soon faded; he did not have to campaign again. Nevertheless, he never ceased to push the dual themes of military readiness and political unity. Fittingly, he devoted the last letter he ever wrote on public business to a readiness issue. He discussed one more time the need for a national military academy to assure a steady flow of competent army officers. Two days later, on 14 December 1799, he was dead.

John Adams followed George Washington in the presidency "like a fat barge after a battleship," in the colorful phrase of historian John Richard Alden. During his one term, the country came to blows with France in the so-called Quasi-War, an undeclared war that saw considerable fighting at sea. Congress took steps to increase the strength of the navy—to include founding a separate Navy Department—and to raise a huge (for that time) regular army. Having never worn a uniform, Adams wisely decided against trying to command in the field as Washington had done during the Whiskey Rebellion. Instead, he gave the command to Washington. Although the crisis abated before much of the army was enlisted, the resulting war scare impressed on many Americans one more time the need to keep a force in being. It also served to revive fears in others of the dangers inherent in a powerful standing army, largely because of Alexander Hamilton's role in the buildup. Adams lost the presidency in 1800 to Thomas Jefferson, and retired to his home in Massachusetts. He died on the fiftieth anniversary of the Declaration of Independence.

Thomas Jefferson remained in opposition to the Federalists, and had the satisfaction of seeing them fade as his own Republican party—today's Democrats—came to power. He was elected as a Republican to the vice presidency when Federalist John Adams became president. That odd combination sealed the precedent begun with Washington when his vice president was John Adams: the second office in the land continued to have virtually no political power. Tied with Aaron Burr in the 1800 election, Jefferson became president when Alexander Hamilton swung support to him. Hamilton, who believed the intellectual Jefferson was a practical incompetent, explained that he would rather have a fool than a knave as the chief executive. Jefferson surprised his detractors. He energetically used the powers of the presidency, expanding them in the process. Notably, he stretched the powers of the commander in chief. Exploring the lands gained in the Louisiana Purchase, walking a path of peace while Europe was consumed in the Napoleonic Wars, waging war on the Barbary pirates—all of that and more required him to employ extensively the army and navy that had been created over his former objections. Although he reduced the size and altered the composition of the military establishment he inherited, he worked to make it more efficient and, especially, to assure that the officers were primarily loyal to the country. From that imperative flowed his founding of the Military Academy at West Point in 1802. He lived to see Republicans James Madison and James Monroe follow him to the White House, and watched painfully Madison's ineptness as commander in chief in the War of 1812. Like Adams, he died on the fiftieth anniversary of the Declaration of Independence.

James Madison, having been initially enormously influential as a trusted advisor of President Washington's, settled into the role as a leader of the opposition during most of Washington's administration and all of Adams's. He became Jefferson's secretary of state, and then succeeded him in the presidency in the election of 1808. Having transitioned from staunch Federalist to thoroughgoing Republican, Madison had compiled a long record in Congress of opposing most military measures. All too often those who take a prominent role in fomenting unreadiness are not around when the inevitably tragic price is to be paid. Not so in Madison's case. He was in the White House when the War of 1812 erupted. It became known disapprovingly as "Mr. Madison's War." The country, unready militarily and disunited politically, performed abominably. Only rare good fortune and England's fixation with Napoleon kept the results from being as terrible as the performance. Madison left office in 1817, his reputation severely tarnished. He died in 1836.

Alexander Hamilton left Washington's cabinet early in 1795 to return to the practice of law in New York, where he was quite successful. Washington continued to rely on him for advice, and Hamilton had a major hand in writing the president's famous "Farewell Address." He also continued to work energetically during the rest of Washington's last term and through the Adams administration for a strong defense establishment, especially during the Quasi-War from 1798 to 1800. He specifically pushed for the formal founding of a military academy. When Congress authorized the raising of a large army in 1798, he became, at Washington's insistence, its inspector general, with the rank of major general. He served in that capacity for two years. As the leader of the Federalist party, Hamilton had major roles in the elections of 1796 and 1800, although he himself was too unpopular in certain regions ever to be a candidate. For years he had battled to keep Aaron Burr out of any office whatsoever, considering him to be "a dangerous man and one who ought not to be trusted with the reins of government." Though history has shown how right he was in thwarting Burr, there is some irony in that posture, for many at the time had similar thoughts about Hamilton. The enmity between the two men ended in July 1804, when Burr killed him in a duel.

Elbridge Gerry dropped out of national view for a while after the ratification of the Constitution, but he never lost his interest in politics. When France and the United States veered toward war in the late 1790s, he went to Paris and worked with some success to help paste over the differences. He became the governor of Massachusetts in 1810, running as a Democrat-Republican. Under his administration, lawmakers redistricted the state into weird patterns in order to assure that the maximum number of candidates from his party would be elected. One district looked like a salamander; thus entered into the language the term "gerrymander." He won election as vice president in 1812, just in time to be a part of Madison's ineffective wartime administration, and to see firsthand the sobering results of military unpreparedness. Had Hamilton been alive, he might have remarked about the poetic justice of it all. Gerry died suddenly in 1814.

Henry Knox resigned from Washington's cabinet early in 1795 to return to his home to try to sort out his tangled financial affairs. He had been secretary of war for the entire tumultuous decade up to and through 1794, bridging the last years of government under the Articles of Confederation and the first six under the Constitution. Gargantuan in size, worn out after nearly twenty years of war or near war, and financially strapped because of bad investments, he was not thereafter a factor on the national scene, even though he was only forty-five years old when he left government service. He died in 1806 after swallowing a chicken bone.

Gouverneur Morris, staunch Federalist to the end, saw his career go into eclipse when the Democrat-Republicans gained power. After a decade in Europe, during which time he had been the only foreign diplomat to remain in Paris through the Terror, he returned to the United States and was elected to the Senate. By the time he left office in 1802, he had become thoroughly disenchanted with Jefferson and the Democrat-Republicans. He despaired for the nation's future. The man who had done so much to shape the Constitution, and who had actually put much of it into words, died in 1816 unreconciled and bitter at the way the country had evolved.

Josiah Harmar served as adjutant general of the Pennsylvania militia until 1799, when he resigned, partly because of poor health and partly to be able to spend more time in business ventures. He was deeply involved in land speculation, a pursuit he had begun while still the commanding general of U.S. forces in the West. Despite his years of service in uniform, from the Revolutionary War on, and for all his accomplishments with meager resources, his reputation never overcame the blow it received in his ill-fated 1790 campaign. He died in 1813 near Philadelphia, with the country in the midst of another war. He was accorded elaborate military honors.

Arthur St. Clair never overcame the odium of having engineered America's first great military disaster. He remained the governor of the Northwest Territory until he was dismissed by President Jefferson in 1802. Those were stormy years for St. Clair, who was, to put it mildly, not a popular governor because of the roadblocks he threw into the path of statehood for Ohio and other territories. Broken financially, worn out physically, his reputation in tatters, he spent the rest of his life in poverty. He lived in a small cabin and operated a tavern. He died in 1818 from injuries sustained in a wagon accident.

Little Turtle was the last major chief to sign the Treaty of Greeneville in 1795. But once he did commit himself, he fought no more. His daughter married a white man, William Wells, who had spent part of his early life living as an Indian in Little Turtle's family. Wells had fought alongside Little Turtle in the defeat of St. Clair and, after switching sides, against him in 1794. Little Turtle lived out his years with his daughter and Wells, dying peacefully in July 1812. Legend has it that he was buried with a sword given to him by George Washington. Wells died a month later, killed in action at Fort Dearborn in the War of 1812. His son, Little Turtle's grandson, graduated from West Point in 1821.

Anthony Wayne did not long survive his victory at Fallen Timbers. A year after that campaign he consolidated his battlefield success by completing the Treaty of Greeneville with the tribes of the Northwest Territory. When the scheming of James Wilkinson finally burst into the open between the two men, Wayne rather easily won out in the short run over his unethical second in command. But Wilkinson was the eventual winner; he was still the second ranking general in the army when Wayne died suddenly in Erie, Pennsylvania, in 1796.

James Wilkinson achieved his ambition of becoming the commanding general of the U.S. Army, succeeding to that position upon Wayne's death. His Democrat-Republican party benefactors came to regret their support of him—a lifelong plotter, he could hardly have been expected to change upon promotion to high position. A lack of character is a devastating flaw in any leader, especially a senior military officer. As the commanding general of the army he continued to accept money from Spain, and he was involved with Aaron Burr in a scheme to create an inland empire with New Orleans as its capital. President Jefferson failed in an attempt to court-martial and cashier him. He was slippery, as rascals are wont to be, and so was still around to lead U.S. forces in the War of 1812, where he did so poorly that he was removed. He went to Mexico City looking for a land grant (incredibly, he was sponsored in his quest by the American Bible Society!) and died there in 1825. He is buried in an unmarked grave.

Henry "Light-Horse Harry" Lee had a checkered career after leading militia forces in the Whiskey Rebellion. He left the Virginia governor's chair in 1795, and returned to Congress in 1799. His high point may have been the eulogy he delivered for George Washington, in which he framed the phrase, "first in war, first in peace, and first in the hearts of his countrymen." Thereafter his life slid downward. Failing in business, he spent time in a debtors' prison. He was disfigured by a mob in Baltimore in 1812, and left shortly thereafter for the Caribbean, where he hoped to regain his health. He never did. He died in 1818 on his way back. In a final and ironic echo from the generation that wrote and established the Constitution to prevent the splintering of the United States, Henry Lee's famous son, Robert E. Lee, would choose Virginia over the Union in the Civil War. Not until that costly conflict had run its bloody course would the principle of perpetual union finally be established once and for all.

SUGGESTED READING

Bibliographies abound covering source material from and about the era central to this book. Scholars of the period are already familiar with them, and students of different times or disciplines can locate them rather easily. It therefore seems unnecessary to burden either the publisher or the reader with another one. In similar vein, given the audience for which this book is aimed, I have concluded that end notes were not needed. They would not be particularly useful, and might distract attention from the story itself.

There are, however, several works I would like to single out. They are recommended to general readers who may become interested in exploring more deeply one facet or another of the narrative.

One of the earliest—and, in my view, now verging on becoming a classic—of the modern books on the military and the early Republic is Richard H. Kohn's *Eagle and Sword: The Federalists and the Creation of the Military Establishment in America, 1783–1802* (The Free Press, 1975). Details of people and events related to the raising of the army in the 1780s and 1790s, including the printing of many of the original documents, can be found in a compilation by Robert K. Wright, Jr., and Morris J. MacGregor, Jr.: *Soldier-Statesmen of the Constitution* (Center of Military History, 1987). To place the army of the era in the context of its overall evolution, see Russell F. Weigley's *History of the United States Army* (Macmillan, 1967). Many fine works came out around the two hundredth anniversary of the writing of the Constitution, but my favorite for sheer readability is an earlier one: Catherine Drinker Bowen's *Miracle at Philadelphia* (Little, Brown, 1966). Shays's Rebellion and the Whiskey Rebellion, as well as the background for employing military force in domestic disturbances, are treated concisely and well in Robert W. Coakley's *The Role of Federal Military Forces in Domestic Disorder, 1789–1878* (Center of Military History, 1988). The Whiskey Rebellion itself is examined at book length in Thomas P. Slaughter's *The Whiskey Rebellion: Frontier Epilogue to the American Revolution* (Oxford University Press, 1986). The contest for the Northwest is the subject of Wiley Sword's *President Washington's Indian War: The Struggle for the Old Northwest, 1790–1795* (University of Oklahoma Press, 1985). For more of a focus on Anthony Wayne, see Paul David Nelson's *Anthony Wayne: Soldier of the Early Republic* (Indiana University Press, 1985). Perhaps the best way to get into more depth on the roles of George Washington, Henry Knox, Alexander Hamilton, and Thomas Jefferson is to start with volumes III and IV of James Thomas Flexner's *George Washington* (Little, Brown, 1969–70). Of the writings describing affairs from the Indian viewpoint, Gregory Evans Dowd's *A Spirited Resistance* (Johns Hopkins University Press, 1992) provides an insightful overall perspective. An interesting book combining both the birth of the navy and the conflict with the Barbary pirates is A. B. C. Whipple's *To the Shores of Tripoli* (Morrow, 1991). Finally, for an understanding of the evolving culture of the U.S. Army from its birth, two works will be useful: Edward A. Coffman's *The Old Army* (Oxford University Press, 1986) and William B. Skelton's *An American Profession of Arms: The Army Officer Corps, 1784–1861* (University Press of Kansas, 1992).